The Humanitarian Code

A Book on Consciousness

J Thomsen

Copyright © 2013 by J. Thomsen.

ISBN: Softcover   978-1-4931-2887-7
             eBook   978-1-4931-2888-4

All rights reserved. No part of this book may be reproduced or transmitted in any form or by any means, electronic or mechanical, including photocopying, recording, or by any information storage and retrieval system, without permission in writing from the copyright owner.

This book was printed in the United States of America.

Rev. date: 11/12/2013

To order additional copies of this book, contact:
Xlibris LLC
1-888-795-4274
www.Xlibris.com
Orders@Xlibris.com
143514

The Humanitarian Code

A Book on Consciousness

⇨ The Humanitarian Code is the first book endorsed by The Personal Achievement Institute, incorporated 6 October 1978.

Note:

If you are the nature of person who is content to do nothing in times requiring awareness, then this book may not be for you.

- This is, The Humanitarian Code; Copyright Registered, All Rights Reserved.

Gloria in Excelsis Deo!

This book is dedicated to:
The Creator of All that Is.

Through honoring planet earth
and a lot of reasonable people
discovering their true Humanity,

By God,
we're gonna make it!

Insights within this book

In 1776, our language was much clearer than it is today. That clarity yielded better communication and less confusion—and less of that confusion's resulting conflict and madness. In honor of George Orwell, and to clear up vast amounts of carefully engineered chaos and spin, this book clears up the deceit—and thus the confusion and conflict, as related to the following concepts:

- What is Consciousness.
- What is American.
- What is Humanitarian.
- What is Awareness.
- What is Freedom.
- What is Human Teleology.
- What is the Humanitarian Code.
- What is Human Success.
- What is The Great Healing.
- What is the future of the planet.
- What is the future of the human race.
- What is being done about it.
- What *you* can do about it.
- Why it is important.
- Why human advancement **is** Creator Consciousness.

- How all of the above is   **The Human Event.**

A Reasonable Life

The basis of life is freedom.

The power of life is love.

The purpose of life is joy.

Wherever I am, life is.

All is as I am.

And we are One.

And this is, *The Human Event*.

J. Thomsen

CR ARR 2013

What is Human Teleology?

The subject of this book <u>and the function of the human race</u>, is Human Teleology {pronounced Tee-lee-all-o-gee}, meaning abundantly inevitable, Creator Designed, Creator Intended, or Creator Qualitied. It has two definitions for the purposes of this book and field of endeavor:

1 The profoundly beneficial experience of the advanced human.

2 The profoundly beneficial experience of the advanced human race.

In short, human teleology is Creator Consciousness in action or Creator Consciousness as experienced. To arrive at that observation quickly, one must pose this question; is the Creator of All that IS, the author and perpetrator of human slavery *as is,* <u>or</u> did the Creator through representation demand: 'Let my people go'. And as John Lennon said: "It is, just that simple." All we are saying; *is give non-violence a chance.*

For the function of human teleology, this means:

"End human slavery **now!**"

Therefore, the fury of human slavery **as driven by the various cabals, cartels and monopolies,** *completed by their political lap dog,* is also the subject of this book.

The path of human teleology and the present condition of human slavery are both examined thoughtfully in this book. The experience is ***extremely*** empowering. That is the intent.

This is not the empty and used up power to the people gig. Human teleology reveals that ***you*** are the power. The outcome is a full world of difference. The *final* separation of the present experience of human slavery and our path into Evolution—is our own awakening into the power and unlimited ability we *Are.*

This book strongly advances that awareness.

Foreword

Welcome to the extraordinary. This book is intended to change the course of human experience for the better.

All of us can name something that advanced our awareness, and thus our lives into consciousness. The words and concepts herein are rapidly accomplishing that shift. This book is a focused and energetic setting of intent from, through, and into a magnificent and extremely potent synchronicity. The objective is to move all that is, *toward the Light of the Creator.*

Together, we closely examine Consciousness. This is our greatest gift to All that Is, (particularly ourselves). We also attend to consciousness seared with a hot iron. First, we behold the heart, and thus the home of the indomitable human spirit, the *You* that is you. Then, we jerk back the soiled covers of politics and view the pathology that fouled them. I call it the curtain of Oz because it is <u>*strictly*</u>, an illusion. And we examine the spot where the two directions meet.

We will do two things: 1, fully decode every step of modern politics to uncover the how and why of the what. Such unholy axis has been in need of demystifying for many generations. And, 2, from the above confluence, we witness, cause and experience the New Energy. This is the calling and course of the Humanitarian with a big H as Creator sourced and centered.

We shall define American once and for all. And straight from Creator Consciousness, we introduce *The Humanitarian Code.*

This much I know: You have made the winning bet that the concepts within this book will save the human race. By default, something must.

Millennia before you were born, your fortune, health, spiritual wellbeing, *and life* were wagered on this specific outcome. I encourage you to find out how-that-happened.

This expanded worldview is easy and rewarding to read. *More fun has yet to be invented.* We joke well at modern politics, for modern politics *is* the joke. Perhaps one in a hundred do not share the same conclusion. We do however switch the outcome from victimhood **to empowerment**.

This is the book you have long waited for.

I honor your enjoyment.

Acknowledgements

Ayn Rand and Thomas Paine, in a tie for the second most influential writer in human history, co-inspired this book. Frederic Douglass is featured throughout this book. *All three spoke extensively on human respect.*

If you have considered the self-evident truth of the God given Right to human freedom, you shall enjoy your thoughts contained in this book.

That puts us in very good company as we gratefully acknowledge and honor **you**, the initiators, creators and co-authors of this book.

Numerous New Era writers are present in this book. You might identify their energy and style. Each is focused on one very clear Intent:

Freedom, blessed, beautiful Freedom.

That is to say; Consciousness.

Exceptional merit is honored with editing team Sharon R. Dudley and Burt Dubin. This book could not have been completed without them.

This book was a huge team effort. The greater team included a world of students of Consciousness and ironically, another world of students of non-consciousness. Another world was an understatement. The first group indispensably contributed by their *awareness*. The second group contributed indispensably with their unawareness *and errors a dog 'd be ashamed of*.

The real irony is that each offered equal value *by example*. I know which group I shall choose to associate with. This book will sort the wheat from the chaff in *both* camps. <u>Behold as the chaff scatters *itself* to the wind, just as it is now doing *and precisely as foretold*.</u>

Outlaws, in-laws, scofflaws, horse-traders and straight-shooters, one way or t'other, *you made this exist*. Y'all know who ya are, and I thank ya kindly.

Jeff

The Reasonable Experience

- All oppression resides upon assumed approval.
- We now have the ability to eradicate that form of suicide.
- Welcome one and all to Human Evolution, *the experience worth living in.*
- Thank you for your presence here and now.
- We absolutely are the winning team.

- **Because this is, the Human Event!**

Disclaimer

This book is inspired information. It is channeled from several sources. Each source is Truth tested to be representative of the Light of the Creator. Every objective is to advance the human race into Creator Consciousness. In addition, it is amazing how my own research was pointed in just the right direction. That eliminated untold oceans of guesswork and wrong turns. The synchronicity experienced was without measure.

Unwinding the thought blocks and concepts and placing them into words was a formidable challenge. Although I made every effort to hold a rigorous degree of fidelity, any errors, belong to myself, the scribe.

Except for obvious exaggerations to interject humor, <u>all *qualified* descriptions</u> are derived from public opinion. In other words, the characterizations came straight from the people of the United States of America. You exhibited an astonishing consistency. It was as if the entire nation spoke with a single voice declaring modern politics the house of the devil. I am honored and delighted to place your voice into this book. I thank each voice that contributed to thirty plus years of research. In many locations in this book, I often employed the feelings and sparingly, a wee touch of the language of the public, even when I personally, sometimes, did not agree with such adamant *and terse* descriptions.

<u>This is far more your book than my book.</u> It is written honoring that condition.

The effort in writing this evolutionary manual was pure joy. Even re-reading it countless times to weed out error was joy—owing to a strong consciousness calibration. In short, what an amazing effect that never ceases to surprise me.

Every word in this book shall be regarded as preceded with "In my opinion…" or "As I feel…". Every word in this book is to be regarded as educational. No person, business, or organization assumes liability for the use or misuse of anything in this book. This book is presented as science entertainment, and shall be legally regarded as such at all times, locations and circumstances.

No liability for any reason shall exceed the price of one book, CD or download.

The intent of this book is *strictly and exclusively,* nonviolent communication.

This author insists upon a 30 day unconditional money back guarantee.

As we honor every human as unique, we also realize each person owns a diverse experience. Therefore, this book may not be understood by all, as each person is graduated within their own evolution into awareness.

This book was written in love, joy, fun and great humor. Please receive it in joy, and if returning it or burning it brings you joy, we honor that equally.

I am thankful this book has become a treasure trove and resource to evolving humans. As the veil between the dimensions lifts, we move into greater awareness, understanding, wisdom, benefit *and personal empowerment* constituting,

The Human Event.

You have my gratitude for causing it.

Index, **Part One**

Prolog, pages 3 through 12

Pg 13	Ch 1	**Introducing The Humanitarian Code**

Pg 21	Ch 2	Countering Invalidation with Validation
Pg 25	Ch 3	The Old and The New
Pg 32	Ch 4	Oppression and Evolution
Pg 36	Ch 5	The Decision
Pg 41	Ch 6	Vision and Joy
Pg 52	Ch 7	What Was and What Is
Pg 59	Ch 8	Some General Guidelines
Pg 90	Ch 9	Of Bankers and Warfare
Pg 93	Ch 10	Unspoken Patterns
Pg 111	Ch 11	The Increase in Consciousness
Pg 119	Ch12	Specific Directions
Pg 123	Ch13	Conclusion

The Humanitarian Code

Copyright 2013 J Thomsen

Index, **Part Two**

Pg 125		Introduction
Pg 133	Ch 1	A Reasonable Checklist
Pg 144	Ch 2	Roll Call
Pg 161	Ch 3	Claiming Our Voice
Pg 178	Ch 4	Evolutionary Action
Pg 188	Ch 5	The How and Why of Voting
Pg 199	Ch 6	Term Limits
Pg 213	Ch 7	The Four Levels of Awareness
Pg 220	Ch 8	Third Rails and Compromised Organizations
Pg 224	Ch 9	Slavery Versus Consciousness
Pg 245	Ch 10	Cloture and Metamorphosis
Pg 273	Ch 11	CAFRs And The End of Taxation
Pg 284	Ch 12	The Final Chapter of Human Slavery
Pg 330	Ch 13	This Shall Be Done

The Humanitarian Code
Copyright 2013 J Thomsen

Part One

Chapter One

Introducing The Humanitarian Code

The path of human teleology is defined by The Three Principles of Successful Human Society:

Introducing The Humanitarian Code:

1 The only legitimate function of government is to uphold, protect and defend Individual Human Rights.

2 We stand at One with the Creator in the Humanity of Liberty, the condition of Human Evolution.

3 We stand united in the American definition of smaller government, fewer taxes, and greatest personal freedom.

- We hold these Truths to be brilliantly self-evident as the foundation of all human success.

- We thereby uphold Life and the conditions of Life in harmony and unity with All that Is.

- We literally are the Human Event and the Bringers of the Dawn of Humanity.

- This is, and we are, *the New Energy.*

- The Humanitarian Code is the unbreakable foundation and guiding principle of the Reasonable Political Party and the evolved human experience.

- **We—are the humanitarian outcome of Peace and Freedom.**

- Anything else, is perusing a dead end road.

Our constituency consists of those who are **awake and aware**, thus moving toward a vastly brighter and better experience. We shall enjoy that outcome by way of bringing forth the Human Event *by example*.

Our candidates and office holders have our highest regard and support, working with our membership all:

- Shall uphold, example, *and consistently present* The Three Basic Truths of Human Evolution.

- Shall not present or vote any agenda in opposition to that Truth, or the Oath of Office to uphold the Constitution.

- Platform planks and advocating to move society in the direction of human respect and non-violence is expressly encouraged.

- All Party planks are optional, and employing none or other is valid.

- We do not compromise in spirit, deed or presentation, the first three principles of human teleology.

- Throughout this book, we dissect that which has proven to be non functional and its opposite, human validation. *From a keen and clear awareness of both*, we advance the functional and moral.

- From the Energy of human success and the time and truth tested principles of Consciousness, we now advance *The Reasonable Human Movement and Party*.

- And it is so.

In harmony with Creator and Nature, our Mission is to present, cause and enjoy **The Three Basic Truths of Functional Society** comprising the Humanitarian Code®.

- Reasonable is the Energy of transmuting human slavery *by way of awareness*, into Human Success.

- **We are Reasonable; observing that human slavery is unconditionally without reason.**

Our platform process is:

- A full membership debate and vote is open electronically each quarter on Reasonable goals at: TheReasonableParty.US.

- All proposals must support The Three Conditions of Human Evolution, comprising The Humanitarian Code.

- Debate on platform planks should fall within the concepts presented throughout this book.

- Generalized perspectives and vote totals are to be web published and archived.

- A similar vote is open to the public, and public opinion is fully honored in our debate process.

- Top planks in order, are those passing the Party standards of human respect and enjoying the most support.

- Goals are added and removed through voted results.

- Everything published is subject to content approval and Party ownership.

These principles and voting construct, correct several prevailing shortfalls congenital to all other political movements and parties. They are:

1. The overriding practice is an astonishing disconnect between membership and the leadership and platform both. Such ill treatment is a process of an inside few, forcing a Hobson's choice upon the membership. Such a dictated paradigm ever more often, bears little or no resemblance to choices the membership themselves would make. For example, how many party members upon repeatedly suffering mainstream platform, empty speeches and *excruciatingly repugnant* nominees have said: "What the *hell* are they thinking?"

- The far more accurate question would have been: **"Who paid them to do that?"**

- Ah-ha!

The platform revision processes are so cumbersome, as to roadblock the content from review. The process is designed to alienate those who would offer beneficial reform. *The whole paradigm is rigorously tailored to protect a uni-directional set of cartel driven dictates defining human slavery.*

Beyond that process, lie massively entrenched policies, practices, candidates, office holders and platform planks **at direct odds** against outwardly advertized objectives. Such process, as complete as it is, lays full waste to mission, cause, moral, principle and truth. Short of an aggravated conspiracy theory, such overwhelming evidence makes no sense whatsoever.

This begs the question: To what end does such an *exclusively destructive* direction, actually serve? **It is very clearly not at all in humanitarian interest.**

Within predominate parties, this deeply resident pattern has bewildered, divided, angered, cast out, and rudely abandoned an ever growing profusion of former stalwarts. Such conduct showcases a comprehensive disdain for lower ranked members by the fully sold out party controllership.

- By no stretch of the imagination, is this revelation new.

Given that most political parties are conducting the business **of human invalidation**, such contempt both inward and outward directed, comes as no surprise to virtually anyone. Such woeful management is to most folks, both afflictive and wildly un-American. Such bullying **and despotism** matches only a riot of non-palatable platform planks and violence backed votes. The only product is divisive, coercive, and *consummately destructive* outcomes.

- Reasonable's New Energy of human respect as defined by The Humanitarian Code, reverses and sets right the above inversion of sanity, justice and livability.

- Through holding open and ongoing platform debate, a solid communication link is kept current throughout the organization.

- Equally as importantly, each member is honored for who they are, and as they are.

- This is a rarity to be sure, as it is the diametric opposite of Mainstream political intention and product.

Every perspective born of intuition and experience with the intent of the Transition into Success, forms a whole greater than the sum of the parts. It is this gathering of human respect that achieves the desired results.

The Humanitarian Code is the one and only process by which worlds are awakened and moved from past to present; thus from the pain of hate and slavery, to the Omni-benefit of peace and freedom.

- Our Creator and all Creation inspired Calling is the Evolution into safety, peace and freedom.

Such is entirely Reasonable. The Three Central Laws of Human Respect, The Humanitarian Code, constitute our undivided and unbreakable moral principle. *Thereby we cause human and world evolution.*

We place this Truth and Light up front, first, foremost and without reservation. We see it as utterly unshakeable. We then reflect Human Ascension. It is through this advanced co-Creation Energy that we can and will, transform life from half existence to full human membership **and the unlimited prosperity of peace and freedom.**

As for our methodology, it is the same New Energy of human validation that forms the Reasonable Movement. The same Energy of empowerment *is* the Evolution. Human manumission is every inch as profoundly beneficial, (and valid), as it is now profoundly unstoppable and thoroughly welcome.

- The most important point to note is that Reasonable thinking is in producing the unlimited benefit of upward evolution **now**.

- We see no logic in idly awaiting, and thus suffering multitudes of grievous, pointless and preventable spiritual, economic, personal, family, community, national and planetary injuries **later**.

- The Evolution into Peace and Freedom is unstoppable *anyway*, and it is underway *presently*. **The people *have spoken*.**

It is through our process as presenter *and practitioner* of human validation, that our platform is born. Each platform plank into Human Evolution is intended to honor each perspective as valid, worthy and vote recorded. And unique to this party, your perspective is *actually considered*.

In today's world, such concept is innovative and unique. We call it being Reasonable as we move from invalidation **and into empowerment**.

- Achieving our unlimited upward human potential of empowerment, is the difference between the politics of colossal and conclusively proven failure, or the path to Human Success.

- The Reasonable movement is transmuting the human condition from serfdom to success, from failure to enlightenment, from weakness to empowerment, from strife to cooperation, from harm to safety, from chaos to sanity, *and from hate to humanity*.

- And it is so.

- This is what the human species is now *demanding*.

Chapter Two

Countering Invalidation with Validation

2.   The second problem, in much deeper degree than the first, is from *the identical pattern of human invalidation*. This daily practice is an expanding disconnect from, and reveals venomous disdain toward humanity in general. This requirement as it were, *appears to saturate all mainstream political leadership*. <u>It reflects the unlimited purchasing power of the cartel</u>.

    The disinherited voter now approaching 100%, and the often livid non-voter, each own a keen awareness of this modern political insane asylum. The just plain NO! voter, (the non-voter), holds forth the intuitive *and correct* understanding that such **contempt for human**, has proven to be the *all consuming* mainstream political paradigm for many generations.

    The one location where the politics of raving dishonesty is morphodited into a rose colored picture is across the television. The results of such total loss politics has finally surpassed the obvious and egregious. This is in spite of oceans of televised kabuki failing to convince us otherwise.

    Because of an upward jump in **world consciousness**, human slavery *no matter the cover up name,* is now harder to hide. Many have said this basic of all basic awareness is considerably overdue. As *the awakening* is superbly beneficial, we therefore observe it to be Reasonable.

- Again, the New Energy honors everyone.

- Through opposing human slavery, Evolution honors the human condition.

- **This means you.**

- We believe this is a concept whose time has arrived.

- We hold that human freedom is an exceptional **and exponentially beneficial** experience.

- By way of your discovery of this advanced Energy and reading this far, we can see that your intuition agrees.

- *Together, we are creating an obviously more Reasonable outcome.*

No matter how 'modern' or cartel driven a political goal is, the public's well being is simply not considered. The public is ripped off and *savagely* left in the cold by today's politics. The trend is rapidly gaining worse. *As of this moment, there is no remaining illusion otherwise.*

More and more of the public is sniffing out the not so hidden **intent of human slavery** in the <u>cartel purchased</u> platforms, sales pitches, laws, prohibitions and restrictions. It is then that the owner of such awareness knows without doubt, they are left out of the process *as if they simply did-not-exist.* The public is treated as if they were worms or meat fit for slaughter.

In addition to that morally absent course of conduct, apparently any tall tale whatsoever will be spun up to smoke the bottom dollar out of the mainstream voting, and thus cartel supporting *political infant*. At that juncture *all* scruples vanish. Your intuition is again correct.

To make some humor out of a tragic situation, we will now share the sharply growing definition of the modern politician: The only one who would steal the nickels out of a dead man's eyes! This is thought to be a Will Rogers quote circa 1920's.

The energy there is not new at all, and that's the whole point. The energy is not <u>N</u>ew. As with all old energy, it is as ever, "<u>something traded for nothing.</u>" [ibid]. **The previous quote contains the most important real-world lesson anyone will ever learn about mainstream politics,** *lifetime.*

Again your intuition is 100% correct. Your intuition was likely telling you that message *your entire life.* We call that the world's largest clue. Some heads are now bobbing in agreement. This particular truth ignites political wisdom. *It is the foundation of correct understanding.*

The whole trick of course is in seeing the old energy of omni-destroyment for what it is, and thus its inverse, Human Evolution. One <u>e</u>nergy is of the easily mislead standard political **idiot.** The more beneficial <u>E</u>nergy is of awareness and humanitarian compassion.

Human slavery cannot define compassion. The old energy is human hate. It is the outcome of ever increasing oppression that has come to define mainstream politics for over one hundred and fifty years.

- The New Energy is the humane treatment of humans.

- This, is the wisdom to acquire in order to achieve human race and planetary **continuation.**
- And it is inescapably so.

To be crystal clear, the old energy *is a much dirtier version of the company store*. It's Uncle Tom's cabin on all of us. It's the back of the bus for the human race, and it's Jim Crow for those who walk upright. The old energy is the animal farm for humans, and it's 1984 for all who saw the movie. *It is live human sacrifice to world controlling cartel.*

Today's mainstream politics is no more than a plastic trinket decorated prison cage for those who breathe air. It's the endlessly proven madness of the bridge over the river Quai. It is the lifelong making of bricks with no straw.

It is the squalid captivity of lies, illusions and limitations serving only a preeminent *and rabid* contempt for all life on earth.

- What you are reading right now, is the opportunity to end the politics of human hate.

- **This is in <u>absolute fact</u>; Human Evolution.**

- Exactly and only that, is both Reasonable and moral.

- Ironically, it is positively nothing whatsoever that is <u>not</u> Reasonable and moral.

Chapter Three

The Old and the New

3. The third old energy problem, and yet another grand opportunity, is found in a question: How many dying-party planks are not only fantastically nonsensical, (evidently cooked up in drug dens), but also so outdated as to belong to homo homopterous at best?

How endlessly many of their planks and "legal" policies are so non-operationally vague, that any attempt to root out actual meaning is akin to cutting out a chunk of fog with a paring knife?!! That same snake energy is the twin of any mainstream political speech is it not? Should anything of substance, truth or logic be found by happy accident or miracle, buy out the lotto!

- **The real injury, is that those vacant planks and policies are defended by your life force spilled onto the ground in <u>unlimited violence</u>.**
- <u>This is the key *and correct* understanding of modern politics</u>.

Corruption and danger placed together fail to span half the distance thus represented. Even more insidious, is the *carefully coached* fact that such perpetual say-nothing fetor is <u>intentional</u>.

All of the mainstream *snake oil* represents an ever slicker refinement of the bait and switch ploy. It is the intention of saying the outward appearance of something, the Oath of Office for example, and then voting an opposite direction, somewhere almost without exception, *drastically* virulent to humans. The cause however, <u>is the cartel</u>.

When laws of this underhanded nature are passed, it represents not only a blank check, but an open season license and invitation for every known abuse. *Human slavery is simply that demand fulfilled.* This is the danger of a cabal purchased sales force of professional, lifetime **liars**.

- It is also the destruction of the concept of checks and balance.

Mainstream political practice is morbidly outdated in the sense that the world of dishonor that defines mainstream politics is distantly below present human consciousness. Not only has this condition held true for one hundred and fifty years straight, but this gulf is rapidly expanding in of all things, *both directions*.

Lest there be any error, the overall direction of modern, mainstream politics is intentionally toward human oppression. The evidence is now perfected and in overwhelming preponderance. **As a broad hint Human Evolution shall not contain human slavery!** Ergo, modern politics is aggressively decaying *and cannot survive the shift in consciousness.*

Such treating of humans as feedstock, the planks, the empty speeches, and particularly as voted in chamber, is none other than candy coated, Simon pure **human slavery output.** The big trick to make that human hate go away is to recognize it as it is. The trick to that is found in the present knowledge that it is universally opposite of how it is advertised. Such craven intent and outcome defines modern politics in the flesh, being semper flagrante.

- **Mainstream politics has come to define itself as the procedure by which you get thrown under the bus.**

The process of full recognition is the method by which tears of helpless anguish can be transformed into the tears of powerful joy. Quite often, the whole freedom process defaults to humor and the deep realizations placed within humor. Knowing that, and placing such readymade leverage onto our side, the wanton dishonesty of modern politics can be gracefully transmuted into human respect by the permanent *self-abatement* of modern politics.

The keys to living that empowerment are quality political jokes, the much keener insight of a New Energy perspective and good old fashioned Yankee ingenuity. They are relentless and focused moral action, top notch organization, and informed, awake, aware, proactive, and enlightened voters.

Indeed, it is from the choice to be fully human, that human friendly Energy shall flow. The human friendly part is the Evolution. This primer for example, aptly *and correctly,* provides long forgotten basic directions on how actual humans are treated. Behold: **The Three Basic Truths of Human Evolution:**

1 The only legitimate function of government is to uphold, protect and defend Individual Human Rights.

2　We stand at One with the Creator in the Humanity of Liberty, the condition of Human Evolution.

3　We stand united in the American definition of smaller government, fewer taxes and greatest personal freedom.

- It doesn't get any more Reasonable or beneficial than that.
- *Right there, is the Evolved future of the human race.*

Therefore our Reasonable Energy is right on the mark. It is up to date and serves **present** human consciousness. Every goal is from and toward Creator Consciousness. Every plank is responsive not only to the Reb (for short) membership, but also to the full public—any age, status or uniqueness which we celebrate. Now that is New Energy!

Even the Indigo children, whether manipulated with government forced drugs or not, can participate and vote. As it turns out, the Indigo are *nowhere near* as easily fooled as the mainstream voter! Their intuition and discernment are considerably more functional. *That's why they're Indigo.*

From the government's viewpoint, that con-artist paradigm is decidedly not moral, however it is keenly logical. That's the "new math" by the way. In terms of modern politics, it is also the "new morality" as well. As it turns out, these concepts are important to understand.

What do you think? How many lives are going to be trashed in the human-to-robot-process by truly, truly, *despisable* politicians?

These are the same oligarchs, who from a formidable fear of loss of [thought] control, are vehemently opposed to the successful, cost effective, and rapidly growing, private sector schooling movement. This includes small scale private sector anything.

It is the same lifetime politicians and for the same reasons, who are *violently* opposed to the nation sweeping wave of home schooling. As it turns out, home schooling has proven to be a burning political embarrassment. It far better prepares the student for a rewarding, successful, balanced, functional, productive, *thinking,* and responsible life.

Such human destroyment represents a fully anti-Oath political action. It is not the *slightest hint* moral or American, yet it is famously logical. Is this subject a side track from our main theme? It is not because:

- THE planetary wide debate is the abject failure of human slavery versus the Success of human freedom.

- From a moral viewpoint, there is no debate, **as only one direction defines,** *or can produce*, **human Evolution.**

- For those paying attention, there is an all important key right here:

- Human Evolution is all inclusive.

- By definition, everyone is honored and treated as human.

On the other end, call it unbecoming human or human de-evolution, human slavery and the politics of human slavery is the embodiment of exclusion. It is the treatment by **legal fiat** and coercion, of humans as not human. People are specifically excluded *by the violence of gun point force* from human race participation. This is done by cartel driven genocide **and the procedures of human genocide**, that we call "modern politics".

- The understanding of *inclusiveness*, of treating humans as worthy of humanity defines all that is Reasonable.

- Such is the very key to the human future.

- **It is absolutely THE key to any future worth living in.**

For one old energy example, let's end the requirement to first be an insider's insider and funded to no end to move human policy one tenth of a grain. The leverage in that model is geared directly against the human race. It is a stacked deck being dealt by a very crooked house. The entire concept is to exclude you from participation. ***You therefore become a guaranteed target.*** † *This is rule number one of modern politics.* †

For yet another brass knuckle punch, virtually all policy pushed or voted by the mainstream politician, is *conclusively* toward **human slavery**. Combined with a standard and ubiquitous political non-probity, this becomes the apogee, study, science, art, practice, age and era of a very, very, **raw deal**. † *This is rule number two of modern politics.* †

- Welcome to modern politics—*you're being eaten alive!*

And sadly, you actually *did* get what you paid for—human destruction.

Today, the established worldwide system is engineered specifically to deny your human potential and virtually all your Human Rights. This is particularly true of laws and legislatures. Such raw iniquity constitutes the art of mainstream politics. Human Teleology is its opposite. *It is the absence of human slavery.*

Modern government is now correctly defined as the great conundrum by which the upper level know they serve Slavery, and the lower levels only suspect it. *All of it is headed directly to utterly brutal tyranny unless the human race can muster enough self respect to stop it cold and <u>forever</u>.*

The opposite of that authentic dead end essence, would be not only Reasonable but Evolutionary, causing human freedom and therefore Human Success. *"There is not a man under the canopy of heaven who does not know that human slavery is wrong!"* (Quoting Frederick Douglass.)

Therefore, for the function of humanity, our <u>N</u>ew platform process causes every goal to be of human compatibility. It is not only common sense, but a welcome world *whose time has now arrived:* **It is The Human Event.**

- The time to be blinded with hate is over with.

- The time to be activated by awareness is upon us.

- This is the function of the Code book, (The Humanitarian Code).

- *We are doing something other than burying our heads in the sand.*

- **We are in the process of restoring the Creator's faith in the human race!**

Just as we are aware of the inoperable, we are now engaged in the workable. Just as we *understand* human slavery, we are *living* The Humanitarian Code. Just as we discard who we are not, we become who we Are. As we reduce slavery and its politics of violence to dust, **we join the Universe as humans.** The New Energy is therefore *strictly* humanitarian; the humane treatment of humans, and **not** the endless blood sacrifice to cartel.

- We are now within success because we **are** the New Energy.

As this book advances each newer concept upon the foundation of prior concepts, it is written in an intentionally novel manner. This **textbook for the New Paradigm**, is intended to be read in order. I have discarded as many rules as humanly possible and yet maintain a book. In that sense, the read is much more entertaining.

Had I not been strong-armed into pagination, that would have been tossed also. But don't feel too put out as none of my handwritten drafts suffered a single page number. Notice also that the "chapters" are not chapters at all, but only break points between concepts. Later on, even that gets tossed. Keep each of the foundational concepts in mind, and it will all drop neatly into the Human Event *which is your personal empowerment.*

- Because it is *absolutely* so.

- Your personal empowerment, is the outcome you wanted the most.

- *This is the process by which it shall be experienced.*

Chapter Four

Oppression and Evolution

4. Taking all of the thus far presented concepts one step deeper into wisdom, human slavery, (that is to say and define modern politics), is the result of a larger and heretofore hidden condition: That Devil's game is debt instrument, non-Treasury, and non sense international banking. *Here is where there is no room whatsoever to make the error of underestimating the incomparable destructiveness of international fiat based banking.*

As long as such practice exists, all other considerations across the human spectrum become null, and without meaning. We can "elect" and thoroughly suffer a dozen Presidents and unfit Congresses at a **single digit approval rate**—and not modify the modern political outcome of exponentially increasing oppression. <u>*Now you know the reason why*</u>.

The reason for that condition, the set-up, is called an IOU. That model is not only what you owe directly to foreign cartel, it is now far beyond the amount most can pay across their lifetime. You know whose life – *and – blood - line* is consigned to pay the ever increasing balance.

Worse, *the* unspeakable evil, is the ungodly sum now owed by the young and unborn who will experience a slavery *they did not commit*. This is an amount none of them will *intentionally* ever have the means to pay. It is not possible in the standard political model **of abject poverty.**

The balance of this debt against *imaginary money* is to be paid up *directly as designed*, in conditions of ever increasing human oppression. This is observed in virtually every new law in several generations. Such is the world, the catch, and the squalor, of old energy. <u>It is exactly human slavery.</u> The modern political construct of human disembowelment is a relentless downward spiral into a living hell of dehumanization, oppression, injury, disability, destabilization, despotism, no hope and no return.

Although more or less fully etheric beyond the resultant laws and violence, the sum of political and mechanical methodology standing directly behind human slavery was just given. Very few institutions have presented such information in truth. We think we did a Reasonable job of it.

As a suggestion, a very commonsense goal might be to eliminate *forever*, that non-Constitutional, and therefore non-legal, non-American, **human usury process**. That step alone would stop cold, the main cartel driven engine of human butchery worldwide. Such astounding benefit is eminently Reasonable and underway *presently*.

- As a tremendous benefit and bonus to the human race, the above step would also kill the much hated, *(and unneeded)*, Income Tax.

- That Marxist world of woe runs like clockwork at a 70 to 90+ percent disapproval rate depending upon which survey addressing that ruinous subject is employed.

- As it turns out, few would <u>not</u> call such a substantial life improvement **Reasonable**.

- By the IRS' own statistics, it is now approaching *the majority* who are in significant disobedience of that law rendering it null.

- The worst part is that anyone, *without exception,* can easily be "interpreted" to be in criminal risk and thus politically attacked as has been the slightly hidden standard practice for generations.

- The Income Tax is a page out of some horrid science fiction nightmare as well as Karl Marx' book, The Communist Manifesto. *Common sense demands its end.*

- **Evolution will not entertain the income tax *A-T A-L-L.***

- Also within that step, is a heads up lesson <u>*and experience*</u> in drastic, *revolutionizing*, instant, and long term economic improvement.

- *Do not expect any modern dirt-bag politician to admit any of this.*

- Now you know beyond any shadow of doubt why: **They never were on your side.**

- I also believe you already knew every inch and dollar of that much.

- It has been left up to you to do or undo any of this, or make it a Reasonable goal.

- The canvas of Creation, the Matrix, is yours to paint every outcome upon.
- It ever was.
- *The difference is awareness.*
- Welcome to Human Evolution.
- Welcome to your **empowerment**.

For example, envision your benefit *in the absence of the greatly hated income tax*. What a beautiful and glorious day that shall be. The good news is that it is definitely on its way. You have demanded it, **and that condition** *is being delivered*.

- Ending the *mechanisms* of human slavery might be a highly sane move for those who hold that ending human ruination and the profoundly destructive politics and policies that go with it, as beneficial.
- We observe that the current political direction of human slavery is malevolent, costly, painful, immoral, wrong, violent, destructive, un-American, dehumanizing, corrupt, disrespectful, racist, bigoted, *and utterly inexcusable.*

- *Therefore, the direction of human success is always Reasonable.*

Chapter Five

The Decision

5. Onward to the solution.   (The Decision)

"We sense that an extraordinary spiritual shift is within reach. This is the awakening and transition into the Evolutionary Self...with all the power and potential that entails."

Craig Hamilton, Enlightenment counselor

<u>When we make the decision to be human,</u> *to be treated as human,* <u>All that Is—can, must, and will, become that decision.</u>   Not only is that the start to your evolution into co-Creation, it is the center, being compassion, of Evolution itself. *This is the Reasonable message.* This we quote commit to both head and heart. We read this together at every meeting.

We hold that the human race has now evolved to where we can no longer be mollified with anything less than truth, or anything short of humane treatment. The three Truths of Human Evolution and the Reasonable Party are indeed *the correct* vehicles to that experience. Yet it cannot substitute for the key and individual decision **to be Humanitarian**.

We can in total blindness continue to patch up the symptoms of politically delivered inhumanity to mankind such as landmines, bombs, warfare, manufactured contention and economic servitude **or**, we can remove the *cause* of the un-humanity. Such a practical move would directly result in a thousand fold leverage in human benefit, and a thousand fold reduction in pan-world human cost. This is awareness, again Reasonable, as directly opposed to the ever-present *amplified ostrich syndrome* that defines every inch of modern, grave bound and *exclusively* **suicide bent politics.**

It is our belief in separation from Creator, Creation, and each other that holds our humanity away from us. This is the system wide domesticated illusion *that 100% of all modern politics is based upon*.

There are illusions upon illusions and false fears upon false fears, but nothing that would not vanish in an instant upon exposure. This lifting away of the world's heaviest burden is called Human Evolution. Such is the exact reason for Reasonable: *We are the living opposite of physical, spiritual and economic human harm.*

- It is the decision to live in humanity, and the decision to **Live**, that becomes the renewal of the Spirit.

- All, then flows into that construct.

- Shakespeare instructs this concept best: "Our remedies in ourselves do lay, that we ascribe to Heaven."

- Here is the Reasonable message: Should we desire either; any future, *or*, any future worth living in, we shall create both.

- *The Destroyers of the human future must not be allowed to write that future.*

- The primary method by far needed to create a beneficial future, is through **the loss of illusion**.

- The good news is that such evolution is not anywhere near as difficult, *by several magnitudes,* as it may at first seem.

    The key to human success comes right back to the decision to join the human race! Or, continue to remain lorded over by a rapidly sinking rat pack of endless political lies. The awareness needed to break the mainstream political illusion to dust, should it by some miracle not do so on its own, is rather simple: It is the politically amplified *illusion of separation,* the big lie, that drives every aspect of the vast collection of outright lies known as, *mainstream politics.*

- When the mocked up control drama the television duns at us falls against the Light of reality, then all the other falsehoods manifested as endless forms of political strife and theft *can no longer exist*.

- Hate then becomes displaced and replaced with the unifying Energy of reality **that is a lot more Reasonable and livable.**

- Right there, dissolves most of the lies that plague humanity.

- Any other challenges now have the same unifying Oneness and co-respectful method of resolution.

- Such is the difference between human respect and human slavery.

- With no irony, this is also the key to planetary survival.

- Therefore, Reasonable is <u>not</u> the black hole of modern politics from which nothing returns.

- Rather, we are the distance <u>away</u> <u>from</u> modern polemics, that destituted anti-energy *yielding no earthly benefit.*

- Reasonable, is therefore defined as both the human spirit *and living condition*, **advancing into the benefits of Consciousness.**

We may do many of the items required of politics when at our choice and advantage. However with great resolve, we shall never condone human slavery. Human injury is not by any accord Reasonable, moral or beneficial. Rather, we are fully within Human Evolution. We hold that invitation up for all *by living the example*.

We see all the way through the bought off politics of human destroyment. And it is, just-that-simple. This is not rocket science.

- Modern government has devolved to become the only train-wreck on the planet large enough to induce *everyone* to search for the off button. *We have a lot of company in this regard.*

Therefore the whole concept of Evolution is a matter of perspective, namely obtaining a viewpoint from the beneficial and possible, as directly opposed to a self made prison of fear. Recall then why you are reading or hearing these words. Recall also that the function of this book is to change the perspective from the impossible to the possible, <u>for that step gains the Creator's co-authorship into empowerment.</u> *This is what every one of you demanded;* ***a way out of the blood soaked hell of modern politics.***

- Every objective then, is to take each next step forward with joy, resolve, vision, fun, self-respect and courage.

- Such method is Reasonable and workable.

- *This* **is why we have chosen this time to be alive**.

- We are the witnesses, benefactors, definers *and deliverers,* of Human Teleology.

- And *this* realization moves us one step further into the Human Event which is the utilization of **your** empowerment.

- Because this is *absolutely* The Dawn of Humanity.

Chapter Six

Vision and Joy

6. The key to Evolution is to actively contemplate the direction this Life Energy is headed. The method is to boldly envision **and emotionally enjoy** the vast benefits of Human Success above and beyond the science of human slavery. When this step is done in fun and delight, the pleasure and magnitude of the co-Creation process is in strength.

This part, being in the vibration, vision, emotional enjoyment *and moment* of an exquisitely beneficial outcome, is a one step, highly effective, co-Creation *technology*. I encourage you to use it because it works.

- All reality started with this nature of Creator vision.

- That would be the proof that it works.

Feel all the way, the beauty and grace of the beneficial outcomes of the Human Event. If you can accomplish this one step healing practice, feeling the essence of your personal choice, voice **and empowerment**, the human race has a future! Nothing then can stop Human Success. *Fear itself is vanished.*

- The controllers then, have lost their grip over your thoughts—**and thus over *you*.**

From that vision of great joy, the heart will compel any and all flight into Evolution even as your own power and magnificence of co-Creatorhood takes wing. Sense that unlimited beauty. <u>Live</u> that unlimited beauty. *Feel the Great Healing of all that is.*

- This is the causation *of an advanced living experience.*

- **As fully Reasonable, we believe human slavery no longer has either chance or location.**

If that exercise was thought and cheer expanding for you, then you had it correct on the first try. Such is just how easy and human friendly the Reasonable process is. At every level our process is about you empowering *you*. In understanding that, you understand Evolution, where life is sacred, **and there is no human slavery.**

Therefore this feeling of joy and harmony, this freedom and saneness causing process, is all about how tremendously fun moving into a vastly better life actually is. All powerlessness is an illusion. In fact, such is THE illusion—*a meager and dumb coin trick once seen as is.*

- As evolved, we choose to empower vision and disempower fear.
- And thus we break the chains of human slavery.

All oppression in fact resides upon a foundation of vapor. Seeing it for what it is erases the illusion. This leaves only Truth, human advancement, peace, freedom and harmony with Creator, Creation and fellow human.

With zero fanfare, apology or regret, this discourse in Evolution now firmly addresses the pathetic quagmire of modern politics. As you already know, it is *damned ugly*. We do not sugar coat it.

- *Nothing it seems, is as destructive as modern politics.*

Simple truth (and math) has conclusively proven the mainstream outcome of human slavery as likely the most immoral and corrosive chapter in human history. <u>Nearly all of you see it that way right now</u>. That collection of utter insanity has long earned its place as the most dishonest chapter *in all history of Creation,* bar none!   † And this is rule #3 of modern politics. †

From this moment forward, slavery is bereft of its candy coating. The reason for rummaging that garbage pit of hell is to recognize it *as it is*. Until one correctly understands the problem it cannot be repaired. "Reform" has wasted immense resource—to *no change or gain whatsoever*. **And that's the problem—cartel owned politicians!**

- It is in non-understanding, the dictatorship has managed to survive.

As you may have noticed, I freely interchange the ill understood terms of mainstream politics, modern politics, Marxism, and human slavery. The insight that clears up the understanding of the above terms is; the energy, the dishonesty, the intent, direction, M.O. and outcome are, *in spite of the labels*, **identical**. Subsequently, each <u>dictatorship</u> is interchangeable and indistinguishable when completed to its end. Every day this truth becomes more self-evident. Ergo, I toss those sick terms about like the fecal rags they **absolutely** are.

- Notice that I could have used the term 'bought off' and not changed the meaning of mainstream politics *in the slightest.*
- Nearly all American population over grade school age knows this.
- Nearly 100% of the world's adult population outside of America is *adamant* in this conclusion: Modern American politics is a *thoroughly purchased* **whorehouse**.
- The system can no longer hide its dishonor, damage, hate, failure, violence, theft, prostitution, insanity or ceaseless lying.
- *This is one of our chief advantages.*

Marxism and Fascism are only the technical gee-whiz labels. *Human destroyment is the actual output.* Anything other than that *specific* understanding of interchangeable results is directly born of, and constitutes the deception of modern politics. <u>It is very important to get that right.</u> *No healing can arise from continued ignorance.*

- *This* **clarification is the starting point of healing the human and world condition.**

True healing arises from Awareness and Compassion. Our humanity comes from the desire to right wrongs, to find justice, balance, peace and harmony—to make the world a better place. *The public has stated that establishment politics is clearly the opposite direction.*

- To actually be a healing source, a Lightworker, is to be Reasonable.

- We are in fact, the Bringers of the Dawn of Humanity *in no uncertain terms.*

The trade of the healer is to walk the fine line of awareness so the repair is accurately directed. Yet we do not dwell within the problem, for such error winds up empowering the illusion, *the opposite* of healing.

An important realization is that the non-healer and the unwell spend major time and thought *upon the problem.* This dwelling in fear and imparting of thought, attention and energy into fear, directly causes the manifestation of that which is <u>*not*</u> wanted. If such error describes you, read the above concept as many times as it takes until you fully get it. The resulting life improvement *will-be-drastic.*

Far more destructive than the above error, is that both the intent and product of television is to <u>massively amplify</u> strife and suffering. The result is to continuously draw the hapless viewer (multiplied by millions) into hate and fear. Such crap steals the viewer's attention and emotional energy and misdirects it to further perpetrate hate and fear. If you get that, then you understand that it is a self-generating, downward spiral. <u>*It's a set up*</u>. All of it, is the exception in hate and harm rather than the rule of peace and wellness. *It is designed to misuse **you**, to cause the old energy.*

Removing the power cord to the **idiot** [manufacturing] **box** represents for most, the single largest life improvement generally available on this planet today. Virtually all Human Evolution writers have made the same appeal. Such is the reason for that. Now you know. Removing one's excuses is the first step to sanity. It is definitely the first step to empowerment. You <u>*can*</u> unplug **the time and life theft device.**

Obviously, the solution is to place time, effort, thought, word, deed, vision, energy, skill and thankfulness into the positive and beneficial direction of the solution. The more inspired and enthusiastic, the better.

It is the God-within-ism, the enthusiasm, that is your personal empowerment and effectiveness multiplier. Here is where, as a result of an inspired upward jump in consciousness, your attention and intention can outweigh and outperform **the herd mentality**—trapped in the old and lower fear vibration. <u>*It is unlimited leverage in practice*</u>. It is God working within you.

- Every enlightened master in human history taught and exampled that same nature of empowerment.
- Inspiration is also the road sign from within, as a clear indication of the correct direction to proceed.
- This is why Freedom *vastly* outperforms slavery—it is because of freedom's vastly higher level **of consciousness**.
- Now you know.
- This is why Consciousness and Freedom are one and the same. Both exemplify *and are* human respect.
- This is why human slavery, suffering, non-consciousness and modern politics are one and the same—each is the absence of the Creator's light and wisdom. **Each is wrapped in human hate.**
- This is why we are now called to be the healers of humans, nations and worlds.

An appropriate definition of the Energy healer (of any nature), is one who uses the ability to hold vision and gratitude upon specific, yet omni-beneficial outcomes. Such is the trade, the joy, and the functional plane of the energetically fit and the healer.

- If you can do that at all, you are needed.
- Right <u>here</u> is your Grand opportunity to evolve this entire world.
- For many of you reading this, you have found the reason *why you are here*.
- See and feel the Grand absence of human slavery, and the *directly resultant* Grand Human Success.
- Envision and then live, your own co-Creatorhood.
- **Know that numerous other evolved humans are doing the same.**
- Taking action in concert, we cause the experience of the Evolution; *coming out of Slavery and poverty, and moving into Human Success.*

- And *that*, is Reasonable.

There you have the New Energy of Human Success. Such intent, attention, and action defines Human Evolution. This is an important realization. For the robust and the healer this is an everyday modality. For the truly advanced this is an every moment modality.

An equally important realization is that human freedom is the natural state of the human. It is human slavery that represents the extremely destructive *not* natural.

- Ask yourself which one **you** prefer.

Therefore, the distinction between normal and Natural is vital. Reasonable is therefore in the experiencing of that which is Natural. It is Creator Design. It is Human Teleology. It is your higher Consciousness.

- This is the Great Healing. *It is the Calling of the human race.*

Here are some suggested energetic steps in this magnificently rewarding area of Evolved living:

Step one: Carefully and intentionally lend **no support of any sort** [that rhymes] **to the Beast** (of mainstream politics)!

- This is the single most important stand the evolved human can take.
- This first step is an *exquisitely clear* case of **"Learn not to burn"**.
- This is likely the clearest case of learn not to burn *in human history*.
- Call this first step the smartest and most profitable move humanly possible.

- As a double bonus, this *specific* shift demonstrates that you can no longer be taken as a fool.

- This move demonstrates that you are awake, aware **and shall no longer endorse human slavery.**

- Anything other than this condition is by now, a *painfully obvious* total loss.

- If you are reading this, you **are**, smarter than the total loss trap of mainstream politics.

- That's why *you* are reading this.

This move also comes down to both arithmetic and profit. By not supporting the professional thief, that leaves money in your pocket and your life force intact. This is so as the mainstream voting record at any level is hell bent *in a **very** fanatic sense*, directly upon stealing **your money**—and forcibly bringing ever larger parts of your life **to ruin**.

There is no part of your life that the mainstream political yeggman is not assigned to utterly destroy. It is the errand and means of human genocide. Today there are drastically fewer who cannot readily see and describe this operation.

- No!, is therefore the *only* answer.

- *Use it.*

B. Mentally see and feel the old energy as a closed and distant chapter. Or view it as swept away by awareness and truth. See it as shorted out and de-energized. Or observe it as vanished into nothingness. Or envision the old energy of human hate as flooded away with Light. This is precisely what we do. Or do all of the above. Or, do whatever celebrates you that is legal and harms none.

- Common sense is booting modern politics out the door even as we speak.
- An army of people are now 'forward assisting' that departure.
- **This plainly instructs us: The Evolution *is in full progress!***

    C. Then quickly move into the harmonic, human compatible feeling of Human Evolution, *our existence without human slavery.*

    See and feel your benefit in an evolved world with far less oppression in it. Picture your model of success and abundance <u>*in the absence of the modern political model of engineered human destruction*</u>. For example, what would it feel like to triple or quadruple your take home pay in value? That may turn out to be a prime example. See the difference between the old energy of enforced failure and the New Energy of empowered success. Enjoy the *feeling* of your empowerment.

- This advanced existence we now know is possible, necessary, welcome, appropriate, underway, **and Creator guaranteed.**
- It is Human Teleology. It is unstoppable. And we give thanks.

    D. Intentionally dwell in, bask in, and explore in every direction, the emotion of true evolution and empowerment. We thus energize and co-Create that unlimited beauty, grace and harmony. Explore that world again and again and again. Carve out, and deeply enjoy your slice of Heaven as often as possible. *Now expand it again and again.*   <u>That's</u> how it's done!

    E. Do not then, lend any part of the old energy a second thought.

    The same instant the old energy is chased out of your life, it is gone. You then are the healer *and the restored.* You are now the hologram of the

New Energy. No force can stand against your Light and Power of knowing that truth. **The great illusion of powerlessness is now smashed and gone.** You may now celebrate. *You,* are the transforming consciousness.

This combination instructs your subconscious *and the world*, that you are 100% done with being jerked around by the nose, as so many are, by a gang chain of filthy, honorless, hate centered, Monoparty and purchased <u>outright</u> lies. By freeing yourself from that cesspit *from hell,* you gain the self-respect and dignity you are worthy of.

- And you *are,* fully worthy of that evolution.

F. **Invest in your own future. It is by far the most Reasonable investment in existence.**

- And it is so.

The old, representing a hellish nightmare at every turn or government in general, defines the archetype of death, suffering and dying, and of squalor, bullying, continuous hassle and constant loss. What future is that? One hundred years of sordid and sorry mainstream policy has caused that violence saturated tribulation. The catch is that you are *the everyday pay dirt and punching bag* for every misfeasance possible. Such purchased virulence makes pap and nullitude of every known moral and value. That however is the entire world *and definition*, of modern politics.

- When mainstream politics can be correctly described as Satan's personal scapegrace, then it is time **to end it.**

In stark contrast, our platform process allows everyone voice and vote—a respect not elsewhere found. Our process advances the redeeming <u>E</u>nergy of human freedom. Evolution itself can be charged with your perspective and participation. You can now directly cause Human Success **with membership**, the all important exponing of voice into real-world *empowerment.*

- This do, for it is Consciousness placed into reality.

- There is a simple formula Reasonable goes by: *Membership equals empowerment.*
- We use this formula because it works. It is *your* empowerment.

To provide a mental picture of the importance of freedom, the following quote is from *The Code* by Tony Burroughs, a book I gift out and recommend. "We are the ones who must step forward, with courage and dignity, and set our course for freedom and abundance. We must come to understand; that we didn't come here to be enslaved or to live under a dark cloud of debt. True freedom and the abundance that goes along with it—is as close as our next thought. It's time now, for all of us who long to experience our highest calling to reach out for it, and grab hold with all our strength, and to cherish it for the gift that it truly is."

- *In regard to Evolution, human freedom is correctly observed to be THE single product, more so than any other in the full span of human history, that sells itself.*

- We call it Reasonable.

- ***It is, and we are, the Human Event.***

Chapter Seven

What Was and What Is

7.   The concepts presented here are not only New in human ascendancy, they are also new in time. We are addressing platform planks into Human Success; yet none appear at the re-birth of that which is moral, Reasonable, common sense, beneficial, workable, livable and American.

In trust for you, there are no shove it down you, preset, 'for your own good', bullroar and hidden Marxist, pie in the sky, half baked—politician cartel, and banker serving **doublespeak**. Neither are there any of their sunken, dead end, morally empty, dishonest, purchased and wacked out <u>spin fests</u> **unerringly advancing violence, poverty and slavery**.

- We have left that domain to the mainstream.
- And they have unabashedly, made it their home!

Being more Reasonable, and honest, and American, we gladly honor your IQ, experience and intuition. In contrast, by way of do as we claim integrity, we honor you as Reasonable. Such event and intent is indeed <u>N</u>ew, very new.

The whole Reasonable process of upholding The Three Truths of Human Evolution is live, now, inspired, real and organic. It emanates from possibility itself. Should you wish a Reasonable goal, or to state it just so, or to move it about in status, you cause it to be. The Energy is of your ownership. It ever was.

- The whole Reasonable concept is your real-world empowerment at every level of experience.
- **There is no excuse for anything less than that.**

Should you wish the experience of Human Success composing the Evolution, then you choose it. The Key; is simply the choice to Be. Shakespeare told us that also, both instructions being of the same <u>E</u>nergy.

Numerous masters have pointed out the co-Creation process of the hologram. Healing results from discernment, <u>followed by defining decision</u>. In this case, powerful healing flows from Is-ness, that which **Is**.

- "Become the change you wish to see."

Mahatma Gandhi gave us the same instruction, **and for the identical cause of Freedom.** *These are the very specific directions as to how the hologram of Creation works.* Here is where gaining the mindset of Being human, as a result of defining decision, <u>makes all the difference there is</u>.

Much of that difference then flows from our unwavering action to co-Create the condition of human. From such life defining decision backed by resolute determination, all doors will swing wide open for you to Co-Create your Self. And who you are is Human, *should you make that decision.*

- The key is: *The decision* **is the technology.**

Consider that Creator sourced and directed Energy into Consciousness to be multiplied by the thoughtful, informed, alert, aware, **Humanitarian**, and determined individuals who have made the same Human defining decision to be Free. Therein is created Human Success.

- **This is the Creator Consciousness Humanitarian** *Choice.*
- **It is expressed through the Humanitarian** *Code.*

Hopefully none screw up and slip backward into the illusion and destitution of the cesspit of mainstream political **unconsciousness.** Such seduction is nothing other than a cheaply appointed **rat trap.** We now know that trap snaps violently shut upon the neck, wallet, *and humanness* of the asleep and unaware. Call that the world's *gaudiest* trap.

Here is where the power of an aware decision is more effective than most folks can fathom. As it turns out, the aware decision is the source of all human empowerment. It gives the hands of Creation employment. And that momentum is begun *immediately.*

Goethe and the Marine Corps in their own way, instruct that "all providence conforms to the firm decision." Now you know how any successful person became that way.

- This also teaches us that virtually nothing is impossible, including Freedom. **And this is, The Worldwide Evolution.**
- **True humanity, Reasonable teaches, awaits only the decision only you can make.**

Should one wish to continue in oppression and the unabated political lie science of omni-destroyment, that is equally as easy. The half-life trick there is to stop Creator Consciousness flowthrough. ...And then allow the null consciousness of television to dictate your level of life experience. We do however respectfully ask you to observe what those two very common standards have so far produced: **It is not freedom or humanity.**

In the contrast of being Life Energy, Reasonable, the direction and experience of Consciousness, asks that every goal honor and uphold Human Evolution, the direction of Freedom and humanity. Our Life process is the creation, in realization and experience, our *vastly* greater potential and membership into the fully alive, fully awake and fully human.

Reasonable then, is defined as Integrity. Our whole process and Mission is being and living that Integrity. **We do that which honors Life.**

Often we employ large letters to designate that which is from Source such as Inspiration, Consciousness, Freedom, and Evolution, all the same from that View. Let's include Respect, Love, Laughter, Kindness, Joy, Harmony, Health, Wholeness, Prosperity, Success and Freedom, as they are One and the same. They are utterly inseparable.

That paragraph was required to clean up the grand confusion about freedom. It is a pernicious confusion carefully designed by the tailors of woe to reduce freedom to only a word, **lest we forget our heritage as human**. Human, is a condition and experience *of oppression free existence.*

For example, pull freedom away from any other Source quality, and the scant crumbs that are "allowed" by some Marxist decree of infliction to remain, quickly shrink to become so hollow and shallow as to be rendered effectively non-existent. Call that devil's process now decoded and sorted out by intent and results, *both of which are human slavery.* Such is THE example of **absence** of the Creator's Light and Consciousness.

- We have thus *correctly* defined all mainstream politics.

Somewhere within Evolution, we shall transition to Human, that which is free. Let's examine the inverse: **Slavery fails to define any part of human.**

- Does the condition of slavery feel humane or human like to you?
- We feel the same way.
- That's why we are Creator Sourced and Centered **Humanitarians.**

Frederick Douglass is absolutely correct, probably now more than ever. *He correctly understood the foundation of Evolution.* From there, we have the formula for human success: **It is not additional slavery.**

Most of us have been rote instructed that we are [small h] human, that meaning not necessarily either free or worthy of freedom. Yet we have endless spiritual experiences within the vision of freedom. But, within this limited paradigm and illusion, the shoe is on the wrong foot isn't it? Does this not explain the painful limping as opposed to bounding forward?

Spiritually speaking, that was no pun. One of the many problems in the non-human model is that God gets waxed out of the picture and replaced by something with no care or concept of that which is human. It becomes 'lost' that human and freedom are one and the same. Where in the paragon of iniquity, is the Truth that an individual cannot be one without the other?

- *Pull freedom, and there remains no human.*
- This is the precise process by which humans are devalued to meat, fit only for injury, robbery, servitude, extortion and slaughter.
- **That is precisely where mainstream politics throws <u>YOU</u> under the bus without a second thought.**

I think, that in general, modern society does not instruct the truth of what we are, or of that which we are composed. Yet, a society that does not know, cannot be held to blame. In its spiritual poverty, it is unaware of its poorness—or the riches so easily available. Therefore, the Living Truth of the Creator Connection, or Spirit if you prefer, shall be conveyed forward here: It is freedom, for what is slavery, _except human hate?_

Within the Reasonable process, that is to say the Human Evolvement process, we become first that which is worthy of sacred Freedom. To do that, we make the defining decision to be human. Secondly, we become Human, that which is in the condition and experience of Freedom, that which is not slave or serf or vassal or in non-voluntary servitude. To manifest that condition, we practice, are, think, speak, act *and vote* **human**.

To think such is any part of mainstream voting presently, is to think in grievous error, for it is not. That highway to hell has run the wrong direction for well over a century. It is insanity to think that such a clearly marked road to ruin will go in any other direction than every sign has clearly shown us.

- Perhaps the objective is to learn how to read*!*

- Mainstream politics has now come to define itself as the mindless juggernaut of finely purified defilement.

- **Mainstream politics is that great march into the oven while plainly viewing the outcome.**

Within the mainstream voting procedure, we have made the unwitting error to permit, continue, and advance human slavery. The textbook insanity comes in with the realization that it is us, upon whom the oppression rests. Yet because of that realization, it may now heal. As it does, this is **the Great Healing** into human and planetary wholeness, wellness, harmony *and sanity*.

Modern politics has turned all of our elections into Chinese fire drills that serve no actual purpose whatsoever. Right now, our "election" process is steadily being exposed the most obvious deception of modern mankind. That of course was Satan's plan all along, *again defining mainstream politics*.

What happens when we put God into the picture, when we put the shoes of Foundation on the correct feet? Let's contemplate that for a while:

I have found that in the same Glorious instant we make the first true Creator Connection within our own personal Evolution, the Light comes on, and the Big realization hits: We are Spirit, an Energetic part of Creator and

Creation, having a human experience!   We are Daughters and Sons, Offspring, Heir and portions of God!

- Are we then worthy of Freedom?

I would suggest that the non-reason the human race yet permits and practices slavery, and in fact vote concatenated our own destroyment, is that each of us has not made the right decision to respect and represent **Life.**

- As Reasonable, we do respect and represent Life.

- And, we know why we do.

- **We respect ourselves as Human.**

- That my friend, *is Empowerment.*

Chapter Eight

Some General Guidelines

8. Platform guidelines as follows, are provided to assist you equal to the amount observed to achieve Reasonable goals: Allow the First Energy to be **The Three Truths of Human Evolution**, for such is Reasonable. Allow the same Code Energy to be equal respect and treatment for all humans, for anything Reasonable lives no other possibility. With that Creator Consciousness and View, Healing begins.

From that pattern, we live a deep respect for all Life, personal property, Nature and Resource, for that is fully Reasonable. We also state each goal with clarity, and minimum words simply because we are Reasonable. As Reasonable, we observe that falsehood and deception are typically very complex, requiring endless, circular, vague, and infolded laws that dispense political favor through violence unequally among people. We observe that truth is simple, principled, honest, and self-evident. It is easy to state and easy to understand. It is fully grounded in cooperation and common sense and applies to everyone equally.

- These are the Truths Reasonable lives, enjoys, benefits from, and instructs at all times.

Notice well that each Truth above is *patently* the opposite of modern politics. This is a key concept to take into awareness as it proficiently exposes the unlimited hypocrisy now defining mainstream politics. It also exposes the unconscionable *and* unending abuse, fraud, theft and outright malevolence intrinsic to that entirely Marxist-Fascist slavery *consignment*.

- **Mainstream politics has come to define itself as the endless festival** *celebrating personal injury.*

A Reasonable Truth is, that the foremost key to human and planetary continuation is a new way of thinking, even while we suffer political conditions and abuses that directly and direly threaten all life on earth. Therefore, Reasonable is defined as informed and aware humans who have made the decision to uphold the conditions of Life.

This decision to thrive includes every aspect of human and planetary life as a fully integrated whole, viz an energetic, biological, practical and spiritual Oneness. Our existence is utterly inseparable from the fabric of Life itself. Reasonable is One with Nature, One with all life and One with the planet and everything on it. It is our viewpoint *and way of Life*. We intend enlightened balance and harmony with All that Is, all the time.

- This excludes the practice of the worldwide cartels.
- It also excludes the practices of their prostitution force of mainstream politics.
- Reasonable is therefore stewardship, balance and harmony by way of enlightened awareness.
- This includes everything within the realm of human contact.

Reasonable recognizes that energetically, anything and everything performed outwardly is reflected in kind. Therefore in careful consideration and harmony do we choose our actions.

Reasonable action enslaves nothing and no one. It does not produce cruelty to any life form. We do not wish such old energy to be upon our hands or heads, or reflected within our own experience. *The Reasonable human being is smarter than that.*

- This is also a key to ending Slavery by no longer being its source.
- This answers *why* the practice of the cartel is not sustainable.

Anything Reasonable is the Energy of respect. This enlightened Energy is given so that it may also be received, for it is the Creator's Love and Harmony placed into experience. It matters not the object of kindness, be it air, earth, plant, animal, human, or any other form **of Creator Experience.** That which matters, is the intent of harmony or not harmony—*that we likewise experience in equal measure.*

- The Laws of Creation and Nature are simple, just as they are inviolable.
- We honor that.

- It is the politics of man that are intentionally complex enough to hide every manner of corruption and hypocrisy, *just as they now do.*

That which is not working or workable, or Reasonable, is the lie fest of counterfeit morality through legislation. Such legerdemain has so far produced only deeply twisted, and political power serving obliques, *strictly* in name only, of "morality".

- *The problem is, that it is not actually related to morality.*

- Without exception, all old energy can be traced directly to a kickback, the one and only modern political 'moral'.

- Such underhanded dispensing of economic political favoritism has thus far murderously damaged its own advertised cause.

So far, the crooked politics of "environmentalism" or any "morality", *the same as all modern politics*, has been a study in the firestorm destruction of common sense and truth. That such debacle has utterly destroyed its own *stated* cause, is merely a by-product of the insatiable fury to advance human slavery through the process of **predatory deception.**

- This is done unerringly under the bellicose and intellectually offensive banner of feel-good politics.

What has now become obvious, is that the old energy of self-serving, grandstanding and self-congratulatory politics, {*Is there any other kind?*} has caused the opposite outcome of the slick and inverted sales pitch virtually every time it has ever been employed.

- All of the above **intention to deceive** is <u>THE</u> defining disposition of all mainstream politics.

- It is the dead opposite of advertised, **no matter the advertisement!** (Nearly 100% of you made this statement.)

- And this is the function of all modern politics—selling human slavery **by way of deceit,** *as purchased by international cartel.*

Any exceptions are indeed rare, and pretty much limited to politically ruined economy and higher taxes in the same breath. Although quite true, notice well that the proposed "solution" as ever, is **the exact,** wrong course of action for the stated condition. Yet again, as if many trillion lost samples were somehow not enough, this proves the outcome of all old energy in a nutshell; dishonesty and destroyment. Thank you for correcting me by adding theft and slavery—*which is the actual point.*

- A reasonable observation is that any initiation of force or the use of fraud or theft is not, nor can it be, a sustainable condition. This fact has been proven to be without exception.

That is human slavery. The key is that it has not in any way, been openly named as such. Yet the tyranny of force and fraud can be *temporarily* propped up **through *ever increasing brutality*.**

- This is precisely what we now observe throughout modern government.
- **The fact remains that it is human slavery.**

The fraudulent practices of modern politics as excused by some poorly defined, feel good 'morality', have notoriously and savagely retrograded nearly every paradigm addressed by government in any of our lifetimes.

- History has shown nothing more defined or consistent than that!

Our Reasonable methods are the *direct opposite* of the standard political skullduggery, graft, corruption, back room deals, fraud, hate, theft, backstab, **legal witchcraft**, and ruination *that now define modern politics.*

- We are the New Energy that serves Humanity, Earth and Life.

All told, the sum of modern government evinces a clear design of no respect for, and no clue or care of that which is human or humane. To that list could well be added common sense, proper accounting, responsibility of any nature, and that which is just, honest, beneficial or functional. Tragically it seems the same list gains a new characteristic daily, as forced backed political abuse of power has grown into an aggressively malignant cancer.

Every portion of the old energy serves to divide, conquer, and subduct the human species, a task that it has carried out to perfection. Where force cannot work fraud has. Where fraud fails violence is employed. All old energy is founded upon two themes; the amplification of the illusion of separation, and the dividing, conquering and continuously maiming of the human race to keep our species away from Evolvement. Such inhuman subjugation is readily observed at both the intent and results.

For each intent of injury to both human and nature by old energy, there exists its counter, the intent and outcome of wellness. For each political harm possible, The Reasonable Process draws from Consciousness, and produces the beneficial condition of harmony, the opposite of that harm.

For every falsehood produced by modern politics, there exists an inner intuitive truth. For each political insanity, there exists its counter Energy of common sense. For every illusion of powerlessness, there exists a re-discovery of our *actual* ability. For every systemized lie of separation, there is a thousandfold evidence found in the Truth of commonality.

A Reasonable start begins there, for such is the foundation of healing—and seeing right through the house of illusions of modern, hate, theft and injury centered politics. The same moment the big illusion, the illusion of separation falls, the remaining mountains of illusion defining modern politics, begins to internally vanish as well for total lack of foundation. At that moment, <u>realization</u> catches up to, and meets <u>intuition</u>. And the Truth is seen.

From that moment of the Creator's Glory and Light, modern politics can be seen the same as the crooked and cowardly warden at Shawshank. From there, mainstream politics is only something to escape **and <u>forever be done with</u>**. {*That was the clearly stated top of the line wish for everyone.*}

Thankfully, the New Energy methodology gives us all, the remarkable insight that most of the escape from slavery is **internal**. It is as close as our next decision: *Am I human or not?*

Let's examine that devil's illusion of separation and a touch of the ten thousandfold greater common ground—from red blood to the ever present inner drive **by Creator Design** toward Freedom. Let us see if we can yet identify the "need" for repulsive, twisted, psychotic, immature, power starved, abusive, habitually lying and lifetime condescending mad-people found with clockwork regularity throughout modern politics. That Satanism has and uses tactics from landmines to NBC weapons *and now medical weapons*, all of human destruction—and *strictly* political origin and deployment.

Reasonable is, and examples, that we exist in a world of people who all strongly desire the same peace, prosperity, dignity, respect, freedom, safety and Creator Connection. Most of us now see, that modern politics has delivered the opposite of that.

In our natural politically unmolested state, we all desire to honor each other, Earth and Nature. All of us have much the same errors, challenges, hopes, wishes, dreams, and the perpetual attraction toward Evolution that is our Creator Connection.

Every individual needs, and is willing to give appreciation, respect, kindness, friendship and companionship. We desire at heart to count, to make a positive difference in the human and planetary condition. The Reasonable Movement is that opportunity *and vehicle*. **Reasonable is the example and present worldwide leadership into human Evolution.**

At our core truth, in an environment free of force and fraud, no rational human wishes to harm another, and remarkably few do so anyhow.

Fundamentally all humans desire, and will attempt any peaceful means of conflict resolution prior to considering methods of proven fewer returns. This process is now made magnitudes easier by seeing through both the illusion of separation, no matter how media amplified, and the politics *or* hate centered religions financially dependent upon, *and therefore relentlessly advancing the* **outright lie** *of person to person separation.*

- We sense the potential of the human experience being far more harmonious than it is.

- Knowing what stands in the way of that, *we can now proceed to rectify it.*

- **You are now learning the *correct* directions of how to do that.**
- Human Teleology moves us out of the experience of system programmed strife, and into the evolution of unity and cooperation.
- This is a slight taste of the cornucopia of the benefits of Evolution.
- And it is so.

The function of the mainstream media is the opposite of that. You knew that. A very easy observation is that the media's function is to report the negative. We find that not only does the media strictly serve the cartel, the media *is* the cartel of human slavery. Unless something is deemed as meaningless foppery, it will not be reported as good.

The negative reporting arrives with several functions: Fear and the illusion of separation are primary among them. Then comes the tin horn blowing of the politico with some fantastic *but standard*, statistical maneuver defying even the laugh test. ...And *that* gets broadcast as a "positive". The person relying on the mainstream media thus <u>gets sold down the road</u> only to be sheered of even more of their life force *by the system of human slavery*.

This sets up the second "positive'. Here we have political promises and sloganeering that defy both the laugh test *and* the truth test. ...And the mentally zombied mainstream voter buys right into it time after time. ...And will again the next time—just like the last time and the time before that.

We see different names and faces—**and the same sorry ass lies** over and over and over. The real irony is that as long as it is 'their' side doing the lying, it's ok. In fact, the outcome may *never* be classified as a lie if it is their side doing the lying. "Read my lips" wasn't a lie. "The era of big government is over" wasn't a lie. "Mission Accomplished" wasn't a lie. "Hope and change" wasn't a lie. And "Whatever the shit" won't be a lie either. The mainstream political lying machinery extends in both time directions. **<u>The lying will continue for as long as mainstream politics exists</u>.**

So much for the obvious. The false negative sets up the false positive. That truth tests. <u>*Seeing the illusion ends the illusion*</u>. ...And now we move *forward* in truth:

Every human desires to be loved, heard, understood and trusted, just as every *AWARE* human on this earth desires vastly smaller **and greatly more truthful government.** All of this, including the desire for freedom itself straight from our DNA, defines the New Energy, the direction of Human Evolution. It is the direction of a vastly better, brighter expression of safety, peace, grace, wholeness, cooperation, dignity, prosperity and harmony.

All of us cherish our own family, culture, creed and Nation. We are now rapidly evolving to honor, celebrate, understand and appreciate our minor, and mostly language only, surface differences. This is also the New Energy—and *none too late!*

- A dress code on the outside does not change the DNA *or the ever present drive toward freedom found on the inside*.

- It is that realization that forms an enlightened relationship to our fellow humans.

- Reasonable instructs these truths of upward Evolution *by living them*.

If even one precious human can climb the gentle slope of Awareness away from the old thought cesspit of *system programmed* fear, division, animosity and strife, then the Way is made easy for others. The Path of Consciousness becomes brightly lit by the joy of escaping human slavery and its deeply underhanded politics and religions *of purchased divisiveness.*

- That Truth is immaculately Reasonable.

The whole key is in being human, worthy of humanity, as much as it is in the process of becoming fully human. We become evolved by leaving behind the sorry energy of hate and slavery within our own past. Such is not overpowered by force or lawyerly acumination. It is simply recoded and left behind as errors made and lessons learned.

- *Worthiness can be salvaged from any error—under the condition that the awareness created by the error is subsequently converted into action leading to an improved experience.*

The same moment one is cleared of human hate, <u>the politics of human hate has lost its grip over that individual</u>. Human Ascension is gained through this understanding and process of respect, common sense, honesty and dignity; the Creator's model of Human Success.

- This is the Great Healing. *It is now defined.*

Our process begins with and simply is Self-respect, ending that which harms humans. **The whole function of Evolution is ending that which harms humans.** Our Calling is to provide and live the pathway of human safety, respect, and Success, *for such is the Human Event.*

What person does not deeply desire peace, harmony and Freedom, with the prosperity that goes with it? Yet, these are the very qualities mainstream politics must not, and cannot provide. *It is not in their interest to do so.* The reason why; is that mainstream politics is the concubine and boot lick to *vicious* international cabal, cartel and monopoly. This has held true for numerous generations. This is also the True Bill from virtually everyone guided to read this. *The standard politician will not escape this.*

- How else do they get elected when every election is purchased?

Technically, it is a worldwide corporate aristocracy. However that does not in any way modify the fact that it is human slavery. It is simply purchased politics. At that point, *any* name given to the process is irrelevant.

- Any name given to the damnation it produces is also irrelevant.

- **The intent, methodology and results are human slavery.** *It is now rapidly approaching human genocide.*

Mainstream political leadership is keenly aware of that fact. Nothing is plainer. The mainstream voter is precisely the opposite, at thought and perception, thinking up is down, in is out, good is bad, and every insane televised falsehood is gospel. It would be a joke of cosmic proportions, <u>except for the injuries done at voted gunpoint.</u> Those injuries are now contesting for the most depraved, senseless, damaging and widespread in all human history.

<u>Modern politics requires division and strife to exist</u>. This is true even if nearly all of it is manufactured—in order to bring forth a deeply perverted and authoritarian 'utopia'. Modern politics *is* division and strife. All of it is intended toward ever greater oppression that, by its actual name **is human slavery.** We have witnessed this direction as having virtually no exception.

- It is the *manufactured* division and strife that creates the illusion of the 'need' for ever greater oppression.

The oppression must be preceded by the televised illusion of division, difference, animosity, strife, and warfare. **The manufactured divisiveness is seen as the 'cause', and the dystopian oppression is seen as the 'cure'.**

- <u>That is how the entire present system works</u>.
- We now know the results. <u>**You**</u> have placed the realization of that process into this book.
- These realizations are present so that the procedures of human slavery may be seen **as is**.
- This is how we stop human genocide, **by *crushing* the illusions standing behind it.**

We also see **profoundly corrupt** bureaucratic decrees backed by nearly unlimited brutality. We are evolving to understand this model of savagery with clarity. We also experience this process with ever increasing frequency. It is now the norm associated with nearly any government interaction beyond the surface. The term "jack booted thugs" was heard *routinely*.

The typical path to such understanding is by way of government lawlessness and injuries from that lawlessness. Most of you reading this have had that experience and often more than once. This condition was extremely consistent across America. The contributors to this book were adamant in this regard: Government lawlessness was the standout theme in every part of America and is heard in virtually any daily conversation.

- Many more will suffer and perish until it is stopped cold.

To see what is in the mainstream politician's interest, one needs to look no further than the endless flood of perfectly un-American laws of the last 150 years. The anti-personnel intent of virtually all of those laws is less human freedom, ever more government intervention, expense and insanity—and the directly resulting sharp increase**s** in governmental waste, fraud, theft, total failure, violence, lawlessness *and abuse.* **This list is now accepted as the singular definition of modern government.**

The above anti-human conditions are now openly run away and unarguably progressing worse. Sadly, the jury is in on this. All doubt has been removed. The chief paradigm shift here is that we are no longer in denial of the above condition. This observation is also consistent across America. *That is why it is in this book.*

- Fortunately for the human race, the ivory tower of political old thought is falling apart at all speed.

- That we shall celebrate—and hasten.

- It appears to be a matter of human race survival.

- Sadly, it is of sheer **and all consuming desperation,** that modern politics is, and does, *exactly what we experience today*.

- This we shall understand—and end.

- This also appears to be a matter of human race survival.

My editors will kick my rear end for this many adjectives, but here it goes:

The squalid and thorough collapse of mainstream politics is irretrievable, not reversible, unrecoverable, well earned like nothing else, greatly just, consummately appropriate, highly welcome, amazingly overdue, **and absolutely final.** Whoooo! I liked it. *I'll bet you do to.*

- That condition also sums up many years of well known and clearly understood, *but not yet televised,* public knowledge.

- The above condition is as observation of that which is. It is not a guess of that which might be.
- As such condition is phenomenally human and planetary beneficial, it is therefore eminently Reasonable.

The beauty of it all,

is that you have the satisfaction of causing it.

The observations behind the mainstream political implosion are cogent and practical:

1 The human race is done with being fed political lies—while at the same time, every day brings forth yet another batch of outright, deliberate, hideous, condescending ***and asinine*** lies.

2 The human race is done with excessive government, now beyond the extreme, and done with ever growing government sourced abuse.

3 The human race is done with insanely excessive taxes, many of which have proven of little or no benefit, often causing flagrant degeneration of the causes the taxes were advertised to repair.

4 We are done with the purchased terrorism of modern government.

5 *We are humans, not horsemeat!*

The condition of being human is self-ownership. The condition of human slavery is not self-ownership, whether by force, fraud, or the complete anarchy of some invisible bureaucrat in charge of dispensing or withholding their personal and illegal extrapolation of political bullying.

- How many of those bureaucrats have not proven to be two faced, fully comatose, arrogant, hopelessly inept, one way, anal, and/or the usual; ***devastatingly lazy.***
- This observation was unanimous.

- How many government employees seem to have a singular mission of causing as much suffering, hate and discontent, misery, injury, theft, strife, malice and abuse as humanly possible?
- How many times have you said that?
- How much more of it shall we incur *prior to ending it?*

    The top levels of modern politics own a keen understanding that fraud and fear are their weapons of imprisonment. **They use them well**. However, fraud and fear *can only influence the mind*. It is <u>the awareness</u> of the manipulation tactics of fraud and fear <u>that clears them away</u> for the imaginations they are composed of.

- **The human race is in the business of ending human slavery. Indeed, that is why we are human!**
- Through escaping the mental and spiritual chains of force and fraud within ourselves first, and then others through sharing this information, we transmute human slavery into the success, safety, self-ownership, sanity and the livability *we now create*.

    The empowerment transition takes place at the <u>lifetime abandonment</u> of mainstream politics. It is a liberating experience. Envision it as the cutting away of the brutal and inhumane mental, spiritual, financial, and physical chains of human slavery.

- For it is *absolutely* so.

    The transition is an enlightening experience. It is the ***knowing,*** you can no longer be fooled by the hate, fraud, malice, dishonor and abundantly proven *intentional destructiveness* that constitutes mainstream politics.

We encourage you to test the Human transition and see what is meant. What is felt? What becomes revealed when inner, outer and Higher self portions work in harmony to produce self-ownership?

As it is both human and world beneficial, we call it The Reasonable Experience. It is no longer living in fear. It is your vision, causation and ownership of a vastly better, brighter, freer and advanced human *experience*. It is *very* Reasonable indeed.

- "To understand reality, one must be willing to give up unreality."

- This quotes Vernon Howard and many other Masters of Truth.

Precisely that, is the ticket into Human Advancement. By seeing through, and giving up, the lies and unabated destructiveness of modern politics, we walk the pathway into self-ownership and Human Success.

By definition and practice, the Energy of transmuting human slavery into Human Success is Reasonable. Should you hold the outcome of self-ownership to be desirable, you are invited to join us in membership, *thus producing your empowerment.*

We strongly believe this is a mighty good deal. This deal is a great deal better than the old "deal", that was no deal at all—*and you know it!*

Your life essence is simply **not valid** in the old energy, again defining that model. That was the "deal" you were dealt by the system. It makes **zero** difference, which meaningless large animal symbol is employed to swindle the eye teeth out of mainstream, partisan, hate blinded *and revenge centered*, politically uneducated **dingbats**. The mainstream Uniparty swims in time proven hypocrisy. *It is time to provide its well earned drop kick.*

Thankfully, you knew the zero difference beyond any shadow of doubt. <u>This was the most consistent theme across America</u>. It is an amazingly high percentage. The difference between yesterday and today is that the above condition is in writing. You put it there. Now it can heal. The mainstream dog and pony show *crap* **is where we employ the word; NO!**

- Nearly everyone I spoke to felt the same way.

- You also know you are not alone in causing Evolution.
- **Turn the mental table, and gladly feel the Empowerment.**
- Such Energy, is a Reasonable gift to you *for being awake!*

In 20-20 retrospect, it is easy to observe that mainstream politics is filthy, broken, miserable, hollow, shallow as spit, base, cankered throughout, utterly destructive, *and consummately disingenuous*. Such condition is scientifically known as dishonorable. Be it friend or foe, history has spoken with an authority *as not ever before.* It's ok to quote that, because the Truth belongs to everyone.

- Any modification to politics that **escapes** the constant mainstream partisan lying, theft and hate, will result in upward motion.
- *Evolution is the only and last direction left untouched by* **the utter wretchedness** *of mainstream politics.*

There is virtually no one who cannot accurately describe the causes *and results* of mainstream politics. Strangely, this also includes the partisan illusion of sides. One 'side' calls the other side insane, purchased, dishonest, morally bankrupt, prostituted, self-centered, dishonorable, controlled, brain washed, **genetically incapable of accepting responsibility** {proven a thousand times} *and ritualistically destructive*.

- Right now the public agrees with both **'sides'**!
- The public now sees in overwhelming majority, that both "sides" are identical, identically poisonous and identically repugnant.
- *If you have achieved this realization, and you undoubtedly have, congratulations* **you are part of the solution.**
- Thank you for being awake.
- **Right here is your grand opportunity.**
- *This book provides the long awaited solution to the very problem the human race has endured for generations.*

The anti-personnel <u>mainstream political outcome</u> smacks of an insanity that cannot be described if it is allowed to continue another moment. **We are looking human genocide <u>right in the face</u> if it is not stopped.**

- All across America, mainstream politics was described as *shockingly reprehensible*. A profusion of four letter words were employed virtually every time. The feelings ran strong.

- Consequently, much of the power lies in viewing our not-aloneness in *demanding* a vastly better expression.

- And we are doing precisely that. It is not overdue another moment. **It is delivered.**

The universe of mainstream politics is of human execration no matter which way it is hidden. The paradigm of slavery is rooted in the assumption that humans, *and particularly you,* are so dumb as to actually need to be relentlessly oppressed [and ultimately slaughtered] in a condescending manner identical to feedlot pork.

Every moment of television and all the way through school, we are rote instructed dire political falsehoods. Most of those untruths are so illogical and inane as to defy the imagination. In any other setting, they would be convicted in felony. The damage done would be the overwhelming evidence.

- Modern politics is not technically human slavery, it *is* human slavery.

- It takes a special mentality, <u>a consciousness seared with a hot iron</u>, to knowingly produce human genocide in trade for the next election.

- However, that's the case.

- **It is *precisely* how all mainstream politics functions.**

- Nearly all of you described that condition to a "T".

The real tragedy is this: When human hate is the only item on the political shelf, that is what is purchased. And right there is the problem; human hate. It is not so much a lack of thinking outside the box (of human slavery), **it is a lack of thinking at all.** The whole "deal" turns out to be the spiritual equal to following the witless throng—*directly into a burning building!* (*...through mindlessly believing the television*)

- And there you have the modern political paradox.
- America has clearly stated: Mainstream politics is the rabid marplot that needs to be put out of its stinkin' misery.
- Modern politics et al., is simply the soulless mercenary of an élite cartel, *centered directly in human destroyment.*
- Once we have that *correct* realization, we can walk away from that self made hell by leaving that error behind ***forever.***

Only through seeing, realizing, and embracing the reality of modern politics, can we then cause a different and better outcome. The river of de-Nile has yet to flow prosperity. It would seem that through enough experiencing of unbridled ruination, the definition of modern politics, one can then envision, appreciate, and cause salvation.

By understanding the politics of half-human, one can then demand full human. Through seeing that which does not work, we can then form a Mission—and experience what does work. Reasonable is in the transformation of human slavery, into the functional and workable. That means Human Success, ***the absence of human slavery.***

- There is the Cause: It is Human Teleology. It is who we ***are***.

The human race has again and again endured the experience of dissolute governance by corruption, fraud, misrule, theft, injustice, bad faith, bankruptcy, perfidy, malice, odium, ponzi and scam of every known invention. We have seen their wrenching failure, brutality, domestic terrorism, senseless violence and daily Judas kiss. We have experienced crooked and criminal governance that fails to understand or recognize Human Rights, common sense, decency, justice, equality, truth or mathematical principle.

We have witnessed endless bureaucracy fail to recognize their own law and for that matter, any law. Nearly any involved contact with government brings out this condition of anarchy. We have witnessed these repeated bureaucratic nightmares grow more profuse and more injurious by the day.

The readership has provided this author with an overwhelming preponderance of evidence. Such process is no longer the exception. It is the norm. *All doubt as to whether or not it is human slavery has been thoroughly removed*.

- Modern politics now stands convicted.

We have witnessed shame saturated governance replete with professional liars, thieves, swindlers and cowardly political felons. We see them engaged in every orgy of voted debauchery known.

We have seen public officials, both appointed and 'elected' with felony records indistinguishable from prison population. We have seen their willingness to lie and swindle without the slightest reservation. We see this evidence in profusion. We have witnessed them complicate our laws enough to render them meaningless. We have witnessed every hate, butchery, cold blooded murder and serial crime known performed under the color of law.

We have observed their life's mission to destroy the Constitution. We have observed them mouth human rights, yet destroy those rights with every single vote. We see these offences *daily*.

As needed, we have examined the roots, intents and mode of modern politics. This is not to in any way dwell upon the problem. Rather this examination is to identify human slavery and thus from Consciousness, its opposite, Human Teleology. *We view one, in order to see the other.*

We have caught mainstream politics with their hand in the cookie jar in unlimited felony violation of Oath of Office. The same goes for selling their soul to international cartel. The latter is the cause of the former. *This is the standard and defining mode of operation **of all modern politics***.

Marxist bent politicians often mouth the theatrical words of human respect, yet that is where it ends. It is their actions that tell the truth of the intent of human slavery. Thankfully we are no longer blinded by their various spins, lies and scam tactics—*most of which a monkey could see through*.

As human, we are keepers of the flame, the inspired creative fire that can never be extinguished. Each of us is an extremely powerful creator with a nearly unlimited ability to manifest once discovered. <u>This is the realization the system has striven for thousands of years to suppress</u>. Our Constitution with its exclusive focus on Individual Human Rights is the exception to the system. *It opposes the rule of history's oppression.*

To showcase the importance of this power and ability, *I shall provide its contrast:* All those in old energy have made a trade: It is the identical trade for the world's power that was offered to Christ. In that deal, that the mainstream politician gladly accepted, there was a trade off.

It is well to remember that The Devil could not make the offer of power unless it was *in his possession*. Now you know *who* has been running the political structures of the world. Now you also know ***how***.

The trade was the handed over ability to *manipulate*. The trade off was the loss of the ability to *create*. The trade itself is a severing of the Creator connection. This is done through the joining of various organizations who have as their central theme, the termination of Human Rights. You are the ones who told this author the names and methods of those organizations. We now have a much clearer understanding of their satanic intents, practices and outcomes. They are centered directly in human genocide.

This particular trade is consummated by the receiving of cartel sourced campaign finance. Presently, there are almost no exceptions within the world of mainstream politics. They have finagled cartel sourced bribes that, in grievous error, we call legal.

- Now you know the name of the mousetrap and its *correct* origin.

- The readership identified this game to near perfection <u>from intuition</u>, both *with and without knowing the details.*

Those in power who only have the ability to manipulate have throughout history, made every effort to ferociously suppress both the ability and far more importantly, <u>the realization of that unlimited ability,</u> of co-Creatorhood housed within all of us. *We have also just defined the function of Marxism.*

- Our job is to simply call the game of oppression (loudly)—***and be forever done with it.***
- <u>The benefits of ending oppression are safety and empowerment</u>.

The worldwide shift in consciousness is primarily in rediscovering the ability we had all along. *This means the human race is slipping the chains of Satanism that have run this world for nearly all recorded history.*

- With that, The American population has now judged the mainstream politician to be wholesale unfit to rule man or beast.
- *<u>This</u> realization is the transition into political **sanity**.*

The reason is this: Slavery, theft and injury is placed upon our backs with no regard, relief, or second thought. It is as if the human race were a personal pack mule to be cursed and cropped to blood.

Is the human race to be forever mendicant, beggars on our own land? Are we to forever be limited to the tasks of servility? Are we to forever suffer half wages and triple taxes? Is our every move and our every thought to be dictated to us by those who hold us in scorn clear to the point of seeing us broken and dead? Are we to suffer these things while our controllers **howl in laughter** at our willingness to put up with it?

Could it be of our own shame, that we continue to mislabel the intent and outcome of human slavery? Is such savagery made any the less savage by coy title, fluffed bow, *or the spew and swindle of talking heads?*

We have witnessed taxes go from small and bible sworn temporary, to concreted monstrosities of ten thousand misuses and an equal number of thefts. We have experienced unrestrained societal destruction through tens of thousands of anti-Constitutional laws. Each of these laws specifically protects the politically connected cut-throat monopolies of barbary, malevolence, ruination, slavery, murder, rape, poison and death.

We have seen our population imprisoned to a degree more than any other nation on earth. We are now spied upon to nearly the same degree. We have witnessed crimes of consciousness replace crimes of injury. We have witnessed our Freedom, our Life Force, and our Sacred Honor being thrown away to cause after cause indistinguishable from utter nonsense.

We have seen our future whimsically mortgaged into the unknown even as an unthinkable reckoning has been drawn to us by the bought off politics of human destroyment. We live these violations of soul, even as every day's news yields up new affirmations of an ever worse, and ever bolder **river** of thoroughly instituted government sourced abuses.

- The intent of subjugation now appears at once to be both omni-present and omni-sourced throughout modern government.
- *Who among us can stand and say; it is not so?*
- **Modern government has come to define itself as** *that great body of shame;* **producing slavery, violence and anarchy at the command of worldwide cartel.**
- The public now holds modern government as thoroughly convicted.
- You are now reading the results of a nationwide Grand Jury.
- Thank you for bringing this author into that awareness.

From the failure of slavery and its anarchy, rises the Awakening into the meaning of human. The New Energy is the transitioning of causation into an empowered existence of health, grace and wholeness. It is none other than THE Human Evolution. *It is the dawning of true humanity.*

- **There factually is, no greater kindness or benefit to the human or planet.**
- *Now,* is the moment we move from servitude to shareholder in the game of life.
- This is Human Teleology. It is who we *are*.

The beauty of the present increase in Consciousness and from that, the Humanitarian Code is this: Once an individual achieves awareness, they can never be stepped backward into ignorance. That is why we are the winning team. The math is in our favor. This is why it is Human Teleology: The Humanitarian Code is now and forever changing the human race from slavery to Success, from injury to Freedom and from illusion to Empowerment. **We, are the conduit of Creator Consciousness.**

- *Reasonable holds that it is time to awaken.*
- Freedom is inspired, whereas slavery is only suffered.
- Neither the human nor the planet has the option of ongoing political non-awareness.
- We can no longer abandon humanitarian thought processes.
- Slavery cannot be allowed to continue.
- *This is the reason we are here.*
- Most of you reading this know that, and we thank you.
- *As far as politics is concerned, Reasonable thinking holds that the only thing that should be deviled is eggs.*

Reasonable thinking cannot blame the ceaselessly corrupt politician for the famous non-attention of the general voter who in blindness of sleep, casts his or her own downfall to chains **and then**, finances their own destruction! For those yet the slightest bit offguarded by ever worse politics, now you know how it got that way. The professional liar only wheedles sidefaced up to that foolish, tragic, and as you know, utterly wasted mainstream non-vote. <u>Oddly, every political question presently in existence, is correctly answered in this paragraph</u>.

Have we not called the old energy in truth? Have we not spoken it as it is? If we have well given this truth, then we are Reasonable. The human race no longer has the option **at all,** of allowing that omni-destroyment to continue. Savagely dirty politics, deals and deeds is the old energy. All of that nonfunctional devilry is *<u>right now</u>*—*being* uprooted and cast aside by the New Energy of human empowerment and wellness, **the Evolution**. It is the Evolution into awareness, wholesomeness, prosperity and success.

- The awareness and empowerment belong to you.

- **It is time to claim it.**

From the unlimited lunacy that *any* mainstream politician and thus automated liar and Statist, is by some miracle on your side, arises the counter-concept that Reasonable is. The old energy is bent and proven by <u>an unbroken track record</u>, to destroy Individual Human Rights. Our Reasonable Energy is specifically set to uphold <u>the condition of human</u>.

- To the point, our much more Reasonable Energy is specifically set to uphold Individual Human Rights, *the condition of human*.

To be Reasonable, intake that key concept into intuition. That is how the New Energy works. That is how to "work" it. When done correctly, it is without effort—<u>for one can never be stepped backward into unknowing.</u>

- The next individual achieving awareness is also moved upward in consciousness *forever*, (...placing the math in our favor.)

Only the New Energy can and will segue the human and planetary experience into Success. One energy is exclusively of human and planetary destroyment. The other <u>E</u>nergy, that of Consciousness, is exclusively of human and planetary **compassion**. Only the latter is of the Creator's Design and Intent. The Reasonable voice reflects that knowledge and humanitarian consideration to Humankind and Nature.

Please allow the voice of Life itself, of human and planetary respect and ascension to guide and overview every step of our process. May our platform reflect that which is respectful and beneficial to All, for *only that* is of upward Evolution.

- Politically speaking, we say; drop the pollution and join the Evolution!
- For it is so assured.

It must be CLEARLY stated that Reasonable and all related to Reasonable, is an absolutely non-violent movement into political sane-hood and Human Success. It is of upmost importance that we not repay violence with violence beyond self-defense. The amount of violence initiation is presently intolerable as it is. When government answers peaceful protest with **murder**, it is time to awaken *to the absolute fact of human slavery.*

The initiation of violence or the use of hate, lies or fraud to achieve political ends, does these {old energy} things:

1 It is a reduction to the same spiritual level of bestiality as those engaged in human slavery.

2 One can never solve any problem by the same thinking that produced the problem in the first place. *The stratagems of hate centered politics cannot solve the stratagems of hate centered politics.*

3 Violence, lies and fraud produce the opposite of the stated advertisement. <u>This is precisely as it is right now with all mainstream politics</u>. We have witnessed that dishonor for generations of political lying, bullying, fraud, coercion, violence, and *profound failure.*

4 Above all, such bonehead action would be the precise excuse so desperately sought after, to unleash the unlimited brutality and murder the system is well known for. **Thou shall not provide that excuse!!!**

Any and all such action or suggestion, possibly even in jest, will quickly result in dismissal from the Reasonable membership. It is directly opposed to anything a Reasonable human being stands for.

Force, fraud, backstab, slavery, lying, bullying, coercion and total failure is the sum, limit *and definition* of the modern, mainstream political world*!* Such abject poorness is pointedly not our limitation or paradigm.

Being Reasonable, we share the nexus that we are <u>not</u> spiritually limited to the dusty nadir on the Scale of Consciousness. For only above that *by equal measure*, is your personal effectivity as human and as co-Creator. This is your freedom and empowerment.

For those who are to make a beneficial difference, there are your directions and methodology. Such is also Reasonable; meaning **your personal empowerment**.

- And it is *axiomatically* so.

It is already hazardous to be right when government is wrong. What we do not do, is make the situation worse than it already is. The objective is to make the situation better. Truth is an infinitely more potent weapon than violence. *Learn how to use truth,* **<u>simply by being it</u>**.

For decades now, people's intuition has been telling them the same thing contained in this book. All we are doing is providing solutions. The only difference between now and yesterday is that ever more people are ready to understand the cause, and implement the cure.

- It is only falsehood that must be supported by violence.
- *Such is the most reliable identifier of political falsehood.*

- Truth is self-evident and stands on its own.
- **And that is our method of achieving peace and freedom.**
- It is very Reasonable. *It is also several magnitudes easier.*

Violence is so useless, and so pointless, that we do not employ even the thought and thus, the vibration of it. The vibrational frequency of thoughts upon Human Success forms both a shield of strength and a quantum cloak. This renders strong immunity from the endlessly self-destructive energies of lower consciousness. Example: Luke 10:19.

Predators within their lower energy, must first find easy and ***perceived defenseless*** targets. Cowardice knows no other world. This is the explanation behind most governmental acts of violence. Such outright cravenness is the hallmark of Fascism. There are enough examples that you are probably aware of many or have had first-hand experience or both.

Secondly, the energy of coercion must first find targets of equal vibration. *Only that is visible* and thus able to be recognized. An example would be fear, hate and violence. Such is also several things that by definition, Reasonable *absolutely,* **is not.**

Force, fraud, cowardice, injury, backstab and mayhem is the realm of the underworld, <u>and that is where the human race will leave them.</u> May those so enthralled, have the "freedom" to tax, hate, maim, abuse, exploit, injure, murder, rape and enslave themselves as much as they please! Human Ascension is anywhere above that pit of Hell, and so is Human Success!

- If you learn nothing else in this lifetime, *please get that much right!*

In the identical Light of Awareness, Reasonable does not condone, and will remove any energy of the supremacist. All of the above reasons apply equally and fully. Read them as many times as needed. *Any* display of such old energy, word or deed shall result in loss of membership.

Such small minded, short sighted, selfish, bigoted, racist, sexist, pious, footshot and fungus bound, mentally and morally unbred, unbrotherly, unchristian, un-Christ like, wrong, base, and crass energy of **hate**, is the **exact** <u>illusion</u> **of human spiritual separation** ALL modern politics *is directly built on, and directly dependent on.* We ask if that statement is Reasonably clear.

Such lost at sea, Big Lie old energy of <u>**human versus human**</u>, is the never changing methodology by which all mainstream politicians swindle money, support and vote off the politically unaware **stooge**. Anyone who provides the mainstream politician vote, money or verbal support has been taken straight to the cleaners. They are politically pre-educated and pre-awake. No damn clue might be a better description of such woeful and led around by the nose, omni-destroying *fantastic ignorance.*

- The old energy is identical to being politically asleep at the wheel, oblivious to a dozen screaming warning horns.

- The drunk driver has greatly better odds, and they get rightly jailed for that mistake!

The drunk driver is at least aware of where they are *supposed* to be going! The mainstream voter *most decidedly* **is not**. It is as the song goes: When will they ever learn, when will they ev-er learn? As you know, it is so.

- All you did was call it.

To agonizing modern political embarrassment, Reasonable recognizes that such bigoted, sexist, stupid, racist and counter-productive, victimhood and hate driven human to human separation energy, cuts in equal amounts through all race, color, creed, religion, sexual orientation, age, gender, location, hair color, and handicap, health, employment, education, or economic status. Such old energy represents those whose' internal thought patterns and vibrations draws unto themselves every manner of harm and self-destruction they typically experience. Such old energy <u>is all about being the continual victim</u>—*and the Universe answers!*

- That's the catch.

Bottom line: We are smarter than that! Such dilapidated and self-checkmated old energy is *the illusion of separation.* It embodies and defines, all modern politics. It is the opposite of anything Reasonable. It demonstrates no understanding of that which Reasonable is or stands for: We are Unity, harmony, respect and cooperation with All that Is.

Removing the bitter and disgusting old energy that is the **INJURE EVERYONE ELSE LIFEBLOOD** of mainstream politics, thus removes the excuse and stupidity foundation that feeds the coercion of human slavery.

That is the entire world of modern politics. The moment you understand that, really understand it, you gain a Reasonable understanding. *It might pay well to read the previous paragraph a dozen times*.

- It is time to awaken the sleeper.
- We do that through recognizing and removing the old energy.

Through removing such dismal and immature energy from every aspect of our lives, the true healer transmutes, with a touch of judo, human disrespect into human respect. Human harm and its political arm are thereby broken by its own hate-momentum, and transformed *by its absence*, into Human Success. This is most fully Reasonable.

- This is a simple concept, and we are thankful that it is a simple concept.

Writing that bigotry noise had the feel of rubbing a puppy's nose in poop. Yet there are a few childish, hate saturated losers, some in every human subgroup, who are still blindly immersed in non-consciousness. Their whole paradigm is of human spiritual separation, *the illusion*.

- Through that view of separation, the human race is played like a fiddle, continuously, one against the other.
- *That is the-entire-theme-of-modern-politics,* **without exception**.

Thereby we are **tricked**, and thus locked into subhuman bondage through the ever gaining brutality and life force theft directly resulting from modern politics. **This is the reality of all mainstream politics.** You have done well to see it as it is. *That is why it is in this book!*

It is the thought and act of separation that is the source of human coercion. That is the illusion and its results. It is the Unity of Oneness, <u>the awakening</u>, that results in freedom, safety and empowerment. Ascension is **the absence** of the every moment coercion of human slavery.

- Reasonable wisdom is in the clear comprehension of *both* conditions.

We reject the anserine self-injury of hate in favor of Freedom and Success. One can embody the injury of human slavery or of the unlimited benefit of Peace and Freedom. Only one is Reasonable, workable, conscionable, humanitarian, livable, likeable, successful, prosperous, or worthy of the human race.

- Only one condition is worthy of planet earth or this universe.

The old energy of Slavery is now rejected for its exhaustive failure and its satanic content, intent and outcome. Most of the readers of this book have clearly stated; that's *exactly* what modern politics **is**.

- Recognizing it, is about 90% of the cure, **if** we maintain a voting discipline that reflects that awareness.

- Virtually anything presently on television fails that test.

- You knew that *and called it*. **Now you know the reason why.**

Beyond the bigotry monkeybusiness, weapons and violence are easily defeated by truth. Allow weapons and violence to remain the *consummately tortured* lot of those who defend falsehood with violence, suppression, oppression, dirty tricks, and cutting off debate. We can see their misery and **agonizing desperation** for it is now exposed to the world. It no longer needs explanation owing to its obviousness. Here is where mainstream politics defines itself. The more things change, the more they remain the same.

- The *essence* of mainstream politics is this: "There is none so blind as those who refuse to see."   Anonymous

- Modern politics has come to define itself as the largest plague in all history of the least honor in all history.

Observe how their own political lies have ensnared the mainstream politician ever so tightly. They, <u>for fear of moral lynching</u>, can no longer afford public questioning. *The logic of that is immaculate.* Notice I never said it was the slightest hint of moral.

Truth defends itself. **We are that Truth.** Therefore, we have no need for the self-defeating processes of dishonor, injury and theft as relentlessly maintained by mainstream politics. Such pitiful, mongrel, miserable, sick, twisted *and morbid* energy is left to modern politics for that is what modern politics is. Few do not by now clearly know it. It is however, now stated in English **and placed directly before the Supreme Judge of the Universe.**

Reasonable then is the turntable Energy of human empowerment. We correctly place the raw destructiveness of modern politics into a location it cannot recover from: We expose it to the world.

Mainstream politics now stands as intrinsically **dead**. It is daily gaining horrifying and long traveling stench and *demanding* burial*!*

- Modern politics is the ship of fools being guided by a ship of traitors.
- *And you called it.*

We shall start the turntable Energy with a question. I have heard it asked countless times and from every corner and walk: Why am I not Free and thus fully human and fully successful as God designed the human to be?

- Reasonable asks rather how can you *not be*, that which you so inimitably are?

The first is mentally held, modern society projected, *pure illusion*. It is the illusion of limitation. The second is the Truth of empowerment awaiting only claiming. I think that was Reasonably presented. Such is Truth.

- It is yours, and it is now.
- It is Free, and it is Freeing.
- You know your soul is active when your speech reflects Creator Designed Humanitarian principles.

⇨**Now** you can measure it.⇦

Chapter Nine

Of Bankers and Warfare

9.   (The chains that bind.)   ...Of Bankers and Warfare

Individual Human Rights are the definition, experience, and quality of human. They are the treatment of people *as humans*. It is the condition of livability. It is the condition of humanity. The opposite is butchery.

In the past, our humanity was secured with blood. In all known history, the energy of oppression has understood no other form of communication

Of constraint, the life-spill has been the lifeless blood of tyrants and various other dictatorial élite. As there is a generous supply of such oppressors, several points are well proven. The endless blood spill, be it history's friend or foe, has included vast forces on all sides—*God's side, of course.* Such a strange conundrum is the very riddle of unlimited murder this book addresses *directly*.

The primary goal of warfare is the death and destroyment of the disarmed and defenseless. That outcome is consistent no matter the lie stated for the warfare. That would be men, women, children, elderly and freshborn without so much as a second thought. Such lineage defines and displays both the old energy of wanton human destroyment, and politics as usual. They are identical, inseparable *and cartel demanded*.

From this painfully earned wisdom, a fitting analogy of modern politics is this: If the problem is say mercury poisoning, then stop ingesting mercury! *The same applies to the pure human destruction of mainstream politics!* **This nature of common sense is strictly Reasonable.**

Behold, the riddle of continuous warfare **is now exposed:**

Is it but a strange fluke that the same international banking interest floats quantum inflation tax, and debt engineered *appearance*, of money, to **all** sides of each conflict <u>with no miss</u> in many centuries of human warfare? Have we clearly and perfectly identified the function of war? *Indeed we have!*

- Could cartel driven warfare be defined as the blind exchange of our humanity, for politically orchestrated butchery to—*ourselves?*
- What kind of deal and what kind of animal existence is that?
- By what strange leap or twist is that *not* human slavery?
- Any benefit, if there is any, is toward deeply hidden bank cartel, purely satanic societies, corporate monopolies, the military-industrial complex (Moloch), *and exquisitely dishonorable politicians*.
- There must be a more Reasonable and safer life path. There is.
- We are leading it *by example*.

Behold our Reasonable friends, the following insights presented in this book:

Shall we continue to call the income tax the largest outright hoax in human history? Alas, we can no longer: What paltry scraps such harm becomes against the vastness of the international banking scam standing directly behind both the income tax *and* unending global warfare.

The Universe is cleaning **that human sacrifice *ritual*** up—as not compatible with Consciousness or possible in Evolution. Ever more powerful Energy movers are focused upon this healing process. One healing task brings in awareness. Then choices are real-world, *and not illusion*.

That phase is enjoying stellar success. The majority of people have now sided on the removal of the non legal debt money and against the warfare it causes. This includes its Marxist tax and the ongoing privation it causes. This is an easy conclusion once one sees *it is all one and the same*.

Do we hate the carrot, cow or tree even if we may alter their life path? We do not. Why then fear that which shall abruptly achieve healing and balance? Reasonable does not, even in the knowing of that which is.

Neither hate nor fear is, or describes, the Reasonable human being.

- And it is so.

Chapter Ten

Unspoken Patterns

10. So, we look at the lemming like politics, now over the cliff. And we look at warfare in the knowing *that all warfare is in fact political.* And we see the banking gods directly behind the human sacrifice system. Only now, it is an unmasked illusion—***an illusion without the curtain of Oz.***

We then view smallness itself pulling strings and levers of smoke, flame and movie like political machinations. We now see these illusions are morbidly unnatural fantasies. Every mainstream political oracle has turned out to be centered in the outcome of live human sacrifice.

We observe the mislabels of that holocaust have run rampant. Those labels turn out to be any lie whatsoever the mainstream voter might swallow. We observe **any** psychological twist that will cause the uninformed voter to support the illusion and thus the slaughter.

- It is by this method oppression survives.

From that Truth unveiled, we now observe and can easily understand an enormously clear cut set of **political patterns:**

- The first pattern is both human and human condition destroyment.

However, precisely that has been the unflinching voted **and recorded** track record of mainstream politics *for generations.*

- That pattern is now patently obvious.

- From one end of America to the other, this was <u>the</u> central theme.

Allow into evidence the intent of the Oath of Office to protect the Law of the Land, the Rule of Law forming civilized society. Observe for the record, its diametric opposite, destroying it to ashes and anarchy, as voted daily in chamber. The track record there is its own *exquisitely* damning evidence.

- **Stop endorsing human desecration!!!!!**

You want obvious? Well then here it is: The cure for the hopeless **drug** addict, as the modern politician by practice and definition is, rests <u>not</u> in *"<u>more drugs</u>"*.

- How many generations have we said that?

The addict <u>ever so desperately</u> would have you believe ***any*** lie at their disposal*!* *This is precisely how all modern politics works.* This is a critical *and central* concept to understand if the human race is to survive!

- **Please get this correct because *your* survival could easily depend upon this *specific* understanding.**

Within mainstream politics, we look at a hundred years of blindly voted mayhem—and ask what planet are they from? Do any of them have a pulse? Did a single one of them graduate first grade math? Is there anything in the universe that can explain or excuse their **vast** crashed and burned track record? What insanity possesses the fantastically brain injured, genuflecting and bobble-headed claque associated with such advanced leprosy?

How many times have the en-tire London Bridge, sky pie, moon cheese, fairy dust, toe jam, mouse droppings and dry wells been sold and resold to these truly astounding asses? The same dog that don't hunt, has been sold a thousand times. The bandit-politician who sold it <u>still</u> has all the money! If that is not amazing, well then, I do not know what amazing is.

- Is *amazing,* the right word?

- The evidence shows it to be quite some distance *beyond that*.

The bottom line is that any cartoon character in the world, clearly would have done a far sight better. <u>The awareness test</u> presented at each vote, <u>was clearly flunked</u> by a wide margin, again, and again, and again, and again. *No grading curve reaches that low—or ever should.*

Such an unmitigated debacle is our *second,* **exquisitely clear pattern**.

For crying in a bucket, is it ever obvious! Right there is several lifetimes of completely sick 24/7 jokes and miles of great quality poetry for oodles of easy money! That *authentically defective* emperor, **truly,** has no clothes! The truth is out. You have spoken. <u>*This theme never changed*</u>.

- Nothing excuses the governance we now have, or its abusiveness.

Yet not all is lost! The gate to human Freedom is now wide open. Virtually every telling measure of mainstream politics is hemorrhaging life force by the day. This outrush is advancing daily as voter detestment toward mainstream politics and its nonstop holier than thou bullying skyrockets.

One look at the empty heads of politics today, and the overwhelming urge is to puke! That is the word-for-word impression given from one end of this Nation to the other. As one, we have expressed extreme disgust with modern politics. There remains no choice; *except to put an end to it.*

Such a rational trend is our *third* very clear pattern.

- As of this writing, this movement into Evolution comes as no surprise to anyone.

This third pattern clearly demonstrates awakened awareness. It is rock solid evidence of a jump upward in consciousness as shown by an anathema to the art and science of dishonor that is modern politics.

- The entire planet is awakening. This is the *conclusive* proof.

As humanitarian awareness advances, the spiral of death that defines modern politics, suddenly loses its appeal. The no parachute pattern of mainstream deadfall now stands decoded: It is accelerating as we speak.

In spite of some ups and downs in **the revolting modern political crapfest**, the mainstream bottom is absolutely falling out. Ultimately, there will be no return *whatsoever* from that pattern. You saw it here first. Remember these words. *This*, is the New age and it is *your empowerment.*

Such beneficial condition is Light and it is Reasonable. As we examine political imprisonment, then and only then, can we gain the perspective and wisdom to look upward in consciousness and find the solution. As we *end* the death dealing orgy of lies we call modern politics, **we gain our humanity**.

Human oppression is directly born of, and continues for the moment as the direct result of lack of awareness. More specifically, this means spiritual awareness. **The Great Healing** *is born of, and will take place as a direct result of spiritual advancement: This is the Human Event.*

If you have read this far, you have expressed the desire to become whole, and then the healer of humans, nations and worlds. You have decided to bring forth and experience a better, brighter, safer, and freer existence. You have expressed at some level, achieving the absence of human slavery.

- This is the advancement of humanity.

A big part of our Mission is to place large amounts of fuel, as information and visualization onto that righteous blaze. From that Light of Truth and Empowerment, may our every act follow the gentle example Gandhi instructed, for *only* that, is Reasonable.

Countless Americans contributed to this book and the solutions presented. From that, we now have a set of well proven principles to guide this nation and world into healing. I also heard the unavoidable indictments of modern politics, a *small* few of which are presented (for contrast only). I listened more for the **solutions**—as being a thousand times more important.

- **This book is the compendium and delivery of those solutions.**

- *The main thing;* **is thinking outside of the box of human slavery**.

For the record, *no one* including myself, will escape the responsibility of allowing modern politics to become the hell bound machinery it now is. All of us of voting age share that responsibility. Many of us are now aware of the wrong thinking and errors that allowed that condition. Many more are moving into that awareness *rapidly*.

- The only fatal mistake is not gaining wisdom from experience.

- It is not nearly so fatal—if done in this lifetime!

- **Now *that's* Reasonable!**

For the record, no one including myself, will escape the responsibility for energizing the human and planetary condition into Ascension. This is wisdom in action *as gained from experience*. **We are *that* Reasonable.**

- And it is so.

Now the nastiness of politics you were twice warned about is gaining full swing. I foretold your enjoyment. May our political exposure process now gain its fullness. *Mud shall be slung.*

- This Marine is ok with that.

A related sub-pattern of note is this: As the *pure hate* exuding shrill of mainstream politics goes up, **as it ever does,** then participation rightly goes down. It is a wonder the filth pouring politicos have yet to figure this simple thing out! The dirty downside is that vast oceans of extremely human harmful laws are achieved through advanced known, *and counted on*, **non-participation.** On second thought, perhaps the hate spewing politicos did figure that much out, and it is the general public that has not. *Aho!*

That pervasive pattern is a death spiral *rigorously* inherent to mainstream politics. The very tightly controlled media must have ever increasing shock and awe amounts of grief, strife, embroilment, animosity and enmity, (hate-drama), for its ratings survival. Within the political-Media partnership and cartel, there is not one sleaze bag politico who is not keenly aware of this requirement. The methodology is usually the sound bite. *The endless flood of* **raw hate** *is the cardinal requirement.* Prime examples would be the ceaseless liars inhabiting Lamestream media: The media *needs* their mock-polarized hate-for-hate power plays, **and they all know it.**

As the non-consciousness of the system drops by the day and at the same time the Consciousness of the human race goes up, the system of human destroyment loses its grip upon its own prisoners. That's **exactly** what we're seeing and it doesn't take Sherlock Holmes to figure it out.

Not only is that ever wider gulf understandable and obvious, but, as it ultimately reduces human slavery, it is also Reasonable. In fact, merely seeing this commanding pattern in clear understanding if even for the first time, helps move the awakening human into Reasonable Energy.

From that moment, as the nonstop political **lies** of human slavery get shaken away like so many pesky fleas; one has then earned, and experiences Reasonable thinking. Such awareness is the foundation of Human Freedom, which is Human Success, which is the Human Event. It is unmistakably so. Better yet by far; **the path of Human Evolution is now in writing.**

Even that harmonic of modern politics is now exposed. As related to modern politics, nasty is as nasty does. Nothing in fact is nastier or more divisive. In fact, the nastiest, hate-in'est political talking head of them all, would be all too happy to egotistically tell you: "I told you so". That is employed here as an example spoken by *a textbook model of hypocrisy*.

I hope that is the last time I feel the need to reach into the rag bag and allude to such a thoroughly internecine, **total moral loss**. Such a depraved example is the definition of "obviously part of the problem". Here is where the mainstream punditry shows its polished and ample derriere.

The painful part is that the above description fits nearly every mainstream politico to perfection. Sooner or later, as a measure of IQ if nothing else, the public will **conclusively reject it.** Such healing is already in motion. How can that be? *It is so, because you provided the material for this book!* The contributors to this book have *absolutely* rejected modern politics in total for its chronic and habitual nonstop *lying*.

For the record, the *modern* human sacrifice system began in earnest in 1913, and is roughly 100 years old as of this publication. That marked the start of the Federal Reserve System.

The **fourth** pattern is fully exposed with a question: How many pointless surveys and exit polls have shown us that up to 96% of various candidate vote totals are a NEGATIVE vote? (And was again in 2012)

- *The human race is going to have to do better than that.*

Such total loss vote is to hold the <u>other</u> of <u>two</u> automated, professional, purchased and *morally void* continuous **liars** out of office!

- Call that rubber-headedness the crown joke of all no laugh jokes.

How many times have you said or heard this statement: "They are all liars." Or "They are all liars *and jackasses*." That, is why the negative vote is a total loss paradigm. Such black hole energy is textbook and clinical insanity. It is also imbecilic **beyond comprehension or excuse.**

- There is no possibility of good coming from the negative vote.

That no-conscious situation is a lost cause. It is a dead end road being driven at top speed. The blind corner bridge is all the way out. Such outright lunacy is now decoded: *It is THE hand-basket straight to Hell.*

- The negative vote is <u>not</u> the direction to human Ascension.

The big catch is that even without thermonuclear weaponry, mainstream politics has perpetrated enough wrongdoing and backroom deals to directly and direly threaten all life on earth. No one wins this throw-away vote or any other mainstream vote which *by definition*, is **purely throwaway**. Bloodhanded, lying politics wins every time. **You** *do not*.

- Such complete destitution is the definition of non-awareness.
- Where is ANY proof otherwise?
- *There,* is the precise location where you get thrown under the bus by modern politics.

The awareness level contained within the negative throw-away vote, *spiritually* fails to outweigh the yellow sulfur content of a single sow bug's popcorn fart. It is a loser on the Scale of Consciousness. Yet even that has a good hundred years of long tonnage over the not existent, real-world demonstrated, voted in chamber *and recorded*, **prattle only** difference between the identical twins of tweedldum and tweedledee. There is no point in calling that which you so darn well know, defrocked or demystified. It is however, now stated for the record in the Court of Civilization, that there be <u>positively</u>, <u>no</u> <u>further</u> <u>error</u>.

- The vast majority of the people I spoke to are playing on the same page with the realization there is **zero** difference between tweedledee and tweedldum. (And never was)
- The challenge for the remaining partisan **idiots**, is to point to the candidate that is <u>NOT</u> purchased by cartel.
- ...Or who is <u>not</u> a member of organizations committed to ending Individual Human Rights.
- ...Or a single one that votes their Oath of Office.

- ...And the list goes on and on and on.

Remember the old coin toss of heads—the politicians win, and tails—you lose? That moonshine cod's-wallop precisely defines the profound no-choice of mainstream politics. It is by definition as diabolical, snake oil, and no-win as it gets. Most of you reading this, knew that most of your life. How many times have you said the same thing yourself? Is there any number that big? It's good to know at least *something* surpasses the Federal debt!

- *For all others, that was your wakeup call into the real world!*

Fundamentally, the mainstream no-choice is a perfected exercise in demonstrated delusion. By definition, the further one slides down that well greased path, the further they are immersed in, and caught up in, delusion. **And**, the easier the mousetrap of slavery snaps shut upon them *with the silence of the lambs.*

- That error delivers human slavery on a silver platter.
- *This is the bull elephant in the living room folks!*

Most portions of this book weren't written for you to "like", they were written for you to <u>wake up</u>. This could be one of those portions. I like it a lot. You might not. *I like that even better!*

<u>When the walking dead</u> vote that way, the powers that be do not need a pre-programmed vote 'managing' system to e-dial up their false results. At that juncture it is automatic. *The noose has been voluntarily fitted.*

- The count is limited to; "how many loser-idiots have shot themselves in the foot today?"

The objective here is to grow a brain and <u>not</u> fall for that satanic trap, that heads or tails, **directly produces human imprisonment!**

One of the differences between the past and a vastly more livable future is that the above no-choice political **con-game** is now exposed. Both 'sides' are equally purchased by cartel. Both 'sides' are equally corrupt, equally dishonest, equally destructive, equally Marxist, equally sold out and **religiously dishonorable**—and have been our entire lifetime.

- **The simple truth is there is no mainstream political direction except that of human slavery.**
- And thus we have again correctly defined modern politics.

If by some loony-tunes marvel and wonder, you do not *clearly* understand the above merry-go-round mess and mouse trap, then read it again and again until you *do* understand it.

Understanding that no-choice snake pit is the beginning of the Awakening. This understanding is where the lights are on *and*, somebody is home. *Most of us have concluded the same thing our entire adult life.*

It seems that the en-tire planet except, for the unconscious buffoon of the partisan mainstream voter is aware of this fact. It has been correctly, exhaustively, elaborately, clearly, and ceaselessly convicted in the court of life. It is now accepted as commonly known scientific fact. Even the *slightest* politically awake individual will all too gladly inform anyone of that stone carved gospel **truth**!

- If you think I had fun writing this book, you're right.

The above political truth is *the basic of all basic modern political realizations.* As tragically obvious as it is, and as enigmatically small as it is, it does however mark the all important first step into political **adulthood**. As that old energy no-choice Malthusian pogrom was in desperate need of a 2×4 treatment, we hope it was addressed with Reasonable impact. If so, then this book is serving humanity *correctly.*

In order for the human species to survive, the ***egregiously uninformed*** standard voter simply must evolve far enough to become smart enough *to occasionally consume oxygen!* Precisely that is just how long and far, the taken to the cleaners mainstream voter's head has been firmly stuck in a dank and rank location where the sun does not shine!

Reasonable cuts through that idiocy like taking a buzz saw to a bar of soap! Truth is like that. Consider all that pathetic, miserable, beaten and honor void <u>Uniparty</u> lunacy now exposed to the elements. May the birds and bugs eat it alive! **And how sharply underway that process is!**

By the end of this book *somebody's* parade is going to get rained on. If you are awake *it will not be yours.* Let the rain in your face, or lack of it, be the indicator. Old give 'em hell Harry, {President Truman} put it this way: "I tell them the truth, and they just think it's hell!"

- Said differently; **the mainstream voter dies a thousand deaths**.

It could be just coincidence, however, that is the very same number of times the mainstream voter has been **slam stabbed** square in the back.

Now if the bloodletting were limited to only them, that'd be fine, I'd have no problem with it. They could have all of their sick-twisted back stab and murder by number festivals they wanted. I wouldn't care what they labeled their slut-like *servitude to Satan*. However, it is not limited to them.

- The vote condoning slavery places ruin upon all humanity.
- ...*Which explains a main necessity of this book.*

The **fifth** extremely set pattern, consists of two portions. When added together, this condition has been a dominant reality for a minimum of fifty years. *Horrifying,* doesn't go far enough to describe this pattern either. The danger to society is measurable in terms of *the loss of our humanity.*

- Quite predictably, this is also not a media obvious pattern.
- Not one I could find, said the media cartel was their friend.

Part A, is those who do not register to vote, *usually lifetime*. The catch is that they *could* vote but choose not to. In some precincts, this hell no {no hell} vote *in opposition to* mainstream politics is the majority. This condition is markedly increasing. Many very aware individuals are in this category.

A good many of these folks, and some do vote, are shooting match angry at existing politics for the damage done. This trend is also on the increase. Someone forgot their many Oath of Office undertakings and… someone actually noticed! Although that level of anger is understandable, we never said it was Reasonable. We have only correctly reported *that which is*. This outwardly appears to be by far the quickest growing category worldwide. Very few *anywhere* are now surprised by this pattern.

Part B, the other portion, is voters who do not vote at every chance to do so. This outcome is WAY too routinely the majority. This **no!** vote is often up to a 90% supermajority—notoriously so in many smaller elections. The condition is as predictable as it is pathetic and destructive.

- With both parts added, this is where a tiny fraction of people, *and television advised automatons all,* decide virtually every election.

Quite obviously, this 'round the bend condition demands the Question of just what underhanded grab bag of human hurt was up for vote.

- Whatever it was, ***you can bet your last cent, it wasn't Reasonable!***

The *televised* voting statistics will always appear opposite to the above reality. It is not the portion told—it is the larger portion **not** told. In the court of life, omission of truth holds the same culpability as falsehood.

By way of antipathy, the choice to no! vote on vast collections of trash, is an intended face slap to dirty politics. It is a deeply intuitive (and correct) moral poke <u>at the exemplary non-moral.</u>

- *How many times* is it said and heard: "What is there to vote **for**?"
- We define it as a lack of Reasonable candidates and conditions.

The repugnant crap up for question is either utterly infelicitous candidates of the mainstream anti-American, or defalcation deeply buried in twisted up and lawyer-fied gobbledy-gook. It is usually both. Go ahead and say it aint so and see who believes ya, but know to your last fiber that quantum tragedy now stands decoded and exposed *correctly*.

As one energy pattern by way of the intended **no!** as the message, both no vote portions have added up to the majority for decades. Such sorry outcome, is a hideous and intentional mainstream political execration of anything and everything *even remotely American*.

The non vote is a gut reaction to the exhaustive cesspool of mainstream politics. ...That clearly defines that which is now unquestionably unambiguously and now unarguably, **un-American.**

From the evidence, no and hell no have won nearly every election. The strong majority certainly wish that were so. Most of them will tell you that much gospel *instantly*.   Much of the time in telling the story, politeness will fly right out the window only to be replaced by an unquenchable anger.

- **The non-voter understands the reality of mainstream politics.**

- The tragedy resides in that the average voter **clearly**, *does not*.

The longtime non-voting majority has turned out to be morally, factually, intuitively, and mathematically correct. They have been proven correct for more than a half century, roughly the time frame of their **majority**. There is a fact of life to put in the pipe and smoke!

The no! voter intuitively sees modern politics as a hammer crude pirates' tool where the raw cowardice of **gunpoint force** {get that} is used by A to steal from B, to steal from C, to steal from D, to re-steal from A. …When the only one stealing from everyone is government.

- This nature of cut throat lunacy **is** the modern political cartel.

The human race is now awakening to this fact that explains mainstream politics et al. The Awakening is Reasonable. The rotted left-behinds (and endless armed robbery) *never were*.

The silver lining on the non-vote is at least some expressed awareness. …Even if it is of wholesale disgust and loath of modern politics. Ah, but just ask *any* longtime hell no voter, and they will tell anyone their political standpoint until the air is plenty blue, loud. tense, and hot!

Their opinion of the mainstream politician is **way** not approving, but it is damn certain healthy! It is also split the arrow three times *accurate,* <u>and absolutely worldwide at that!</u>

That information *might* seem personal, depending upon one's voting record. However, it was written as a generalization *only*. That does not make it so much as one quark, less factual. Sometimes I also, have to remind myself that **the majority** rarely votes!

The tragic part, is that the sum total of the no vote illusion is both dishwater weak and of zero effect. The non-vote is fully delusional in spite of its growing popularity. No amount of their bellicose wind will move human slavery the first inch toward freedom. The intention of being freer has not been served by this **blunder**. Make no error that the expressed intent **is** increased freedom, *and this wish is **identical** clear across America.*

The no!-vote, ***and it is a vote***, although normally a clear majority, is not counted at the ballot box or displayed on television. The information is plainly available, however it is swept under the rug by the media cartel. *It is as if it simply does not exist.* The shame is very present. However, we pretend it is not—**in order to preserve the status quo.** *The catch is that the status quo is the destroyment of our humanity.*

Here is where one hand washes the other in a partnership of omission. If this information were to be brought to the attention of the public, modern politics would be on the way out the door at a *much* quicker rate.

That illusion just got blown to **smithereens.** Very soon, all political illusions shall enjoy the same fate. (They're arriving presently.)

The no-vote condition is directly responsible for the silver platter delivering Darkness itself win after win for generations. It is in *the absence* of awareness and Creator Consciousness that we have unintentionally caused the political system of human sacrifice. Proactive *and aware* voting is the cure. To live American, we need to vote American.

The non-voters, God love them for being accurate, is another head in the sand mob that must awaken to political reality and American voting responsibility *if the human race is to survive.* In other words, we as humans need to evolve beyond that peculiarly destructive **dumb tax**.

Ironically, that rarely translates to anything other than a balloted NO! vote on virtually all issues. **But**, *read each one carefully.* Reasonable Energy is being introduced more and more—every-single-day.

Within the act of omission found in the non-vote, the mainstream politician "interprets" that **as an endorsement!** *The gall in that equation is unlimited.* However that is the truth of the non-vote paradigm and modern politics. Unless stopped cold in their tracks the modern politician/*horse's ass*, is trained to take ***everything*** as 'demand' for additional oppression.

- That is the number one reality of all mainstream politics*!*

That utterly calamitous no-vote imbroglio, now stands in pillory where it belongs. May that illusion now cease to exist as we see it for what it is. May we undo the harmful law, and replace the cartel owned bootlicks and prostitutes the above error so regularly caused!

And now we arrive at the true crux of mainstream politics: **Your pick from all the filthy litter *is not the exception.*** This is because every pup has the same fence jumpin' mother called lucre. The father, <u>if there is one</u>, *is a whole lot of theory.*

- Many say the Devil is the father of modern politics.
- ...*And they absolutely mean it.*
- This opinion was heard *continuously*.

To provide a cogent format; there is almost no mainstream politician who has not wholesale opposed the Creator Inspired Constitution. This abandonment of the Constitution serves the intention of ending our Human Rights that is our humanity. This is the modern and purchased function of all mainstream politics. ***Their only commission is to produce human slavery.***

Each mainstream politician has traded constitutional restraints for lock step servility to the international bank and corporate cartel. Corporate cartel is the partner to the world controlling banking cabal. It is this unholy union that effortlessly plucks elections worldwide. There are very few exceptions globally, and virtually none within the United States. Every politician will loudly tell you of their loyalty to you, however their **voting record** *conclusively* provides unlimited disrepute and ignominy with religious regularity.

- The mainstream voting record is universally in direct opposition to the Oath of Office.
- It should be no surprise the same record matches the cartel side of campaign funding.
- Such is the time tested world of dishonor of 100% of **all** current mainstream endorsed political leadership.
- This is an exquisitely clear picture of mainstream political values, actions and outcomes ***once elected***. {The truth test}

The unholy catch is that four of the five patterns are "interpreted" _**by not being stopped cold,**_ as "demanding" additional human slavery. This is done by career politicians _who define and exude continuous dishonor_.

- All five patterns showcase the symptoms of Marxism and/or sold out politics, (whichever label one prefers).
- We no longer have to ask or guess, where, or to what, or to whom they have resolutely sold their conscience;
- _...FOR THERE EVINCES NONE WHATSOEVER REMAINING._

This conclusion is entirely self-evident from the voted results of human oppression, the intentional sawing off of humans at the hips. _None_ of that mainstream track record is made up. Wishing it were, however, does not in any way repair the problem **of the ever increasing theft of our humanity.**

That betrayal to all that is American, <u>done in absolute bad faith</u>, is the outcome to be aware of as related to all mainstream politics. _Every cut and joke has been ten thousand times earned_. Even that hell intent, the largest and most hidden truth of them all, now stands Illuminated before the Court of Mankind. Now, <u>and only now</u>, as of _**this**_ realization, can **the entire world** begin to heal.

There is massive and nuclear pent up energy within these five advancing patterns, and Evolution will be powered by all of it. ...For Reasonable is the New Energy of Truth, Integrity, and the American Way of Life of Freedom and Dignity. **We respect humans as human**. It might be a new concept right now as this is written, however it is the correct concept for planetary healing.

- _**We**_ are the means and method of achieving unity, prosperity, advancement and self-ownership.
- The Humanitarian Code **is** that healing.
- ...Where we forever break the bonds of human slavery.

The solution is straightforward. If you have said it once, you have said it a hundred times: The present task given to the human race concerning politics is to relentlessly, rigorously, furiously, and with all possible discipline, _using <u>any</u> legal means_, **thoroughly,** cut off the mainstream politician's money supply and support. We do this <u>proactively</u> at; 1) the party level; 2) the campaign level; and 3) particularly at the ballot box. Fate, and a prolonged string of terrible errors have left no other choice or timing.

- All three are now decisive to human and planetary survival.
- **This is the American vote.**

An American vote is a Reasonable vote, and a Reasonable vote is an American vote. Both express true anti-slavery Humanitarian principles and The Three **Fully Self-Evident Truths of Human Success** that are:

- The only legitimate function of government is to uphold, protect and defend Individual Human Rights.
- We stand at One with the Creator in **the Humanity of Liberty**, The condition of Human Evolution.
- We stand united in the American definition of smaller government, fewer taxes and greatest personal freedom.

Because:

- We hold these Truths to be brilliantly self-evident as the foundation of all Human Success.

And:

- We thereby uphold Life and the conditions of Life in harmony and unity with All that Is.

And:

- We are, and this is, the New Energy and the Dawn of Humanity.
- Behold, **The Human Event!**

Please consider everything from the first page to now demystified, as has been desperately needed for numerous generations. It is now deciphered, the good, the bad, and the ugly. We have presented the Reasonable, the unreasoning, and every inch of modern politics, *the black hole of consumed life force.* There is a vastly better and brighter future out there awaiting only our resolute action because:

- *True Humanity awaits only the decision only you can make.*

- The time for that awareness has arrived.

Chapter Eleven

The Increase in Consciousness

- Now we further examine Human Success:

11. The next pattern is the clincher. It is by far the most important. **It is human consciousness**. Look closely at each of the five previous patterns and view the *monumental* ground shift in growing consciousness over time.

Which patterns are increasing? Why are they increasing? Which pattern describes *your* relationship to freedom or oppression? What is the intention of each highly dominating pattern? What are the outcomes of these patterns? Why were these political patterns non-existent one hundred years ago? Why did this change with the advent of the Federal Reserve? In your estimation, what is the number of centuries that the élite through bank, street drug, corporate, slave trade or other cartel, controlled governments worldwide?

- Why are these questions now critical to human continuation?
- There's the question.

The first five dominate political patterns alone prove beyond any doubt **the Evolution is on!** The overdue shift in consciousness into the experience of Humanness has well begun! *It did not in any way, start with this book.*

The catch **was** that the overall movement into Consciousness and Humanity struggled on without direction, focus or leadership. Prior to this writing, the Humanitarian Code **as a unit** did not exist. The Humanitarian Code, however, *was ever present*. This book and the Reasonable Party now bring it to fruition as one concise entity serving Humanity *correctly*.

It is the Constitution that set the direction and foundation for the humane treatment of humans. The founding documents of this Nation tell us *precisely* the same principles as the Humanitarian Code. This book only states it in modern English. We clear up the language and with that resolution, we clear away two centuries of Orwellian **spin engineering**—designed *specifically* to enable and advance human slavery.

- The Magna Carta before the Constitution also stipulated the *identical* code of humanitarian treatment of humans.

Prior to the Magna Carta, the Law of Moses placed the King and the subjects under the same requirements. Prior to that, government was above the law and all that existed was live human sacrifice {to depravity}. (The more things change, the more they remain the same.)

- *The near total lack of knowledge of humanitarian principles is directly attributed to the hideous and inexhaustible failure of the government education system.*

- Numerous people have stated to this author that the above failure **will** be recorded *as the worst recorded tragedy in human history*.

- Here is why: (The stolen generations)

- "In proportion as the structure of a government gives force to public opinion, it is essential that the public opinion should be enlightened."

     George Washington

- …And that leaves us with a choice:

- We can do nothing and allow oppression to wax worse—as *has been the trend*.

Eventually the "cure" will be marched in with fife, drums and cannons aplenty. Medals will be pinned on the survivors, and history will repeat itself as the controllers once again win. All the major cartels will prosper as they now do. **It's an absolute guarantee;** *YOU-WILL-NOT.*

- We would prove Revelations, Nostradamus, and a host of other doomsayers correct.

- This threnody, however, no longer has the option of continuation as life on this planet *cannot survive it*.

- This book presents a better choice:

- Reasonable offers *and is*, a peaceful and majestically saner solution.

Everything Reasonable is solidly built upon the principles of respect, unity, Consciousness, and the Three Time Proven Truths of Human Success. The answer is right in front of us. It is simply comprehension, alertness, and insight. It is in the American voice. **It is in God's direction of Peace and Freedom.**

The answer is in discernment, intuition and keener perception. It is in the recognition of that which Is. It is in becoming and being a Reasonable Human being—the Energy, Consciousness *and condition* of Human Success.

Humanity, the quality of humane, is of itself a paradigm demanding spiritual advancement. This is obviously so over the dipole of politically sourced and hate centered human life force theft—the old energy, intent, and experience of division, strife, ceaseless corruption and oppression.

May the voter dig down into their intuition and find the common knowledge presently owned by the hell no, no hell, no to hell non-voter. May the non-voter now vote for Human Success. ...And that ain't mainstream politics—*as you have unequivocally instructed this author.*

May both find, or cause *or be*, something **for a huge change** to vote FOR. We are now causing measures and candidates sharply more American.

As Reasonable, we vote humanitarian. We vote the humane treatment of humans. We may vote Libertarian *if* the candidate is *in practice* actually Libertarian. This is not nearly so hard a task. It can, must and is taking place as we speak in every corner, state, county and berg, *It is in the now!*

- The Human Event is right now, and *absolutely* worldwide.

- Strangely, The United States is *not* the leader in this regard.

- ...Although we should be. {an interesting puzzle there}

- This author has heard *many* labels for the New Energy. It is simply Creator Consciousness as experienced.

- *We call it the Dawn of Humanity.*

- Reasonable holds that Humanity is advancing <u>right now</u>, and probably within **you**—*where it counts*.

Human Freedom shall no longer remain a mere trivia and bone toss from the public face, and a rabidly burning loath from the **actual** face of modern politics. *That,* realization sets the stage for the Great Healing.

The qualities of good are going to win the day over the qualities of bad because Human Freedom will not be stopped *and it can no longer be delayed*. The Grand Shift in Consciousness is directly upon us. ***This is that Shift.*** The Reasonable Movement is both the Human Event and the Great Healing *by way of ending human slavery*. Thereby we cause harmony, balance and success in all aspects of human and planetary involvement.

We can, must and will accomplish The Creator's Design of Peace and Freedom. We now know *beyond any doubt*, we can and will. That realization alone is the single largest difference between the past of unrelenting hell and crashing failure **or**, the experience of freedom, dignity, thriving, harmony, safety and Success.

The old energy of politics as usual, represents the path of human desecration. It is destitution, oppression, theft, slavery, unhealth, injury, rape and murder. The human species has seen one too many days of those cartel driven results. The New Energy is the direct opposite of the old energy. The New Energy is of human freedom, dignity, prosperity, success, wellness, **and the basic Right to be unbullied by the servants of Satan.**

- The New Energy, the un-politburo, by undoing oppression, has transcendentally new levels of Human Success in every possible aspect of human life.

<u>That</u> realization is a central theme of this book. *It is the first conscious step into Human Success*. It is the humanitarian treatment of humans. More information and steps will emerge as the human species evolves. It will come directly from you just as it has thus far. The Reasonable Party is honored to facilitate this experience. That is what we do. **The lid over human ability is being lifted right now,** *even as we speak.*

- **It is your empowerment.**

Therefore, beginning the same transformative moment you read (and share) this book, Individual Human Rights, the real-world, Truth Test passing, and legal condition of human *and quality of humane*, will be won and protected **by Awareness**. Only that condition, outcome *and process*, is of the Creator's Energy of Humanitarian compassion. It is the Energy of common sense, human respect, Success and Prosperity. This is the process and outcome, now in Living motion, through which this book was caused by your desire for Human Success. *The procedure is once again in your care.*

- This is the process of Peace and Freedom.
- **This is Creator Consciousness placed into experience.**

Reasonable is the Energy and direction of Human Evolution. We are of Oneness, Unity, and equality of respect. We are of advancement, truth, integrity, honesty and discernment. No Longer shall the human race be held hostage; **for the time of Healing has now arrived.**

- We are the ones we have been waiting for.
- Because this is, **the Human Event!**
- *Many of you reading this now understand why you are here.*

From Consciousness and awareness you have caused and attracted the Energy of humanitarian principles. Most of you reading this know that without being told. You could have told me *and many of you way have*. **You are aware of your humanitarian calling and mission.**

You knew the truth of Consciousness by the inner energy and feeling reading this book produced. Each positive blend of Creation Energy and inspiration is as unique to each individual as it is unmistakable and thoroughly rewarding. We call it Reasonable.

Such positive, beneficial Energy is the classic to us and Reasonable **signature** the "other side" of absent consciousness, human slavery, *cannot produce*. It is your Inner Self recognizing and informing you of Truth, common sense, and direction that yields maximum personal benefit and the best for all and everything concerned. Such outcome is the Reasonable

Intent. Our **signature Energy-feeling** stems from viewing the location of harmony with All that Is, all the time, *in an environment of truth and honor.*

    Directly from your own valuable and ever evolving awareness, intent, prayer, envisioning, demand, energy, actions, ability, consciousness, knowledge, vibration, thoughts, gratitude, feelings *and existence*, you have fervently wished for and have co-Created this correct for human advancement match-up. This is what we do. As Reasonable, we facilitate *and are* the co-Creation process into Consciousness.

    You are now looking directly at your own creation and nearly all of you reading this are aware of it. The Universe itself holds the belief that you are valuable and worthy of Freedom. We see that as entirely Reasonable.

    From the universal principle of harm no one with hate, a Reasonable translation is: Harm no one with force, fraud or gunpoint theft. How ironic and simple that such a basic principle is the diametric opposite of every detail of Marxism and Mainstream politics. By now, we are also aware of what Marxism has done to humanity throughout the world. That awareness showcases the requirement of consciousness to stop it *everlasting dead.*

    One direction, **cause no harm**, is Reasonable. The other direction is human slavery, a condition enormously spiritually virulent to humans. It is the opposite of how we were designed. As of this document, you are now as equally informed of both directions and outcomes as those who would increase slavery upon you. The one and only difference between the two is your personal moral choice—*the decision to live as beast or as human.*

    Not only is this Energy an inspired gauge of your own evolving humanity, it is also an accurate measure of your awareness. It is **your** commitment to a better, brighter, healthier experience and world that created the words you now read.

    The contents of this book will also help you very accurately measure the amount and direction of your own thinking as to whether it is toward slavery or humanity, hence the name The *Humanitarian* Code.

- The human future, **should we decide one,** honors your choice to have a future.

    The humanitarian choice the future is asking you to make *right now,* will either be forever praised in the very highest esteem for awareness and courage to champion good—or not—for want of humans, or a world, to honor or not honor the incorrect choice.

    As it is your own insight, good fortune and synchronicity that manifested this book, we shall part this section with this ever so valuable perspective: The Universe rewards courage finer and further than all other attributes put together. This is so, because that is who you Are. When you become who you Are, the Inheritance is of course, *yours.*

- *You* get to decide for the remainder of human history:
- Will it be brief or benevolent?
- …For that is the choice providence has provided.
- …And we are most fortunate to have that choice.

    This generation, *and this generation alone and now*, shall decide not only the continuation of the human species *and the planet*, but the quality of experience we shall have. *This* decision reflects the closeness or distance from Creator and each other. The correct choice is motion into Creator Consciousness, **the You that is you.**

- And it is *absolutely,* so.

Chapter Twelve

Specific Directions

12.   Even a single lamp dispels the darkness.
Gandhi

Once you decide to escape the thinking of human slavery to join the human race, never quit. If someone **politically lobotomized** suggests that you need to be one tenth human, gently but clearly inform them: There is a limitlessly better way of living, *and you are living it*.

- This lets your light of Creator Consciousness shine.
- It is the methodology by which we as a species step into the evolution of an infinitely better, brighter, healthier experience.
- To cut through mountains of crap and confusion: It makes no difference what the question is, Peace and Freedom is the answer.
- **Vote that way!**

We pause to ask why we should be subjected <u>**by lethal force**</u>, to live tens of thousands of somebody else's singularly non-applying dictates when: In virtually all instances, it is patently obvious; the would-be dictators fail to live the mandate themselves. ...And for those who do, it is patently obvious; it has not resulted in either happiness or success. ...And without exception; the dictate is the mindlessly parroted slavery intent of the world controlling cartel as passed from bought off establishment, to television, **to brain dead moron and fool**. ...And anyone with a lick of sense sees *right through it*.

- How often is the objective to simply theft your life force?
- *Basically 100%*
- This is also true on several planes of existence.
- Now however, we are aware of it.
- ...And *the correct* solution is in progress.

Therefore, we allow the Energy of full human membership to be reflected and maintained throughout our platform because **Consciousness** is why we exist. May our every thought be in the Humanitarian Energy of God's Design of Peace and Freedom. That is who we *Are*.

Reasonable thinking holds that human slavery has just met its Waterloo. Welcome to Human my friend. As strange as this might at first sound, we do not butcher up and consume humans. It is that *specific* old energy that we have gathered together to stop. We are, *that* Reasonable.

- And it is so.

- Y'all asked me to talk about **Ron Paul** and we'll get there.

- Here are some straight forward directions to Human Success:

1. Sign on board to the existence worth living in. Such is Reasonable. Do it now. In all of Creation, the only Reasonable time is the Now moment. Applications are provided free online at: TheReasonableParty.US.

- **This step is the heart and horsepower of The Human Event.**

2. Fully live and feel in every way, that Glorious celebration of Joy and Humanity as bigger and bolder than all celebrations in history put together and for impeccable reason—Human Evolution! That specific transport feeling, **your** power vision, **your** strength and gratitude vibration, is the causation effect. It is co-Creation itself.

Allow that exhilarating Creator Joy-feeling to course through you, to breath into you, to infuse you deeply with Life Power. Allow that perfect peace and Creator Harmony of Natural Human living and Grand possibility to flow from you, to you, through you, and caused by you, in Love, Peace, Harmony and the celebration of Life. *That* is Consciousness.

- And *that's* how it's done.

- It is, **self-ownership**. *It is your vision experienced*.

Every day then, pause to deeply enjoy your Self to self elevated communication. It is of your own freedom and empowerment to deeply honor both selves—as fully worthy of the Creator Design of Peace and Freedom as fully intended in both worlds. It is as above, as below, as One: It is the *final* chapter of Human Slavery on Earth*!!!*

3. As a huge bonus to you and for you, share this ultra positive, Life facilitating, ultra high energy vibration with a few **actual** American friends in order to make Human Success a done deal. Not too bad for a few minutes of celebration-vibration seeing and feeling it as fulfilled "work"—and a bit of hearty celebration with other awakened individuals. That is how the Light of Human Evolution and the Great Healing becomes organized, energized and accomplished. It is *strictly* **your ownership of you**.

*And that my worthy friend is exactly the Reasonable opportunity, with none other like it in all human history that now begins in Light, Love and massive empowerment. It is *this* very moment, and *this* exact choice.*

- From Consciousness Itself, we readily and plainly observe:

The present Mission of the human race is to conclusively *and forever replace* the violent, brutal, dishonorable, inhuman, cowardly, bought off and mortally failed politics and policies of human hate with the omni-beneficial experience of Human Evolution.

- And it is so.

All human history pivots at this moment and with you. For most reading this, you are well aware of all Creation's calling into the experience worth living in. It is the steps given *in this book,* that shall create your empowerment and a future worth living in *and you now know it.*

The Reasonable objective is to step by step and with every determination humanly possible, move smartly away from the politics of human dismemberment and spiritual evisceration. We then move, by way of Creator Awareness into self-ownership, empowerment, Peace, Freedom and human spiritual wholeness, the all being One and, **The Human Event.**

Chapter Thirteen

Conclusion

13. The Conclusion of Part One:

Via Concia!, is the Motto of the New Energy. [**V** by anonymous request.] When moved from Latin to Usa {pronounced; you-suh}, has two very Reasonable forms: The first is Live Consciousness, for that is our Intent. The second is Life is in Consciousness, **for that is our Truth and celebration.**

- Because this is, *The Dawn of Humanity.*

"The Constitution of the United States, must mark the line of my official conduct."

George Washington

"The government that governs the best, governs the least."

Thomas Jefferson

"**We institute government** , the Declaration of Independence says: **to secure our Rights.**"

- *Therefore:*

1. The only legitimate function of government is to uphold, protect and defend Individual Human Rights.
2. We stand at One with the Creator in the Humanity of Liberty, the condition of Human Evolution.
3. We stand united in the American definition of smaller government, fewer taxes, and greatest personal freedom.

- How can it *not* be so?

For this is, *The Human Event.*

V

Part Two

Introduction

Part two of this book presents some basic concepts and perspectives that bring the Code Book and the Reasonable human movement together.

The movement into Human Evolution is quite time line new, in the sense that it is the one concept neither instructed *nor possible,* within the system wide old energy of human desecration.

- Mainstream politics is now defined as the great cosmic mummery by which we all discover what actually lurks beneath zero credibility.

- *I hear an amen.*

You are the only one who knows if you are Reasonable or unreasonable. The system lacks both the perspective and understanding to, in any honesty, *tell you anything.* The system will vehemently instruct against human empowerment: The system is the lemmings already over the cliff of endless oppression, self destruction, warfare, poverty and *wholesale failure.* Therefore, *value the system's grotesque illusions for what they are worth.*

In the mean time, enjoy the various perspectives offered from here forward and mentally tie them together into your own empowerment, *for such is their function.*

Understanding the Hologram:

"Genius is not IQ, *it is passion.*"
Albert Einstein

The moment you find enthusiasm, your God-within-ism, you have found the You that is you. Along with that Life facilitating condition, you will have found not only what you have set for yourself by your Self to *be*, but also that which you have set for yourself by your Self to *engage*. Your personal Mission for which doors will swing wide open for you is thus identified and enabled.

Whether one knows it or not, this is the Life-Freedom-Success process. All that Is, Creator and Creation, then flows from you, to you, and through you, thus fashioning your world in joy, love, kindness, fun, worth, ease, grace, fulfillment and harmony. It is the *process,* of enthusiasm that brings your experience, and you, into tune with those beneficial conditions.

Cherish then passion, for it is the inner compass of Life itself. Exercising this process then becomes the Freedom you were looking for all along: …For all possibility is patiently awaiting only your firm choice to know which doors to open. *Your decision, is the key.* It ever was.

Understanding the New Earth:

Our Joy, <u>and it is exactly that</u>, is to bring in the Dawn of Humanity. Ours is the conscious *living example*, and therefore the composition, design, DNA, Vortex and outcome of the Matrix. Only this is truly as above, as below, and thus the New Earth.

- Such are Reasonable gifts to you.

Here are two definitions followed by the Three-way, Free-way action plan of the Human Event:

1. Reasonable is when Human Enlightenment catches and surpasses human technology. By what appears to be all known accounts, in order for the human species to survive, that humanitarian condition is said to be in dire need, surpassing all other considerations, to manifest very, very quickly. <u>That very Reasonable moment is very soon, very fortunately for you.</u>

2. It is important to note that when referring to Human Evolution, Human Enlightenment, Human Spirituality, Human Success, or Human Freedom as Creator Designed, the energetic, humanitarian, human safety construct, intent and benefits in this time line, are in every possible sense all encompassing *and identical.* The knowing of that one Truth, will utterly eliminate profound amounts of omni-systemized instructed falsehoods, traps, foolishness, illusions, spin, doublespeak, insanity, pain, suffering, mayhem and confusion. *This will end the present system of human slavery.*

The above concepts, and others that move you, are worth contemplating. They are intended to stretch, exercise, and improve your awareness. When they hit home, they do the same to your *consciousness.* Therefore, please read the above two concepts as many times as needed until they are well understood. Such earned wisdom is the heart of both Human Ascension and a future worth living in.

Nothing in particular has to be memorized. However it does need to achieve placement into intuition. If and when you find agreement with a certain concept, it is thereby placed into intuition. The *concepts* are thereby forever available. *They work best when expressed in your words*.

"You will know the Truth, and the Truth will set you free."
                                                                                    Jesus

The Three-way, Free-way *immediate action plan* of Human Evolution into a vastly better, brighter world:

The following ultra easy and common sense steps, mostly only a small shift *in perception* from victimhood to determined empowerment, are exceptionally positive outcome based expressions anyone who intends to move out from under human slavery can very easily do *right smack now:*

1. Lend no support of any sort {that rhymes}, to <u>any</u> mainstream candidate without exception. This is a rule number two, see rule number one ordeal. The present cause of the human race, *is to break their support to pieces*. This common sense basic freedom step is the same as workplace safety only it is life place safety. This step is how to cause human safety 101. **Any exception is from deception**, *period!*

Stick to this first life-force rule <u>rigorously</u>! These three steps <u>*are, your, empowerment*</u>*!* These steps *are* human freedom. Any exception is continued human slavery. These steps *are* the Evolution—live them. BE them. Gain the benefit of peace and freedom. [Hint: It is ***not*** Bama-Rama]

- Bama-Rama is *the* coin, meaning: **"More of the same, regardless of the name".** Everyone *including the dog catcher* called this one.

- Bama-Rama will exist for as long as mainstream politics exists.

- That is why this Learn not to Burn step, *is the correct procedure.*

Just this first **Learn not to Burn** step, alone would drastically alter the course of human history for the extreme better. <u>This alone would conclusively end human slavery</u>. This trend is already in motion through the awakened human being. Our part is to *greatly add* acceleration through information sharing, mutual support, and sharply focused team participation.

- *Simply picture living as fully human; that should do the trick!*

2. Invest in your own future, by joining and vigorously supporting that which is Reasonable. Your financial support is our budget and therefore what we, working together as a team, shall accomplish.

- This is your empowerment, your organization, your team.

Every dollar and effort is both a vote and a voting *process.* Think of it as energetically voting for you, simply because you probably want to own you. We think that is a pretty good reason to support Reasonable. In fact, that is why we *are* Reasonable. *We are, your self-ownership vehicle.*

Every issue of any nature has an American and an anti-American side. The choice is nearly always clear cut. Discernment of this pattern by correctly understanding that which is American and not American is very easy to learn and practice. For example, supporting The Three Truths of Human Evolution, The Humanitarian Code, is a vote for *you.* It is a <u>very</u> savvy investment in *your* freedom, wellbeing, success *and empowerment*.

To live American, vote American. That is how American happens. By doing so, sends a crystal clear *and clearly understood message;* that you at least, **are awake**. It is also the only known method to transmute an otherwise wasted and meaningless mainstream vote <u>into a beneficial vote</u>. Awareness *and* <u>consistent</u> every day **American** <u>voice</u> is the whole key that causes the experience of Freedom worth living in.

- *Think of both as the New Boston Tea Party, that should do the trick!*

3. Continuously, vigorously and joyously share this Freedom causing information with as many Americans, or those *who could become* American, as many as possible and by any legal means possible. The cheapest and most creative means are the best. The very best is still person to person enthusiasm, for it is *your essence* that is respected. We have all the mass contact items and processes known for your use. *We are the Human Event.* Share and gift this book! Get the word of **the Human Experience** out there!

- Many, *and ever more daily*, are ready in consciousness for fully human, fully alive and fully awake.

A few old energy massively morpholithic {rocks in the head} **genuinely miserable** mud stucks may not yet understand humanitarian, or freedom, or American. Know *with great clarity*, that it is the old cartel sourced energy of the rote programmed <u>robotics</u> at its last few foul, feted and fatal gasps. It is the deathly putrid, dying, cancer riddled and final gasps of mainstream politics and its *bitterly tormented capitulators*.

- Lies upon lies, burden upon burden, injury upon injury, and theft upon theft, *mainstream politics has no honesty left*.

- And that crap ain't goin' anywhere *except the trash can*.

Do not be surprised at either condition, American or anti-American. Who knows how much internal thought is *robot or human*.

Ours is to mass present, and allow folks to choose or not choose *to empower themselves*. Only they can know if they are American or not. If not, our job becomes then to give them space, time and patience to grow into American. Most of them will do exactly that the moment their awareness climbs to anywhere above point zilch—*just as it once did for every one of us*. It is what it is …**and**, it's ok.

- Time will place everyone into political awareness, *one way or another*—**and** **you know it.**

- Said differently, there are *some* not yet brutalized by government.

- As more agencies get their wish, their turn is arriving *shortly*.

- Welcome to modern government.

- **It's nice to know there is now an answer.**

Those who are ready to evolve into Human absolutely will. This information will be *wildly* appealing to them and make you look extremely sharp, because you are. You thus create your own Freedom team. Your team works for your freedom following your example. They absolutely are your Life team, the object being to build it quickly.

The sooner you build your **Life-team**, the quicker we experience peace and freedom. That's how the math works. The objective is to place the math *in your favor*.

It is this step that makes the difference. Concentrate the bulk of your ongoing, day to day Reasonable energy **on this step**. This step is where the real-world leverage in your favor is at. Reasonable and its members, understand well, and put to profitable use, this highly beneficial *leverage point*. This step could be labeled: "How to create Freedom 101."

- No matter what else we may do or not do, we never wander away from this crucial to Human Success step.

- Technically, this step is unstoppable.

- ...Which is *another* leverage point.

- Think of it as being the Bringers of the Dawn of Humanity.

- Because we are exactly that *in no uncertain terms*.

These three steps of demonstrated awareness are the means and methods of <u>conclusively</u> ending human slavery. By the same methods and

Energy, we produce human and planetary survival and Success. **All of these benefits are possible ONLY in the New Energy.**

- The Reasonable Process is simply doing these three steps continuously. (Be found doing the Lord's work.)

We gain our humanity, the humane treatment of humans, the same instant we both internally and externally break to dust the omni-systemized and utterly false illusion of helplessness. The illusion of helplessness is the upmost human destructive lie of them all. Therefore, it is in *the doing* of these three steps <u>with ever growing membership numbers</u>, that crushes the devil's lie of helplessness **to dust.**

It is through reclaiming our power and place as human not slave, that we achieve our inborn and God given empowerment. As we begin to speak with one voice for a Humanitarian and peaceful co-relationship in mutual respect, understanding, cooperation, synergy, success and harmony, we thereby earn and Create heaven on Earth. It is then *as above, as below.*

- **This is the Creator's Intent of Peace and Freedom as opposed to Satan's plan of warfare and slavery.**

All Creation is awaiting these three steps in Consciousness and wisdom. Because these steps are of Consciousness, you place the Universe firmly on your side. The Humanitarian Code is the humane treatment of humans. This is where knowing stems from **with no guess whatsoever, as to which direction is correct.**

The only requirement asked by Consciousness is; that these three common sense steps into empowerment **are actually performed!** To that same degree: 1. We are in good hands. 2. We cause human ascension. 3. We cause our own empowerment. 4. We cause our own ownership. 5. We cause a future worth living in. 6. Fear vanishes, and thereby we become much more Reasonable people, and, 7. **We are the Bringers of the Dawn of Humanity.**

- Because it *absolutely* so.

Chapter One

A Reasonable Checklist

A Reasonable checklist:

The principles of this checklist were adapted from the longtime work of **Dr. Ron Paul**, who is brilliantly Reasonable on most issues.

When we examine any law or proposal at any level, the following checklist is our guide to very accurately measure the human benefit and thus the Reasonableness of any existing or proposed law. This checklist conclusively and forever ***correctly*** answers the larger question of whether or not any law or proposal is intended to, or capable of, moving humanity into an evolution of peace, harmony, cooperation and prosperity.

At the same instant, this list addresses the conclusion of the law or proposition: Does it move humans into additional slavery or toward Success? Is it toward oppression or freedom, inhumanity or humanity, theft or cooperation, poverty or abundance, de-evolution or Evolution, destitution or empowerment, old energy or enlightenment? Are people to be treated as farm animals, collateral, objects, insects, economic digits, robots, work units, vassals, servants, targets, slaves, and debits *or human beings?*

- Within all modern politics, we are spiritually and physically fully exploitable, fully expendable, and fully disposable.

- **And that's exactly what happens.**

To the same extent politically driven insanity, dishonor, larceny and brutality grows in leaps and bounds, humanity shall likewise perish. Endless agencies now embody that ritualized butchery. Through that literally satanic process, we become fully exploitable, fully expendable, and fully disposable.

- On the other hand, the New Energy recognizes and treats humans *as humans*.

- We place value upon Life, wellness and thriving.

- **This is the chief difference between the old and the New.**

Modern human slavery did not arrive by any legal, legitimate or Constitutional means. It did however come into play by the legal ***sounding*** process of modern politics. The illusion works—*as long as the truth is specifically not taken into account.* That is the sum difference between human and human sacrifice to cartel. This very thing, is the Creator's Truth that Frederick Douglass adeptly presented to the human race. Up until this writing, America has forgotten ***the*** Humanitarian Truth:

- **Humans were not constructed to be slaves!**

It is the now defining trend of politically motivated brutality that the human species shall stop and reverse. It was our collective, grievous, and fantastically inexcusable errors in abject political **non-awareness** that allowed hate, greed, brutality and theft centered malevolence to flourish.

- It will be *this* checklist that will forever *and correctly* stop the politician driven virulence against the human race.

A sharp student of Emancipation will notice that each test question is an approximate reflection of The Three Immutable and Eternal Truths of Human Evolution found in the Humanitarian Code. In truth, there is no warrant to proceed further, for such Energy is the direction and vehicle of Consciousness into peace and freedom, safety and harmony.

- This checklist assists you to walk in Light and Life as opposed to the modern standard *of fantastic political ignorance.*

The old outcome is strictly human harm. It is a backward direction now being fully exposed and fully eradicated. Our task is to know that the old energy of mainstream politics, *directly centered in wholesale betrayal*, is on its way out the door even as we now communicate because:

- **We are the Witnesses of the Dawn of Humanity.**

- And it is without a doubt, So.

1! *Does the law or proposal conform to the letter and uncommonly clear intent of the Constitution?*

98% and more of the laws passed by the United States Congress in the full last century, clearly and without doubt, fail this basic test *and fail it miserably*. That action is Felony Violation of Oath of Office. It is the *exact* source of political brutality, slavery, Naziism, and de-evolution straight into a soulless existence of terror. Such direction is the precise reason why government is in a present state of rife to the rafters with waste, fraud, scandal, corruption in biblical magnitudes, and savage abuse of power. The old energy of slavery and human destruction has endless false labels and trite euphemisms to pretend away slavery, but only one source:

- **Violation of the Oath of Office.**

Truth is now told: There is **not one** political or governmental problem that cannot be laid with the Eternal's accuracy directly at the feet of Violation of the Oath of Office. With the same accuracy, there is **not one** political or governmental abuse that cannot be quickly and utterly solved into human benefit by enforcing the Oath of Office to uphold, protect and defend the Constitution.

- The oath to 'uphold' means "to obey" the Constitution.

- *To obey the Constitution.*

- It means the government is restricted in what it can do.

- And that the entire sum of government operation is limited to an enumerated (written) list of a few functions that are ***strictly*** subservient to, and an extension of, our *personal* Human Rights.

- ...Which is a Republic.

- ...Centered upon the preservation of Individual Human Rights.

- This is a reminder that all government employees are subject to this oath.

- For all military personnel, to uphold, protect and defend the Constitution is intended *as lifetime*.

- The **Marine** understands that.

There presently is no challenge facing this Nation that this one step, observing the Oath of Office, would not fully, correctly and quickly repair. Our task is to place *the correction* of present politics into completion.

Therefore our educational process, and the profoundly beneficial outcome it produces, are fully Reasonable.

- And it is so.

2 ! *Does the law or bill cause additional oppression or additional freedom?*

- 100% of laws passed nationwide fall in **one** of the above **two** categories.

- 98%+ fall into the wrong category.

- How then can the process of human damning be classified as good?

- Exactly that lie, is what <u>**profoundly underhanded**</u> mainstream politicians are *demanding* that you believe.

The logic itself is upside down and a good many mainstream voters somehow, <u>call it whatever you will</u>, ***still*** don't get it. That *even further* slaps logic in the face. Did the mainstream voter check their head in along with their hat at the door? You tell me. Right there alone, might be enough material for an entire book.

- Come to think of it, **it is!**

Perhaps the real question should be, is the law or proposal in the direction of humans as animals, chattel, and utterly throw away objects *to be kicked about, clubbed, maced and robbed at will and whim,* or is the law or proposal in the direction of human respect and therefore Enlightenment?

The Constitution was **specifically** formed to uphold, protect and defend Individual Human Rights *as per Creator Design as clearly stated.* Any ***legal*** function of government is strictly and only an extension of, and wholly subservient to, *those definitions and conditions **of human**.* Therefore this second question is a direct reflection of the first question.

Alternatively stated, we ask: Does the law cause greater government size, complexity, expense, invasiveness, intrusiveness or centralization, and thus as *the direct result*, ever greater waste, fraud, abuse, human cost, and growing brutality? Or does the law honor and obey the American Way of Life of smaller government, fewer taxes and greatest personal freedom?

In nearly all cases as the no! voter so clearly knows, the only morally correct vote on law, bill, measure, levy or proposal is H...! NO! That is only because shove it and stick it or go to hell is not yet on the yes/no ballot choice! The numerical supermajority direly wishes that option *were* available and, has *truculently* expressed it.

However, as human consciousness is rapidly changing for the better, **be highly alert** as good, human beneficial, American oriented Energy is now out there. It is unmistakably on the increase. We *know* the New Energy trend is Reasonable:

- *It is placed there by Reasonable people!*

- Ah-ha*!*

3 ! *Can the stated condition to be addressed **by gunpoint force**, be better served using **nonviolent** processes?*

In nearly all conditions in the past 100 years, and vastly more so in the future, the only *conscionable* answer is absolutely! Common sense tells us that naturally occurring cooperation, open debate, barter and negotiation has solved vastly more challenges than the **raw thuggery** and cowardice of gunpoint coercion. This is doubly true when virtually all of the coercion is cartel demanded and completed by the **den of vipers** we unwittingly refer to as "modern politics".

Any time we add a new law, no matter how tempting or easy, *{usually meaning slimy}*, it may at first seem, **it involves the use of gun point force**.

With each law, someone politically connected **uses violence** to pursue political, personal or cartel gain, while those *not* politically connected lose their portion of life that was removed at **armed robbery**. Once one finds themselves on the wrong end of this purchased butchery one too many times, political awareness *automatically happens*. However, that is damn certain learning it the hard way! *The catch is that it may cost you your life*.

- **Reading this book is a much safer and saner way to learn the same lesson that everybody is going to learn anyway.**

- The objective is to gain awareness before it is too late for *YOU*.

- **The larger objective is to end the procedures of human slavery.**

Outwardly, such unlimited **life theft processes** might have the surface appearance of a zero sum equation limited to winners and losers **if** numerous *acute, profuse and monstrous* collateral damage factors are pretended away. The outcome is a lot like using a 500 pounder to get one bad guy when fifty cents of powder will instantly enlighten the same wacked out thug—*as long as a Marine enables it*.

- The law as employed by modern politics punishes the good every inch as harshly as the bad. (Technically, usually worse)

- That is because the design is to protect not people, **but cartel**.

For one example among far too many to choose from, we shall look at the real-world results of nearly all modern "regulations". Within the deeply psychotic world of regulatory law, new law universally translates into the politically entrenched monopoly wins big and monotonously, and all *formerly* potential start-up competitions get violently aborted **at gunpoint cowardice**.

That particularly dishonorable process is a thousand ways masked by windy and fraud saturated feel good **smack talk**. The results however are; the lower *several* steps of the economic ladder get sawed off and any remaining steps thereby become out of reach. The object is to stop any and all competition to the cartel. **And that is *exactly* what happens.**

With few exceptions, the lower socioeconomic class gets hurt the worst and in several rather vicious ways. At the same time, dishonest and purchased politicians break their arms in hearty venal backslap and the raucous public self-plauditing of painted circus clowns and noisy crows. Thus the zero sum *false* appearance is, in real-world *experience*, a few, select, repeat and deep politically inside winners. **The truth** is an entire world society kept in rigid, merciless, permanent and fully intentional gunpoint and vicious, **gang banger style**, thug enforced economic slavehood.

- This is the role of the mercenary, yet up until today we weren't allowed to call it that.

This is facilitated through the cartel purchased modern politician *worldwide*. Any label of the mainstream politician at that point becomes obviously meaningless as their existence has collectively and individually *and conclusively* degraded into a lifetime profession of **hideous dishonor**.

<u>*Modern*</u> political regulations wind up working just like this: Some *monopoly* that makes urinal drain quality, badly overpriced, crooked fitting, and red painted, leaky size 8 spotted owl skin shoes makes the amazing discovery that basically **any** competition will put them out of business. {Sounds like our local utilities} At that point, usually somewhere in-between the second and third generation of mogul-doom and bureaucracy, any and all innovation was long lost to the terminally lazy death of inspiration.

- The bureaucratic process is unfortunately not limited to the keynote maelstrom we refer to as government.

However, the cartels know the mainstream politician can so easily be purchased, they ***are*** two bits a bushel, (and *way* aint worth that). From there, the fate of the human race is sealed. What better way to stop competition than to simply outlaw all shoes, (or utilities), that are *not* gaudily painted, fall-apart, terribly overpriced, throw-away, crummy, red, spray can painted number 8, one size fits all, *actual* spotted owl skin shoes? Got it? {My bad: The technology nomenclature is "engineered obsolesce".}

Now any "regulatory" excuse will do, just make one up. I could think of oodles. Here's one: Size 6 shoes are "dangerous" to size ten feet when skydiving for instance. This of course is proven in a court of law—with endless purchased **junk science** [i.e. government funded] studies. This universally includes enough manufactured, falsified and televised public scare scams and accompanying statistic twists to float a dozen battleships!

The cartel **will supply** the excuse and the modern politician **will obey.** This is *if* they care to enjoy their re-election money! The bureaucrat will obey *if* they like their paycheck. Any counter evidence will be ruthlessly crushed by any means deemed necessary including cold blooded murder *or mass murder.* That's how the system works. That's how to work it.

Not so much as *one* jerk gives the slightest fig about what size feet you own. That completes the pattern of modern political regulatory law. A more accurate name might be "cartel posterior vacuuming law". And that is the trade the modern politician **with malice of forethought** makes: It is very filthy lucre in trade for professionally applied brown nosed bung pucker.

- I hope it was at least Reasonably illustrated if nothing else.

- The right question: Is there *any* cartel the mainstream politician has *not* bootlicked?   {Any utility monopoly either?}

- Tragically, that question is one among far too many to choose from.

The principle one layer *below* the above unlimited happy house insanity and with it, an endless river of *utterly corrupt* judges is this:

Rarely if ever has violence made any problem better. We are continuously and rigorously instructed that concept as applied to interpersonal and societal relationships. History and wisdom has shown us this basic Truth to be a million to one more productive than brutality as applied to the resolution of nearly any circumstance.

Yet, when it comes to modern politics, by some queer to Nature inversion of reality, the *exact opposite* of that universal principle is suddenly advertised as, and generally accepted as *normal*. Within the greed, hate and theft centered doings of mainstream politics, each law states and effects that not only is violence the first solution, <u>but every solution</u>.

- We can now attest that the terrorism and police state of **human slavery** simply cannot cause a beneficial living condition.

From sheer experience, the human race can now affidavit that **live human sacrifice** is not Human Enlightenment. It is not Human Ascension. It is not Success. It is not equality, justice or fairness. It is not common sense, common decency, common respect, or economic prosperity. It is, however, every inch of the intent and uniformed output of modern, *singularly* <u>hate and revenge centered</u> mainstream politics.

The epidemic, intrinsic, systematic, automatic, inherent and defining **despotism** of modern politics is now a worldwide pan-governmental ubiquity and accord. We now know that violence and slavery no longer serve the human race or human condition. At this time the consciousness and truthfulness of modern politics and its results, modern government, is dropping like a rock. Simultaneously, the awakened Humanitarian and the Energy healer have markedly increased the Consciousness of the human race.

- <u>That increase in Consciousness is what we are doing **right now**</u>.

- It is *this* contrast in consciousness the human race is feeling.

- <u>It has now come to dominance over all other considerations</u>.

- **The human race is now aware that for our humanity and human species to survive, modern greed and hate centered politics shall be transcended** *and dumped*.

- **In the specific, mainstream politics as we know it, simply and plainly will not exist, neither by name or by energy or by intent.**

- **Mainstream politics will-simply-be-gone.**

- You saw it stated right here, first *and correctly.*

Mainstream politics is on its way out the door *right now* with all the hang dog slink it can collectively muster. Along with it goes the profoundly human destructive and satanic **idolatry** of government as God, as the *blasphemous and hideously failed* omni-potent end all, do all, be all *and decide all* that defines *and is* human slavery.

So the answer is yes, any condition facing the human race is virtually without exception, vastly better addressed by anything other than government whose track record is replete with rigorous failure, violence, waste, fraud, theft, corruption, brutality and abuse. We ask, where does human slavery serve anyone or anything <u>except</u> cartel?

- Where can human sacrifice *with you on the wrong end,* be defined as a conscious or prosperous act?

- It is not.

Therefore:

This worthy checklist, and it need not be any longer, is indeed an energetic mirror of **The Three Basic Truths of Success, Benefit and Consciousness:**

- The only legitimate function of government is to uphold, protect and defend Individual Human Rights.

- We stand at One with the Creator *in the Humanity of Liberty*, the condition [and Consciousness] of Human Evolution.

- We stand united in the American definition of smaller government, fewer taxes and greatest personal freedom.

- We do so because we are Reasonable human beings!

- *And it is absolutely so.*   - **And right on time!**

Chapter Two

Roll Call

Roll call:

Ayn Rand is correct in this very important detail: One cannot in any way help their fellow human by remaining themselves in [spiritual, mental or physical] poverty, *in spite of every illusion we have been rote instructed otherwise*.

A swarm of already forgotten present day critics have mused in awe, loath, and wonder, as to how Ayn Rand, one person, can <u>still</u> outweigh the political right. That would be a political "right" she tersely, fiercely, vehemently and correctly rejected both in the 1950's and again *in no uncertain terms* in the 2010's.   {the'Tweens}

Come on critics, for God's sake get a clue. The question, if there even was one, answers itself: There is no, then or now, political "right". Any number viewing zero outweighs the political right. My housecat without the fleas, outnumbers **and out-spines** the political right. (But then again, so does a jellyfish.) As near as I can tell with diligent research, a cross-country trek *and a microscope*, the limited government, fiscally conservative, Human Rights upholding **leadership** has self-vanished clean off the face of the earth without a trace or a memory! You would think either bill collectors or John Law was after them for the past hundred years straight!

- Perhaps they owed the fracking oil mafia one too many favors.

- It would make my day if that hit a nerve.

Long ago, there was a book by Barry Goldwater called The Conscience of a Conservative. No more, bud, not no more. *That animal is extinct*. The book lives on, however the contents of the book have been utterly banned from the "conscience of the conservative" **which is simply neither**.

I enjoy a good laugh at those who in crashing error at the pinnacle of delusion, self-label as "conservative" when functionally 100% of their approved leadership is the **dead opposite**.   <u>In fact, their "approved" leadership simply can't get more arrantly un-American or big government Statist</u>. The sheer arrogance and *asininity* emanating from the same blatantly Marxist leadership *knows no bounds*.

I'm talking **real-world voted** here, not the *indescribably* empty headed and hate filled rhetoric and fourth rate acting that spews out like so much banal puke from television and radio. It is *exclusively* 'Television talk'. It is just as preposterously empty-minded, cartel serving, and lifetime hypocritical as the purchased and condom wrapped hand puppets spewing it.

Somehow or another they <u>still</u> don't get it: They are being profusely and prodigiously lied to, and in every which direction but loose. That condition represents mighty, mighty tall evidence of *apparently* little or no comprehension of the English language. They *truly* know not of what they do. The ignorance, hate, hypocrisy **and mouse-think** are *all* off-the-scale.

As but one titanic example of **pure blindness**, (among endless), here is a *real* good one: When *their* President if one has the gall to call him that, is caught <u>on record</u> with his 8 year defining statement sounding like this:

"I don't care about the Constitution.   All it is, is a goddamn piece of paper."

George W. Bush

<u>And</u>, the "conservatives" to the last **blooming idiot** one of them pretend W's repeatedly demonstrated belief, and the floods of <u>*outright* anti-American</u> laws his father and he passed **simply never existed**!   I have a problem with that: And *two too many* **skull and cross-boners** *is the problem!*

How arrogant and unreasonable does the right wing leadership, terminal assholes that they are, have to get before the rank and file stool pigeons **and impeccable imbeciles** finally for God's sakes, wake up? In my **lifetime**, the only thing the entirety of the Republican leadership has gotten mechanically flawless, is *instantly and reflexively* waving the white flag of unconditional surrender at every possible opportunity starting at boo!

- When do the harlequins discover they are being lied to ***ceaselessly?***

- As it turns out, I'm not the only one who noticed the above 150 years worth of right wing backstab and had a problem with it.

- So did Ayn Rand—big-time.

- And she is *still* correct.

Please dear reader, know my intention is to put something in this book that rattles *everyone's* cage. Hopefully it will serve to awaken. Know well that I can gladly rake so called "liberals" who have *officially,* wholesale abandoned any and all of their own classic liberal roots roughly **150** years ago also. I can also do this task along with *effortlessly* raking around <u>utterly fake</u>, sheep brained conservatives from block to block all-day-long.

In fact, the collections of outright illusions the liberals **wallow in**, is now so screamingly obvious and self-evident that I need not elaborate upon them in the slightest, therefore I'd rather not. Rejoice or puke either one, I care not, the same as Ayn Rand when she spoke her opinion.

As it turns out, my Drill Instructors of editors won't let me off the hook without an example. So here it is: My namesake, Thomas Jefferson whose blood evidently flows in my veins, is the *only,* fore-founder claimed as hero by *both* sides of the mainstream Uniparty. If there is a stranger cuckoo-clock madhouse claim in all history than that, I have not yet run across it*, and I hope I never do.* ...And we've experienced **THE Joker**, President-*acting*.

So, what did Thomas Jefferson stand for? How did he *actually* vote? What was the central theme of all his writings (beyond the limited government Constitution of course). He **vehemently** stood for <u>very small and</u> sharply limited government upholding Individual Human Rights. He stood for self-ownership, sound money, fewer taxes and *rigorous* fiscal and debt free accountability, and that of course defines classic liberalism.

- It **damn certain** is not modern liberalism is it?

And there is your example, one of *endless* modern liberal illusions that I could have just as casually shattered to nothing. Notice that the present *American* style of effortlessly debunking mainstream political illusions is not real far from the style of my favorite hero, Ayn Rand.

Another ***outright lie*** applying across all modern politics is the illusion that government is good at anything. History says otherwise, and so does

Ayn Rand. This is a case, one among endless, where modern politics is *morbidly* incorrect, with both history and Ayn Rand being ***pristinely* correct**.

Indeed she is again and again. Yet this part is about the highly talented Ms Rand, not the sanctimonious and self serving complete *assholes* we gratuitously call mainstream politicians.

They for **utter** absence of honor have **not** legally earned the keep of their office. We only have to recall that <u>every one of them</u> swore an Oath to *not* do exactly what they *are* doing. The story need not go any further than that, case closed.

Then I thought, what would Ayn Rand say if she were writing this? *So I asked*. At that point I was on the horns of a dilemma. Do I write or not write the uncomfortable?

Of course I'll write it, however it will be with the proviso that it is what it is. *I'm only the scribe*. So she's a bit rough. I'll guarantee you to the depth of my being *that* was an honor. Any emphasis is mine as I heard it.

{direct quote:} "From this moment forward to their bitter end, the table of politics is turned, the shoe is on the other foot. From here on out, let the mainstream politician, candidate and woodenheaded voter defend if they can, *if they dare*, their brutal oppression of the masses. Let them, nay, make them, force them, to defend vast and endless waste, fraud, theft, abuse, corruption, failure, malfeasance in office, dirty backroom deals and one scandal chained tightly upon the heels of another, for that is what they have become. That is what they represent. That is what they do. That is their nasty little soul if they claim one.

"That is what they deserve, and that is what they now must defend for the eyes of history demand an answer. They have contrived and convened a terrible human sacrifice, and now they must defend that.

"While we produce freedom, let the mainstream defend their utter madness. While we produce peace, let the mainstream defend their results of human destruction. While we produce resonance, let the mainstream defend their division, hate, strife and terror. While we produce economic wholeness, let the mainstream defend their wretched IRS and all its diabolical and contemptible schemes of madmen and drunkards.

"While we produce human advancement, let the mainstream defend their tortured dark ages of oppression. While we convey truth, let the mainstream defend their mountains of hollow make-believe and despicable lies. While we produce well and healthy humans, let the mainstream defend their endless ways to keep humans broke and broken. Make the mainstream hack defend the losing ground of what they are; an anathema, blight and boil upon the {posterior} of human history! Make the howling political hyenas stand upon the intellectual quicksand of their own convoluted making, and tear each other apart like wild and mindless animals!

"Make the mainstream, what's left of them, defend the indefensible horrors that have traveled full circle to define them. Make them explain why they perpetually elect great treasonous rats, criminals and fakes of every nature to office. Make them explain for the world to hear, the acts of their Marxist Comrades who may have never produced an American vote! Make them defend that, the un-American, *their un-American!*

"Make the boot lickers square up and defend the United Nations, that terrible nest of evil with its endless Communists, and vicious Dictators that our person taxes have from their birth supported in every opulence! Yes, make them defend that if they dare, for each moment they do, they defend murder, butchery, rape, warfare, torture, ruin, drug cartel and mass scale slave trade.

"Make the Statist {mainstream politics} defend an America over-regulated to the very teetering brink of economic Armageddon. Make them defend their armies of thugs and jackals, administrators of the first order of brutality who make their rules of thin air as they go! Make them defend their imprisonment society, *the most so of anywhere in the world,* where the innocent are held guilty, and the harmless, homeless and helpless all, as easy prey, are persecuted with a wild vengeance equal to none, not even a Stalin or Hitler, Mao or Pol Pot!

"Make them defend a society where its citizens are brutalized and destroyed to no earthly function and where the poor are reduced to hapless targets for every manner of legalized destruction, harm and debtor's prison. Make them defend their devils of politicians who have sold their being to cartel, and have utterly destroyed the Rule of Law and nearly so equally ***as would be their dream,*** to destroy society to lawlessness, cave dwelling and murder trading over scraps and morsels.

"Yes, make them defend their Statist society where virtue is punished and the vilest of the vile are held in esteem and office. Make them defend a world so dysfunctional and base that the individual and our initiative, the very engine of survival, advancement and prosperity is ridiculed, scorned, held to contempt, and punished out of society. Make them explain one and all to the last remaining mouse, that vicious, crass and upside down world, and make them explain why the Income Tax anywhere yet draws breath amongst civilized humans where it has no place or right!

"Why then do we allow the mainstream voter their strange illusions, the same of the vegetables who laid dying in the opium dens of China, when those illusions enslave the world, kill the innocent and destroy the peace?

"So the task falls to all of us who cherish the humanity of Freedom to make the mainstream politician defend their rabid aversion to Liberty. Make the perpetual liars defend a power drunk and debauched end to end, profligate, dissolute and run-away government of their own soiled origin. Force them in every corner to explain their ugliness, and trap them in every corner to defend if they can, their perfect destructiveness.

"Make the mainstream, pimps of their own mother, defend their own doom of a blinding hailstorm of wildly broken promises and lies unfit for a monkey!

"Again and again, until they repent in well earned shame or slither away, make them defend their own human sacrifice. **They created the burn of slavery from the fire of freedom!** They manufactured a slavery upon themselves, a slavery they wrought and own and appear to cherish. So yes, make the mindless jackals explain their slavery, and make them defend their perfect insanity, their perfect hate."

"*Indeed make the dirty, guilty bloodhanded bastards and pillars of salt whose names in history <u>will defile sewage</u>, defend the ever damning hell they so ardently and greedily made!*" {end quote}

- **Ayn Rand*!***

- *Wow! I could re-read that forever and it would still be pleasurable.*

- *And accurate.*

- **Therefore:**

- It sounds like a plan, and a very, <u>very</u> Reasonable plan at that.

I like what she says and the way she presents it. Both are immensely Reasonable and intensely American. They come from someone who *correctly* understood and deeply appreciated, **American.**

Rand's Objectivism, I would classify as objectively and without bias or prejudice, observing and allowing such processes that work to work, and observing and allowing *away* such processes that do not work. **Modern politics has intentionally failed both aspects of functional society.**

The Objectivist asks: What process benefits humanity and what process does not. From that, the Objectivist concludes that human slavery, the results of mainstream politics, does not benefit either the human or humanity. Human Slavery is not humanitarian to either the human or humanity. Yet its opposite, Peace and Freedom *does* benefit both the human and humanity. *It is the only condition humanitarian to either one.*

Once the labels, illusions, bias and hate blinding are dropped away from the human equation, the above perfect axiom remains as the only Truth there is. From that immutably proven Truth, we then found or formed **The Three Truths of Human Success** that, although presented by Reasonable, do not of themselves belong to Reasonable. They are at once from, of, and leading into Human Success, *the experience worth living in*.

Such is Objectivism. Such is common sense. Such is human Advancement. Such is Empowerment. Such is livability. Such is Enlightenment and Evolution and most fully Inevitable. Such is therefore Reasonable.

- …Aynd, it is entirely so.

- *If there were not thinkers like Ayn Rand, there would remain only the unthinkable.*

- This is why this book honors Ayn Rand.

- The world owes her a debt they can only repay **by thriving.**

Thomas Paine contributed this:

"We pray we can count you among our fellow countrymen, yet we leave the choice to you. You may Live as Human and Free, or exist if you have the shame to call it that as mice, where every thought and every move is dictated through violence by another's will. The Freedom we shall presently take from damnation itself, we shall also leave to those of lost courage and diminished humanity. As for ourselves, we owe this much to our children, and again as much to their progeny for all eternity.

"It has in verity been spoken that the price of slavery by magnitudes untold, outweighs any investment in alertness to maintain Freedom. On this good day, we have well gained the wisdom to know why: The price of slavery includes your Soul, for only the Devil and its servants own slavery. Whilst the price of Freedom is your courage; for how otherwise would either God, Creation or yourself **discern that you were human?"**

Perhaps now, you can see why Thomas Paine, the original author of Common Sense {about 240 years ago} and the *actual* father of this Nation, helped inspire this book. He also understood American.

- The world owes him a debt they can only repay *by living as human*.

George Washington, the reluctantly textbooked father of this Nation, would in silence Truth test your Soul and eye, as he handed you the pen after your resolve was made known. He would see that you were earnest and Reasonable, and thank you with a single firm nod.

- We owe him a debt we can only repay *by living as American*.

Martin Luther King asked us to treat each other with equal respect, through conducting our business with peace and understanding.

- We owe him a debt we can only repay *by living with respect*.

Frederick Douglass our Nation's greatest orator has well stated his part, for he has the greatest Truth of them all. And it stands.

- We owe him a debt we can only repay *by living in Freedom*.

Gandhi gave us the correct instructions:

- "Be the change you wish to see."

- We owe him a debt we can only repay *by living in peace*.

To Be, or not to Be (human) echoed those worthy instructions that every true Master *throughout all time* left for this day, this hour, this moment and *this* instruction on Human Success.

- We owe each of them a debt we can only repay *through being who we Are*.

- I Am, and We Are, Reasonable.

- *And this is*, the Human Event.

- By now you should have a better view of Human Teleology.

- Because you are looking at it.

- **It is the absence of human slavery**.

The individual that I was named after, Thomas Jefferson, elected to contribute the following thoughts. To understand this properly you will have to use your imagination, and for a moment pretend that Thomas Jefferson were currently President. This is how life would proceed *in that case:*

"Be it hereby resolved by the people of the United States of America:

"That our Nation effective immediately shall with all haste, permanently remove all funding, support and participation with the United Nations and all United Nations functions.
"Effective immediately, no United Nations law, resolve, treaty, regulation, ruling or function shall henceforth have any effect or jurisdiction within any portion of our Nation or territories including our foreign

embassies, and in particular, including any American whether home or abroad anywhere in the world.

"No United Nations functionary whether bureaucrat or mercenary, shall henceforth set foot alive upon our soil for any reason whatsoever.

"Any relationship between our Nation or any of the fifty States or any person or business claiming here a home, and any other nation or entity upon this planet, shall from this day forward, be based solely upon force free, mutually beneficial agreements arrived at void of the thoroughly destructive poison of unhonest political coercion in any of its many forms.

"As this Nation was formed exclusively to uphold, protect and defend Individual Human Rights, all future relationships will be solidly built upon synergistic values, cooperation, friendship and voluntary exchange. This enlightened relationship will beyond any doubt, profoundly and immediately improve the lot of all humanity.

"These actions taken today will quickly and permanently obsolete the pandemic siege of government by murder, rape, pillage and naked brutality that has been the bane against humanity from the dawn of our species, yet shall now grind to a short stop *beginning this moment*.

"With resolve to the depth of my soul,

Thomas Jefferson

President"

I rather enjoy his failure to mince words. We owe him a dept that we can only repay *by being honest*.

The general and readily available consensus that I found all across America, is that mainstream politics has degenerated to become so depraved and hateful that the only right thing to do with it is a mercy killing.

That should be all the evidence needed *and it is*. However we have time and again, observed mainstream politics dive into single digit approval. We see that each dive into perdition has a quicker descent than the last one. This pattern has repeated at least since Nixon was in office, and probably long before. It is guaranteed to wax worse for as long as mainstream politics exists. **We have seen it with our eyes, and it is now time to use our minds.**

We have also observed that each adventure into ever lower single digit approval, remains in that condition longer than the last one. We can easily see that each dive is much closer in both nature and time to the revolting leftovers of the previous crash. We see that the names and faces interchange quicker that dirty socks yet the scandals remain, outside of their labels, basically identical. We can easily observe that in every event, one "side" will fail to prosecute the other. This ongoing condition is a direct result of mutual guilt. Everyone has their hand in the same cookie jar.

And we can see that the scandals go on and on and on. We can also see that each mainstream politician over time, gathers ever more scandals. We can see that this gathering of scandals is rapidly gaining momentum. We can readily see that each scandal gathered is at least one notch shittier than the previous one. We are steadily discovering that many of those scandals involve cold blooded, premeditated murder.

A good example is that I would rather be Hillary's enemy than her friend. Her enemies seem to celebrate more birthdays than her friends even though the competition *has edged closer lately*.

- The television is never going to be our ally on any of this information.

Therefore it is time to place the evidence together ourselves without the help of the television, and see the insanely pathetic pattern as it is. It is time to use our minds and see within the endless chain of scandals, the unlimited contempt for the human race. It is our job as human beings to end this cover-up and with it, the stinkin' and pathetic charade of mainstream politics in total and *absolutely forever*.

- This is what I would consider as being honest.

Mr. Jefferson is correct about the United Nations. He also demanded that any use of his name refrain from any and all association with the words democrat, republican, liberal or conservative. Those four words to be spit at until struck from the English language, more than nearly anything else *just piss him off*.

I will explain why: In relationship to each other, those *specific* four words have been rendered meaningless. In relationship to the universe, those same four words have come to mean anti-freedom. If one includes the description anti-American, then one has found the location where Thomas Jefferson and Ayn Rand are in complete agreement.

- And we find these conditions as so.

The roll call includes you, the student of Consciousness. The good news is that fellow students of Life are absolutely worldwide. The body politic of human slavery is presently *and aggressively* being wholesale replaced by Truth to one highly accelerating degree or another on every square inch of Earth. Some of the quicker to catch on locations, not only are not the United States, but started off much worse than the United States.

Why this debacle exists, is strictly due to our own swine like complacency and let's face it, *outright laziness*. Keep in mind that many other's contrast and experience immersed in abject oppression is far worse than in the United States. Ours however, is far more *insidious*. The upside of this story is that The Consciousness Evolution is, in every sense, *absolutely* worldwide with NO exceptions whatsoever.

- Although overdue, the Worldwide Consciousness Transition *of remaining above Integrity*, is now upon us.

- *And it is as Reasonable as it gets!*

Is it not time to dismiss an ark of three penny politicians, allowing them to live in the unemployment lines and thrall that they as evil kings have created? Can a single one of them live by the tyranny they have made and lorded over us? Imagine the twisted and insufferable fat cat pricks who have never worked a day in their entire foul life—faced with a pick and shovel, being forced to buy insurance out of the minimum wage they have not yet earned. Could a single one of them survive the havoc, destroyment and squalor they have so eagerly caused?

- Where would their know-it-all be then?

- Where should it be *now?* **You would be correct on that.**

We no longer ask if we can move mainstream politics into a greater reality. That option was prostituted away long ago. <u>Rather we ask if mainstream politics has moved us into a greater reality that does not include human slavery</u>.

- For the first time in history, we have both the necessity <u>*and the means*</u> to advance in consciousness.

- **We are doing that through sharing this message.**

Do not be set back if someone cannot accept this message. There are some in this world who do not want the cure that will make them whole.

- Rather, *their desire is to feel drugged away by lies* **while dying**.

- Our decision is more fortunate that that.

This roll call would be incomplete if it did not recognize more of the chief players that either caused or contributed to this book. Therefore, a bit reluctantly, I must include the sheer insanity loosely referred to as Mainstream politics:

- **Mainstream politics is the great game of nihilism exclusively arrived at** *through dishonor perfected.*

- We owe the politics of human slavery the mercy of *DUMPING IT.*

Ayn Rand explains the Hologram this way: "Anyone who fights for the future, lives in it today." **So we become Conscious.** We become Human and Free. We become Well, Whole, the Living, and the Healer of self and worlds by casting away failure and its politics, internally, externally, *and forever*. With that beautiful Truth and Humanitarian Respect, **we are set Free!**

- And it is so!

Within Consciousness and its directly resulting Human Success, we see ourselves as the one organization that is firmly on your side, causing your personal freedom, safety, wellness, prosperity and Success. By now, there is every likelihood you have formed the same conclusion.

Therefore, we now ask you to join this, your organization. Joining is free and very freedom causing. We are open to all and request only that you properly inform us of your decision of Human Membership; for Consciousness has arrived so that we may have Life, and have it **magnificently**.

Special thanks to Dr. David R Hawkins, Gregg Braden, Dr. Bruce Lipton, Dr Frank R Wallace, Unity churches worldwide, Vernon Howard, Stewart Wilde, José Silva, Kryon, Pataah, The Galactic Counsel, Lord Sananda, St. Germaine, Carlos Castaneda, Bridger House Publishing for the Handbook for the New Paradigm, EFT, Psych-K, and my friends and teachers at Huna Research. I thank Nightingale-Conant Corporation, and the oodles of New Energy authors inhabiting my overloaded library, who have achieved Consciousness.

- Each is acknowledged for a direct effect on this book.

Extended thanks are owed to the plethora of people who had either a direct or indirect hand in the amazing and providence driven process of this book. Numerous of us took notice that the miracles and protections flowed like rain in this process. Many of those events were nothing short of stunning, and this book clearly could not have happened without them.
Additional thanks goes to the collection of teachers throughout my life who had the amazing constitution to survive me. Somehow, a few did not actually loath my presence when I asked a good many of the wrong questions, often *pointedly.*
Additional thanks to the fantastic people and teachers at Unity who daily work on enlightenment and just keep showing the way by example.
They instruct the Christ Consciousness within. Somehow or another, I have evolved to understand at least, that location is where It is supposed to be. It is a discovered condition that could become *intrinsic.*

I have hopefully broken every norm and still have a book. I have loaded it with as many split infinitives, number disagreements and sentence fragments as I could cram into it. And a score or so dangling chads and purchased judges *installed* a lying weasel as if he were President. With that, we shall move on.

    The kind English teacher (to whom I owe a great debt) that flunked me solidly believe it or not *twice*, four years apart, would have a field day I'm sure. Um, this admission comes as a surprise more to me so than to you Sandy, however, *I was actually more or less listening*.

    I cannot recall if I flunked history three or four times or in which problem child High School, and don't care. By the way I never graduated having been kicked out of two high schools and sentenced into the Marine Corps forty years ago over a few pounds of low grade homegrown leaf (and failure to supply names). Such by the way is the mark of the Indigo. Those who haven't been through the wringer probably aren't. How ironic that later on, history would become one of the things I would write about.

- I'm not so sure if I like *that* irony.

    Here's ya some *real* irony; figure this one out: <u>Both</u> illusory sides of the Big Government Monoparty will *adamantly* tell anyone they can <u>*pay to attend a rally*</u>, that modern politics is absolutely broken and needs to be ***not*** kedged {towed} along as has been the case, but gutted from stem to stern, flag to keel, port to starboard, and from orme to poop deck.

- Or, trashed and replaced in the sense of jacking up the ballast and parking a new boat underneath.
- Now it's awful hard to argue with that, and I do not believe one could.
- The 2012 shift is that nearly every human being **on-this-planet** is saying the same thing.

    However, wait a minute; um, *how did modern politics get that way, and just who got it that way?* If you can audible the correct answer, then congratulations: You have a Reasonable understanding of the prevailing politics of wormwood and bile.

- Indeed it's time to recognize: **It is scrap.**

- **Everyone else has.**

Every now and then, it's time to acquire an at least new to you car, particularly so, when the old car *lays crumpled up in twisted, burning, parts scattered, can't tell what the hay it was, wheels up, recycle bound pollution!*

- And that is how far mainstream politics has abandoned America.

- It is entirely safe to say that there remains *nothing* American within mainstream politics, *nothing*.

The real irony is; this condition applies equally to both sides of the modern Big Brother **Dittoparty**. They have mirrored one another in both policy and vote SO OFTEN, that a new observer has no earthly way to tell one from the other. Ironically, older voters are having the same problem for the same reason. Non voters and the Indigo have had the factual understanding on this from the beginning.

Basically, the entire planet is utterly disgusted with mainstream US politics. It is now estimated that only a percent or two of the *entire earth's population* will proclaim that both sides of mainstream US politics are anything other than *Identical*.

- Both sides loudly proclaim the other side as ***irredeemably corrupt***.

- *And it is inveterately so!*

- Roll Call complete!   I do like this chapter.

Chapter Three

Claiming Our Voice

The modern understanding of modern politics:

There is not one forefounder of this Nation who would not burn modern politics *straight to the ground.*

For them, that is not the least part metaphoric. For us, it shall be. The same result is being achieved by Awareness. What is not in debate, is that would include the United Nations far more popularly known as **The Dictator Support System**, and the banking/corporate gods. *Together these are the three vehicles of human disempowerment worldwide.*

That is what happens when the entire power gaggle has become so profusely depraved, it can no longer be called American anything beyond its hemispheric location. Yet for two of the three above causes of domestic violence against humanity, even *that* does not apply.

Between the three wholesale anti-American outcomes, we have accurately located the source of nearly all human destroyment worldwide. Each one either is, or directly serves, world controlling cartel.

- Within that paradigm, humans are not held as worthy of speaking of other than "to destroy".

As there is no Rule of Law in that model, as with all Marxist despotism, it is simply anarchy. It is cut throat in every effect as only the politically connected profit. This is the same as observed in all Marxist paradigms.

Basically, it is anarchy by way of ever increasing brutality, precisely as we observe right now with the ever more lawless alphabet soup agencies and czarist ministries. Each of these entities is of exclusively Marxist-Fascist intent, methodology, policy, origin and outcome. Ever more of the above agencies have come to define malice in every sense of the word.

On one side of an ever growing political gulf now rivaling the Grand Canyon, are the mercenaries of woe, or simply Mercs. These are the mainstream politicians and the oceans of useless and dictatorial bureaucrats who convey unmitigated injury to humans.

- That is the design of Marxism.

- The correct name for that condition of High Treason, is modern politics.

Very few are now able to find fault with that observation, and the list is shorter daily. That is because ever increasing numbers of humanity are falling prey to politically driven injury, mayhem, slavery and exploitation.

Some have said in relations to modern politics, to not throw the baby out with the bathwater. In most settings that postulation might be fine. However, the same politics presently threatens to extinguish all life on earth. In addition to that, the *exclusive* intent is to **viciously** enslave all life on earth not extinguished.

- At that point, the overall consideration changes.

- Numerous movies of caliber have correctly, repeatedly *and strongly* warned us of these specific slavery intentions.

- *As far as I know, every holy script on earth has warned us of the consequences of what we call modern politics.*

When the energy and intent is the child of perdition, the child of deceit, the child ruination, destruction, anarchy and lawlessness, bearing only the fruit of hate and murder, and now as so many vehemently claim, (rightly or wrongly), the bastard of Lucifer, *then the picture changes.*

Some have asked if I am personally opposed to "regulations" as if every mask should be forcibly stripped from the face of asbestos workers. In spite of the manner in which such self answering *statements* are normally double dipped in acid, the answer is **no**.

What I am attempting to get you to see is that I am opposed to rabidly anti-American and at the same time deliberately anti-competition "regulations" voted into law by the purchased **sluts of politicians** who strictly serve lawless and predatory cartels. The same monopolies seem to be abjectly unable, due to vast internal bureaucratic overload, to produce the slightest wit of innovation or the first new domestic job. As a result of such intrinsic farrago and rot, their economic survival becomes <u>wholly dependent</u> upon purchasing regulations **that preserve and protect their monopoly.**

Sadly, that describes somewhere in the neighborhood of 95% of all modern regulation in the last four generations. I want you to see the difference between the two directions, *and far more importantly,* **the intent behind the process.**

It is very important to note that the same aforementioned empires, often listed in the fortune 500, have yet to produce the sum total of a single NEW domestic job count **in several generations.** At the same instant, *their whole existence* is to stop innovative small business, the only ones who *have* created new jobs **or** made a positive contribution to society.

- The facilitator of that purchased despotism is the mainstream politician, **the holder of the disease of dishonor.**

Therefore, on the side against modern politics and Wall Street, now stand the majority of people on earth. We get to live the detrimental effects of modern politics. We watch the rich get richer, the poor get poorer, and **the middle class extermination** within our modern political system of oppression, ruin, exploitation *and militarized poverty.*

- You have just read the Paul Harvey on all that.

Fortunately in the United States and the younger the more so, the citizenship has stated with every effort **except one voice**, their unambiguous <u>number one political goal and intention</u>:

- "To promote individual freedom by reducing the size and scope of government and its intrusiveness into the lives of its citizens."

Reasonable is that voice: We are One.

As witnesses on this day, the full system and the aggressively decaying institutions within it have but one focus *which is human disempowerment.* Fundamentally, that whole stunk up mess has but one effective tool; the systemized separation of humankind from their true Spirituality, their Greater and true Self, and thus their Human Potential.

- That systematically produced first rift, then translates into fear, hate, and the mindlessly parroted illusions of separation.

The objective of the world controlling Satanists is to remove our humanity **and** our spirituality. Their intended end result being that we devolve to be neither human nor spirit. Whether the process of oppression is named Marxism or a Corporatocracy or uses various religious agenda or nationalist jingoisms is of no matter. The end result however, is.

- The outcome is to use warfare and slavery to slam a wedge between our existence and our humanity.

Unwinding and decoding the endless *and manufactured* illusions of separation, we quickly find they stem from a vastly amplified outward appearance of "difference". Unwinding and investigating even a little further, we quickly find the vast majority of those "differences" turn out to be theatrical and melodramatic costumed stunts and stage plays. They are often exposed as *quite* imitation (brushed in Hollywood dirt).

Upon even a *tiny* amount of further investigation, we find all that Jerry Springer level squabble-trash and manufactured strife, to not one person's surprise, turning out to be tailor made for **television.** That is, the world which is **not**. How 'bout that. Far worse, it just so happens to be the lone zillion to one exception immersed in hate and strife, that makes the utterly {and professionally} ignored rule *and reality* of peace and harmony.

From that deep grab bag of illusions of hate and fear broadcasted, nearly from the day one advent of media, the resulting and extraordinarily predictable cry and hue was for more government intervention. This travesty is directly founded upon the "evidence" of the gazillion to one illusion of division, over the truth of unity. **Because this is the foundation of all mainstream politics,**—*it is very important to understand this particular deception.*

And that is very precisely, what we received. The process itself even without Ayn Rand, caused profound illusions of "government solutions", the ultimate nonsequitur. The catch is that the whole shebang is based directly upon problems that a bazillion to one physically did not exist outside of the bird cage liner newspaper, and the electronic WMD we call television.

To be a tad more accurate, the "problems" virtually never *actually* existed to any measureable real-world extent. At least, that is until Government management, another nonsequitur, stepped in and made the situation whatever it was, genuinely if not exponentially, as usual, worse.

From the tightly controlled media's scare 'em up Halloween grade drama and filth, through the easily predictable sheep like public response, to ever greater government intervention, we at least know how the process works. When the general awareness of that pavlovian manipulation process increases, **the process stops**. And that completes our awareness of the manufactured and ever downward spiral into the living hell of slavery.

- The grand illusion itself is trash grade at best.

- *The objective is to no longer be deceived by it.*

- It is the *absence* of systemized deception, that allows the humanitarian treatment of humans.

- The **absence** of the various deceptions of slavery, is the background from which The Humanitarian Code arises.

Further unraveling the omni-systemized illusion of division and strife **that the slavery system must maintain at any and all cost**, we quickly and tragically find that the religion institutes, right behind television, are the worst offenders at manufacturing division and separation. It is for the same reason of *control-drama*. Virtually all have deliberately substituted their mission of spirituality for an all consuming money racket of human to human separation, churchianity, religiosity, strife, dogma, dictum, scripture twisting, bullying and vigorous holier than thou *ego pumping* that serves neither God nor human.

However, <u>through masterfully stroking the ego</u> with superiority *illusion*, this nature of separation has served mammon rather handsomely. Such is the guilty as charged lower energy of human division, strife, and systemized religious animosity that Rand so clearly saw, and like so vastly many others from intuition, solidly **rejected**.

- Seeing through the divisiveness, greatly eases the rejection of it.

- With 6.000+ years of religion caused wars to their credit, it is time to use another approach; one that involves peace and understanding.

- Ever stop to notice that with both politics and religion, the central theme "<u>that it is the other side's fault</u>" **never changes.**

- With one religion murdering another for 6,000+ years, the human race has finally come to see through the manipulation and genocide.

- This was another common theme from coast to coast.

If fundamentalist religion [of any brand] represents the God of harmony, Oneness and forgiveness as they ever so vociferously boast, then they have unabashedly failed to meet or demonstrate their claim. When there is an entire phone book section with what, a hundred egotistically deep-ended institutions of human separation devices self labeling as the one and only, that picture *just aint right*! Which one does *not* judge the other unworthy? Is it the Christian, or the Jew, or the Muslim? Is it something not yet invented?

And I am not in the least saying that one size should fit all as could be twisted. What I am saying is that the *consciousness* aspect outwardly appears often times to be ***absent***. There is an empty and plastic coated theatrical spirituality and often oodles of it held together with hair spray, cheep suits and lousy perfume, but not <u>Consciousness</u> spirituality, the one that matters, the one that will take you Upward and Homeward and into a far better *<u>and empowered</u>* life experience **right here,** *right now.*

- The *actual* central process of modern religion has two components; **separation and disempowerment**.

- And that is *precisely identical* to modern politics.

Mainstream religions doubly fail their claim as they pour into their liturgy down-looking, judgment, and condemnation of others of non same church or religion and thus hate, fear, strife, animosity, family breaking, enmity, and by proxy, human destruction, torture and the *sanctioned mass murder* piously euphemized as *warfare*.

By the same old or low intent, **that of human disempowerment**, the same failing institutions appear to be the chief offenders at holding humans away from their own and unique Spiritual discovery into their own vastly greater potential, power, connection and Unity with Creator.

This deliberate blockage to the path of Consciousness is accomplished through social and dogmatic intervention and a large host of one way and never negotiable restrictions that saw the budding student of Consciousness in half. It is the spiritual energy of keeping the crabs in the crab pot, all out of fear of losing two mites of tithe. Today, far less people are fooled by such deliberately authoritarian dictum, dogma, and *absolutely* man made divisiveness and disempowerment.

In the New Energy of Spiritual Unity, the <u>actuality</u> of being our brother's keeper and our neighbor's friend increases. At the same time, the human species no longer falls for the institutionalized illusions of human separation and limitation that stand directly behind human slavery.

Allow your inner voice and Creator connection to be your guide in this regard. As a student of Creator Consciousness, should you find yourself in an institution that claims the **only** path and all others to be **wrong**, your heart is in the right location, and your feet are in the wrong location. They need to be removed from there *about as fast as possible*.

Here is an example: Would you be equally honored in church setting if you held different views, labels, dress, skin color, political party, *or the all important and pecking order determining mini-god of income level?* <u>Yea</u> or nay? This is **but one question** that discerns the old energy of separation and hate, from the New Energy of understanding and kindness.

One direction is of divide and conquer and of systematically maintaining powerlessness through enforced separation from the many pathways of discovering Creator Consciousness. This *also* maintains *a* mechanical and *strictly artificial* separation from each other.

The other direction is of Oneness, true empowerment, and a vastly unlimited human potential that has remained rather dormant thus far.

- Without rocket science, one direction is of human slavery, and the other direction is of Human Success.

- *We have been drawn together to understand both.*

- You have instructed the above conditions, and I have written them.

One of my editors pointed out to me to "prove it". I knew the rest of the story regarding religion but had initially left it out, although without a specific reason. So after much reflection, it shall be placed into public record for your benefit:

- This will set easy upon *the Indigo*. (Not a bad way to tell either.)

Out of tens of thousands of government agencies, there is only one agency, *uniquely unqualified* {as per usual} to make the entirely in-accurate **spiritual** determination of precisely *who is and is not, a church*.

- It is not the 'Agency of Consciousness'. (*LOL*)   (That does not exist by the way.) (Even stranger, is that I had to point that out.)

At this juncture, one must pause to ask themselves as to why any government portion or agency could, would, or *would claim the right to*, make ANY determination *at all* within the entirety of the field of spiritual pursuit.

- The question itself is preposterous on its face *and unconstitutional.*

However, the present system belongs to **Satan**. Within that system, the only institutions the system will allow into practice are those *specifically* upholding, protecting and defending **the present system of human slavery**.

The system of slavery has thus far only allowed *license* to those firmly advocating preservation of the system. Presently there are no statistically significant exceptions. That is how the system works. The basic design was not invented by Adolph Hitler. It was however perfected by him and subsequently duplicated here. You can add gun control to that list also.

- If you named the IRS as the church determinant, *you are correct*.

- **The trade is the preservation of the status quo of human slavery.**

- *Now you know.*

It is neither I nor Ayn Rand, but rather the human race that is rejecting the old energy institutions of every ilk. We now see them as they are; little other than highly rusted, decaying, *thoroughly corrupted* and ever more abandoned vestiges of human slavery. They are of **the intent of disempowerment** by one label and methodology or another.

Today, that includes the majority of present institutions. It most conclusively includes every failed and funky thing that your tax money has propped up, funneled money into, bailed out, subsidized, loaned to, or purchased. **These lemons simply cannot make lemonade**. These are universally older institutions and cartels, that have long ago lost the last trace of Creator connection, and *desperately* need to be **buried**.

Most destructive of all, is the endless **subsidizing** schemes and scams that, although magnitudes vaster, are concurrently also far more hidden from public view. How odd and *exquisitely tragic* it is that in sum, this is the bulk of any government's total budget—hidden by a thousand deceptions and mislabels. ...And the middle class, who pays for it all, has in general virtually no clue where the money vanishes in **theft** to, or which method of **theft** caused it to vanish. Picture *that* strange method of larceny in any other setting that, as an example, *should well clear the political vision*.

Such **armed robbery** in its vast plethora of forms and euphemisms, each more nonsensical than the last, is better known as, and spoken of, as **corporate welfare**. It applies to the larger, dirtier, entrenched, stagnated, grave bound older and more politically influential monopolies, institutions and cartels. Most have been clinically dead for generations. Nearly all are in fact government owned, *however you were not informed of that*.

- Why is that insanity *for one moment* allowed to continue?

As a hardened rule, such are the syndicated and soulless corporate structures who, using your money removed with the violence of despotism, purchase mainstream Uniparty politicians by the trainloads and dictate directly to them to steal more of your money!

- *<u>This is precisely how all modern politics works</u>*.

  - None of those direct orders to the modern politician include the intent of human freedom or empowerment *to be sure*.

The same soulless monopolies use **your money** to buy *their laws* that massively profit them, yet *maliciously and malignantly* disfavor you. And the whole time, <u>you fund your own destruction</u>. Ayn Rand really pointed that out by the way, *correctly*.

- <u>**There is not one iota of humanitarian in that model**</u>.

Right now, three deadly and pernicious downward spirals now lay directly at your feet, fully explained, fully de-mystified, and fully exposed. They are the death spiral of Marxism, the dishonor of modern politics and the hellish exploitations inherent to the institutions that buy politicians by the trainload. **These three taken together are human slavery.** The question is, will the human race learn from this in time to save the planet?

- The human race no longer has an option *except* to learn.

The human race in majority now sees clearer and to ever greater depth, the inherent **slavery intention** behind the deceit of modern politics. We are soundly rejecting the dirty and underhanded institutions that perpetrate that slavery. This worldwide and exponentially expanding phenomenon is ironically the slowest to catch on with the mainstream votary owing to the political non-maturity <u>and extreme levels of deception</u>. Once seen, they appear unbelievably excuseless, *which they unequivocally are.*

At one time, the United States was the leader in freedom and the directly resulting overall success. Presently, the reverse is true. The United States (corporation) is ever more aggressively demonstrating leadership in human oppression and viewing the directly resulting ***trail of tears***.

That trail of tears is strictly live human sacrifice. It is that non-legal old energy and intent of ever greater oppression that is being rejected.

- *We are finally seeing human slavery for what it is.*

- **And we are finally calling it by the correct name.**

Here is a hint: Roughly 99% of the sheer hideousness, torture, murder, and to us, unimaginable suffering of Marxism in any of many, many destroyed Nations and Peoples, **never made Western television**.

As a result, the United States citizenry is in wholesale unknowing of the well demonstrated results of human slavery. That particular condition, surpassing all other factors including the ever present runaway greed, and <u>the all consuming frenzy</u> *to inflict injury* **is**, the mainstream vote.

Fundamentally, that utter ignorance of Marxism <u>is</u> the mainstream vote. It is of no matter the station, party *appearance*, or level. It is the very condition Ayn Rand referred to as **the Statist Society**. It is in the thinking, voting, falsehood and sheer profanity of government replacing God.

That condition as per warning is ugly as hell. If angels could weep in heart rending grief, that outright apostasy would cause it. However that *lethal outrage* is now demystified and exposed, and possibly for the first time, *we see it **as it actually is**.*

Only now, can healing begin. Eradicating *that one* illusion {and raw idolatry} of government replacing God, is the location where the Great

Healing begins, for that step unlocks all other steps into Consciousness and Evolution, which is The Human Event.

- The perspective I bring you this day is that of empowerment.

The largest single error of the past was in profound vain and sheer idiocy, attempting to change the mainstream political system from within. **It is a lost cause.**

- *Virtually every one of you made that statement* **and clearly.**

- If that insane error could have worked, it would have worked in the last **one hundred straight years of NOT working.**

- *Right there* is the heart and core of the old energy holding the human race in bondage!

- **It is time to put that insanity** *to end*.

Neither the human race nor the planet earth has the luxury, time or option to continue one moment further in that unbelievable delusion. Undoing *that specific error* is the Road to Human Empowerment. This realization and step, is a political, practical, physical, economic **and moral**, requirement to Human Success.

- *If you get nothing else from this book, please get this part correct.*

- This is a first step into personal empowerment.

- And it is so.

Both the Soul sourced yearn for Freedom, and the ever increasing **rejection** of institutions of human disempowerment with their heavy handed and classically senseless rulings, are greatly more prevalent among the younger third of the population. Various estimates pin the worldwide youth unrest at 70 to 90% *and increasing daily.* Even with that statistical gulf in awakening to success, the general unrest *as related to modern politics* now extends to the growing majority of the entire human race.

That yearning and demand for Freedom emanating from our Design and DNA can be accurately, correctly, and energetically summed up as follows:

"As humans, we are done with the endless institutions of human slavery! We shall no longer be thought of, or treated as numbers, or sheep to be herded rudely to and fro, constantly lied to, looked down at, laughed at, spied upon, abused, imprisoned and dehumanized in every possible way, or mechanically vivisected by science, military and politics."

"We no longer support the human sacrifice systems of utter inhumanity perpetrating human slavery."

"The only Energies we now support shall understand empowerment through Freedom, with that focus singularly and throughout."

The ever increasing majority of the human race, have actively stated the Intent of Emancipation time and time again, almost daily, and with almost one voice.

Reasonable is that voice: We are Human.

As of this day, this moment, this writing, the human race has turned THE corner from asleep to awake, from guessing to knowing, from past to present, from experience to wisdom, from separation to unity and from hate to humanity. Historically and most significantly, against the backdrop of tens of thousands of years of rarely excepted abject oppression, the human species is evolving above the norm of slavery. **We are now entering the probability and unlimited benefit of our own Humanitarian experience.**

- The human race now comprehends that self-ownership is human, and that human is self-ownership.

- Only Creator Intended **Peace and Freedom** can define or produce Success, Compassion or a Humanitarian experience.

We now comprehend that human slavery is not human or the least part humanitarian. We comprehend that Freedom as per Creator Design, *is our humanity*. More than any other possibility, that very specific concept of Awareness, Enlightenment and Ascension, is **the Great Healing**.

- *It is the humane treatment of humans.*

- <u>It is THE understanding and direction of this Age</u>.

- That is why this is **The Age of Truth and Healing.**

Today marks the Age of Truth and Healing. This is because Truth and Healing are the single largest difference between now and <u>all</u> previous ages of recorded human experience. Human history has been dominated by massive and egregious falsehood, illusions, and terrible oppression. We have lived a great and artificial distance from Self, spirituality, innate ability, and the humanity of Freedom. We now see this truth increasingly well.

- We have also commendably awakened ourselves to the New Dawn and a new concept.

That concept is Consciousness. It is best reflected in self-ownership. It is the concept of human respect. The old paradigm was Slavery, an involuntary and insidious servitude to the forces of the greatest falsehood and wickedness ever known. The New concept is the humanitarian treatment of humans. It is the respect for and the facilitation of, the human and the completed human experience: It is *the Human Event*.

As a species and as of this writing, we have now declared our humanness is not in fear or slavery, but in courage and Freedom. That specific concept is the Awakening to Self and self respect—and an infinitely greater, individual, group and species functionality and effectiveness.

As of today, the majority of the human race and in particular, the younger half of the human population have spoken of this specific New Energy with a highly commendable intensity and clarity: **It is human respect.** The New Energy can be correctly and accurately summed up as: *"We are*

Human and we shall be Free." Finally, finally, finally, finally, finally, the majority of <u>the entire planet</u> has spoken a single intent **and**, with all that is possible *except*, one voice.

Reasonable is that voice: We are Free.

To repair anything, it is imperative to *correctly* identify and understand the problem. **The largest single roadblock to Human Ascension today is Satanism [Slavery]** *and its very solid ownership of all mainstream politics.*

The purchased lies and utterly inexpiable dishonor of mainstream politics present oceans of human disregard and endless *Felony* Violations of Oath of Office.

- From coast to coast, we now see it, we now admit it.

Secondly, <u>it is far more imperative to correctly identify the solution</u>. That solution is The Three immutably proven and Self-evident Truths of Consciousness, Empowerment, Enlightenment, and upward Human Evolution found in The Humanitarian Code:

1. **The only legitimate function of government is to uphold, protect and defend Individual Human Rights.**

2. **We stand at One with the Creator in the Humanity of Liberty,** *the condition of Human Evolution.*

3. **We stand united** *and unbreakable* **in the American definition of smaller government, fewer taxes, and greatest personal freedom.**

Thirdly, and even more imperative, simply because it is the one and only thing that counts or matters; is to find *or create* the **level of resolve** with which one will address the problem of human slavery, and *the correct*, peaceful resolution into the benefits of Human Success.

Lastly, the whole enchilada has fully reached, by way of most severe and grave neglect, the point of absolutely no delay. It is either the life or death of the human species and the entire planet, period.

- The time to cause Human Success has chosen of all history **us**, and it has chosen of all time, **right now** and of everyone, **YOU**.

- This is the honor and calling given to us, *here and now.*

And that, my most worthy and appreciated friends, is the full, complete *and correct* understanding of Human Success. Within that, we now draw to close the political era likely **the most shame filled in human history.**

With that, true empowerment and self-ownership are well within reach. Both have remained unrealized *up until right now* and with this New Energy.

- *We can and will restore the Creator's faith in the human race!*

Reasonable looked deeply into that which is human, and found with careful research, **The Three Self-Evident Truths of Human Success**. From this human beneficial Truth that we personally embody and embolden, we formed the three Reasonable action steps into Human Success:

1 Learn not to burn. (Stop feeding the Beast.)

2 Invest in yourself. Support that which is Reasonable.

3 Share this information. **This step**, is how freedom occurs.

By this *specific* process, we create the human experience worth living in, for Human Ascension out of all history has chosen us and *this moment*. We now bond together in our conscious, aware, **Humanitarian choice**, simply and thankfully because: *We are Reasonable Human beings*.

- **We are One. We are Human. We are Free. We are Reasonable.**

- *We stand in uncompromising resolve of Human Success and personal integrity.*

Chapter Four

Evolutionary Action

Evolutionary Action part one; The Tree of Life Process:

I think you'll really like this. As an engineer, this is my favorite chapter of the Reasonable Process.

To honor the evolving human, Our Reasonable plan is planting a tree, the Tree of Life, for each and every sustaining member. As this Earth honoring is both New and new, Reasonable drops the gauntlet of challenge to all businesses, religions, organizations, networks and agencies of any size or nature to do the same. ...**Or**, explain to constituency, public, Creation and Creator, as to why their preference is old energy.

For businesses, organizations or agencies of any nature, Reasonable without bias, offers this Life Energy in the form of a related non-profit service. We view it as elevating consciousness. It is so, for as businesses and organizations grow in consciousness in this manner, many unsolved and outwardly appearing unsolvable challenges solve themselves don't they?

The best part is that there is no worthless, lying, bottom feeding politician or cartel serving gun point threat involved is there? No one first stole something from you, all the while *loudly pretending otherwise*.

This is the correct way of how it is done. Contrast this New Energy and Reasonable methodology to the politically motivated (meaning underhanded) approaches that have cost society direly, yet have solved nothing and can solve nothing. If you can see and understand this contrast clearly, then you also understand Objectivism and *the entire* **Reasonable Life process of peace and harmony.**

Our Life Process is based upon, and is within **Consciousness.** It is an upward spiral into an evolution of human and planetary cooperation. The former and opposite process is based upon **coercion** (violence). It is the intent of ever increasing oppression. It is an ever downward spiral into human and human species destroyment. That downward spiral ends in warfare. Warfare is an integral part of the death-spiral/cartel model. ***The entire standard model is strictly centered on live human sacrifice.***

- It is very important to understand that.

In contrast, the Reasonable Tree of Life Process reflects the rapidly growing membership in aware Consciousness, and the contributing Reasonable members you personally introduce into Evolution, and they the same. **All of us are facilitating *your* personal Life Force.** Therefore, we named the Reasonable Tree of Life Process as such, simply because *we are* the Life Process **moving into Consciousness and personal empowerment**.

Our planting crews are professional, conscientious, experienced and busy. Each tree is carefully located, naturally supported, non-GMO, non-hybrid or graft, and properly blessed with the Intent of Life fulfillment as living witnesses and prayers of the New Energy of evolving Consciousness. The trees are diverse in species and genus. Each is chosen for suitability with wildlife and eco-system. The Tree of Life Process is not flashy or fancy or made for television or politics. *It is simply the right thing to do.* It is most fully Reasonable because:

- *We are the Tree of Life Process.*

- And it is so.

Evolutionary Action part two, Technologies and communications:

Reasonable recognizes and honors the many evolutionary technologies, constructs, and methodologies that uphold and support the American Way of Life *of independence and decentralization*.

We recognize that the foremost human condition issue *worldwide*, is the power centralization of politically facilitated cartel **dictatorships**. This condition stands violently opposed to the human and community empowerment of independence and decentralization. This issue is embedded within all existing issues. Beyond minutia, there are no exceptions.

How many times must the human species suffer the endlessly repeated and inherent horrors, abuses, brutality and malevolence or the astronomical over costs and hideous failures of excessive government and its vicious and pampered prima ballerina monopolies? We do this again and again no matter how cunningly it is mislabeled and television pedaled upon the ***absolutely criminally ill advised*** mainstream voter.

Therefore in rational counterbalance, Reasonable serves as a cyber clearinghouse and New Energy vortex for emerging information that upholds and supports individual, family and community thriving and independence in a wide variety of fields. Each effort will *greatly* benefit the human condition. We view this as simply elevating the human condition **into an experience worth living in.**

- *Reasonable is, the American Way of <u>Life</u> of Freedom and Dignity.*

- And it is so.

Evolutionary Action Part three, Health and Wellness:

Reasonable recognizes and honors the many emerging technologies, constructs and modalities both rediscovered and new, that uphold and support robust health, healing, wellness, longevity and wholeness.

- We support the Reasonable quality of life.

We recognize that a leading human issue is wellness. America has clearly stated that human wholeness is a paradigm devastated by purchased and recreant political depravity of the very lowest possible order.

How long will human health remain in hostage? How long shall it exist as subsidiary to poison and politics? How long shall it endure in thrall to the most brutal and closed monopoly of them all? How long shall the agenda of Cartel and genocide be placed in front of the human race?

- Why is Wall Street health more important than human health?

How long shall wellness ontologies of very low or no cost, vastly superior effectivity, zero side effect, common or energetic non-poison natural construct, and omnipresent, open accessibility be murderously suppressed by perhaps the most heinous, malevolent *and outright destructive* dishonesty to ever tread earth?

- We have been asking ourselves that question for a long time.

- Few have <u>not</u> asked this question.

- We hold that it is time to <u>stop</u> asking that question.

Therefore, Reasonable serves as a cyber clearinghouse and New Energy vortex for emerging information that upholds and examples robust human health, healing, wellness, longevity and energetic wholeness. We view this wellness movement as elevating Consciousness, awareness, and the human condition **into an experience worth living in**.

- *Reasonable is the example, engine and Energy of human wellbeing.*

- **We are anyway.**

This is the monopoly that the American people probably despised the most. It is consistently [*and correctly*] held as several of the most outright *and intentionally* human destructive cartels on earth. The question asked everywhere was: <u>How do we **smash** it</u>.

- You are looking right at the answer:

- Your wellness ends the sickness industry.

- And it is so.

Evolutionary Action Part four, Earth and Environment:

Reasonable also recognizes and honors the numerous emerging technologies, constructs and methods both rediscovered and new, that restore harmony and balance with Nature Herself. Natural intelligence is upheld as an Ideal example. We revere and strive to learn from the Creator's wisdom *as demonstrated in nature*.

We recognize that the debauched and egregiously failed world of rented political favoritism, that by comparison awards sainthood to both prostitution *and* pornography, has not produced harmony or balance in any venue, and in particular with longsuffering Mother Nature.

How long will Earth and Nature be repeatedly raped by the twisted and heinous political warfare state to favor banker and cartel interest? Why is Wall Street more important even than Earth? How long shall the environment remain the pawn of morbid **and asinine,** political football-ism and Hollywood sound bites to win election at any cost, any lie, any cowardice, any backstab, any lawlessness, any corruption, any infamy and any venality?

The old energy of everything as political and violence hostage has miserably failed. It now lays insolvent and exposed to the world. *Its all-encompassing failure and heinous dishonor is now seen as is.*

- The omni-failure of old energy is perhaps best exemplified by the treatment of earth by cartel and politics.

- That failure is another form of Slavery, however it is Slavery.

- **It is time to end it.**

Therefore, it is highly Reasonable to serve both Human and Nature as a cyber clearinghouse and New Energy vortex for emerging information and research that upholds and supports cooperative harmony and balance with Earth and Nature. Within the New Energy, we honor every Design of the Creator **as is**. It is the Creator's Wisdom of Nature that we deeply respect, cherish, depend upon, learn from, uphold, honor, support, *work with* and facilitate. We view this human and planetary essential Energy as also elevating Consciousness, awareness and the world condition **into an experience worth living in.**

- *Reasonable is the example, engine and Energy of planetary well being.*

- We are anyway.
- And thankfully; it is so.

Evolutionary Action Part five, Energy and transportation:

For every one of the above well known reasons and many more, in particular a direct, dramatic and critically needed environmental benefit, Reasonable also serves as the cyber clearinghouse and New Energy vortex for emerging information intending complete energy independence and decentralization **in every possible and existing form and forum.**

This New energy paradigm decidedly includes, yet is in no part limited to; electrical generation and utilization, heating and cooling, food production, every industry known, **and all forms of powered transportation**.

If it can be described, it is intended to evolve into the New Consciousness. *This is the one and only paradigm possible that allows for human and planetary continuation or ascension.* This is also accurately described as a <u>thorough</u> energy independence and decentralization. It is not only freedom of choice that is now direly lacking, it is also just plain human Freedom (*and Reasonable prices*) that have been all but completely *and forcefully* extinguished by politics and cartel.

Like any rational human being, we can readily and abundantly observe the inexhaustible iniquity, and morbid dishonor of mainstream politics <u>vigorously protecting</u> every sordid monopoly interest, not just that of energy production, use and distribution. Can you as a productive, contributing citizen **purchase** 51 minimum US Senators or a House exclusively representing, (*kissing the ass of...*), special interest?
An infinitely better and more workable approach would be to **unpurchase** them! As it turns out, that would be about the single most Reasonable thing a human being could do. Such an action would markedly increase human race and planetary life expectancy! That is why such common-sense action is so *inexorably Reasonable*.

Obviously, the *unlimited corruption* <u>of third world politics</u> has not, *and cannot* beneficially effect the emerging considerations of energy, transporttation, environment, peace, safety, wellness, prosperity **or Consciousness Evolution.** Virtually anywhere mainstream politics is viewed beyond the shallowest of head in the sand superficial, (*the television level*), then horrific failure and internecine **suicide** can be quickly and prodigiously observed.

Planet wide, the modern politician's ear to its citizenry has been every whit stopped up by corruption, dishonesty, greed, dishonor, spoils, **astounding vanity** and *unlimited re-electioneering graft*. Virtually every field touched by modern politics has been deliberately poisoned into a degeneration often criminally worse than if only left alone. Sadly, there are very few exceptions amidst a sea of disasters to choose from. Energy technologies, education and health are three primary examples.

The modern politician's moribund world is that of suppression and oppression. It is now clearly demonstrated. It is beyond any shadow of doubt. Reasonable on the other hand, has heard the clear, unambiguous demand of the supermajority of the human race in requiring **full** energy independence. **The human race** is now demanding to the very last degree, watt, drop, mile and BTU **a complete** independence and non-centralization **and** that the energy or utility dictatorships *of any nature,* be put to *absolute end*.

- Many have stated this is the most overdue and *presently* technically viable process yet.

- We wholeheartedly concur. We have plethora evidence *in hand*.

Therefore, Reasonable serves as a cyber clearinghouse and New Energy vortex for emerging information that upholds and advances energy independence and decentralization. We view this nature of technical harmonizing and energy related restructuring as elevating Consciousness, awareness, and the world condition **into an experience worth living in**.

Such tremendous benefit to the world is *the* Evolution into peace, health, safety, cooperation, human respect, abundance, *Reasonable prices*, environmental benefit and unlimited prosperity. This Consciousness shift alone will result in exceedingly low cost **or free** energy, stunningly efficient energy use technologies, and above all, planetary respect, harmony, continuation, benefit and gratitude! This is the Evolution that is upon our doorstep. It is available *right now.* **It awaits only our resolution.**

- It is entirely Reasonable to get this step well underway *NOW!*

Without guess or surmise, we know beyond any shadow of doubt, *this* movement into Consciousness is an obvious and non-negotiable **requirement** of human race and planetary continuation. It is also the worldwide movement into a war free, peaceful, abundant, cleaner, safer, and vastly more cost effective **experience worth living in**.

Picture a world with *not one* power pole in it, and two or three digits fewer on the electric bill <u>if</u> there is one. Envision a <u>no taxes and fees</u> energy bill. Envision an independent and decentralized power structure that is not only not carbon based, but has no association with the petrochemical model. Picture every vehicle benefiting in fuel economy at the efficiency and cleanliness of **only** the technologies that have *thus far* been suppressed by government and cartel working as a team in the service of perdition.

- <u>That</u> should do the trick!

- **That, should also open one's eyes to modern politics.**

- *Reasonable is the engine and Energy of Evolution into full energy independence and **perfected** energy decentralization.*

- And it is so.

Now, take every established trend in mainstream politics that with effectively **no** exception, is directly into ever greater dishonesty, depravity, and purchased iniquity *greatly to your intended harm*. Ok, now draw a line in the opposite direction into truth, unity, harmony, peace, safety, sanity, and robust wellness, thriving and upward Evolution for both human and Earth.

- That New direction is Reasonable. It is your empowerment.

Many of the conditions just spoken of are nothing less than **absolute** requirements for human and planetary survival. <u>They are no part of optional</u>. And guess what folks, modern politics cannot provide that Evolution into Consciousness *by way of being the direct opposite*, i.e. the massively proven old energy of suppression, Satanism, human sacrifice, **and furious corruption**.

The long time obvious is now stated in English. It is decoded, demystified, untangled, and fully exposed. It is known to nearly all. Now it is being healed. Now we are moving into Consciousness. *Now is our moment.*

We shall cast vote with our word, our example, our actions, money, thoughts, feelings, intent, supplications, creativity, innovation, attention, vision, wit, awareness, Spirit, and the ballot <u>and jury vote</u> *as humans*. We shall cast those votes as Americans, as sane, aware, informed, valuable, appreciated, **self-owned** and finally, finally, *finally* respected.

- We are one. We are Human. We are Free.

- *We are the bringers of the Dawn of Humanity!*

- Therefore, we are in fact Reasonable.

- And it is **absolutely** so.

- Much of the Reasonable fun is taking place *right here*

Because this is, the Human Event*!*

Chapter Five

The How and Why of Voting

The How and Why of Voting

We'll work on the why first so we'll have a better background for the second part, the how of voting.

Be aware that a ship without a direction actually has a direction: Any ship *can find its own way to the bottom*. {As was found somewhere in one of Daniels Quinn's books, presumably referring to modern politics.} So far that has been the experience with mainstream politics.

- *That is the very thing we came here on this planet to change!*

- **The reason why we exist;** *is to end human slavery.*

Here is an example:

The etiology of modern politics: Money and support given to mainstream politics equals corruption, coercion, theft and abuse. That so far, has been the sum and the experience of all modern politics.

And that condition turns out to be semper ubique, every time, ever and always, without exception, never otherwise. In relation to the Oath of Office, the above continuous shame of modern politics is a condition that awards enshrined sainthood to dealers of street drugs, the act of drug dealing, used needles and even the bath tub and old battery acid made drugs themselves. To say modern death-bound politics has not turned out well is the world's largest understatement. I think we are all by now, keenly aware of that gold tableted *fact*.

The following is the modern government conundrum: Modern politics says; you're free. That is to say in reality: "You are free not to be free. Just don't attempt to be free, because we destroy those who do." The IRS is a particularly good example of this—and a "freedom" strictly limited to the endless vapistry of televised, Hollywood designed **spin**.

Here is a very strong example where the Malthusian pogrom of modern politics winds up destroying not only human freedom, but the whole human species, and along with it the planet:

The objective of modern controllers worldwide is to strategically eliminate roughly 96% of the population planet wide. This is a mission it has so far drastically failed, although not for lack of exceptionally determined effort or a vast multitude of *horrid* poisonings. It has instead failed for *dramatically* underestimating the resiliency, Spirit and amazing resourcefulness of the human species that is our Creator Connection (and protection).

At the same time, the objective of modern politics is; *an absolute* elimination of the middle class worldwide. The objective is to very sharply divide the entire planet into two totally **separate and separated** *genetic* species, the higher up haves, who purchase government, and the have-nots who do not purchase government.

- That model is Marxism, Corporate Aristocracy, and all other Totalitarian paradigms **that they all are**.

Needless to say, the have-nots, that describe most of us *including you*, will have *vastly less*. In that model, we would do well to live 10 to 20 in a one toilet, two room mold saturated shack. That model is where anything even remotely resembling stored food, heating, cooling, privacy or powered transportation would be considered a *luxury—by permit only,* (although a permit process is not needed when affordability *is eliminated*).

For those who yet think this cannot happen, or is not happening, one would do well to take notice that the majority of the planetary population lives that way *right now*. At the same time, the government connected few worldwide, continue to enjoy unlimited opulence that we *presently* pay for primarily through the snake pit of the United Nations dictator support system.

That condition is a direct result of what is considered "bad government" by us, and upheld as "a good example" by purchased modern politics. A prime example is that the better known the politician becomes, Career Democrat apologist John McCain for example, the more the later cartel purchased story line of human slavery becomes lock step.

Ah, but all the 'vaccines' that we now know to have contained mercury and 'accidental' live virus would not only be **"free"** but gunpoint and human chip registered *mandatory*. To add awareness within injury, an ever growing body of scientists and doctors are coming forward with very well researched indictments that these vaccines are in *their* quoted words, "worthless", "dangerous" "harmful", "laden with deception" or "a concoction of evil".

- Or "In the service of cartel" to be more accurate.

- Perhaps a more truthful description might be "anti-personnel".

- Are you starting to understand the agenda of modern politics?

The bottom line in that intent; there is no such thing as Human Rights, the legal definition of human. **At best** in that intention, the remaining and mostly forced illiterate have-nots are barely worth the bullet it takes to murder them *at random*. And in that model, they are treated exactly that way. People are treated as utterly beneath contempt and typically only worthy of slaughter. This is the *now* prevailing condition in all Marxist and otherwise totalitarian or dictatorial systems worldwide.

Pointedly roughshod "contraband" searches are a routine practice in that model with such contraband being pretty much *anything*. Yet in particular, it is usually **food**. Travel is by non-available permit only. This does not include discretionary or "unofficial" movement anywhere for any reason. Most offences large or small, would also result in on the spot military or para-military police execution. And like in Russia, Africa and several Middle East locations *right now*, the remaining family is then charged for the bullets, and beaten **savagely** until the debt is paid right then and there, *life savings or not, that most unfortunately, it usually is*.

What luxuries and food there might be, would be given out to those "good folks" who in truth or lie, as it matters not one iota, **turn in** their fellow humans to government for harboring non-system, that is non-slavery, thoughts or words. The above paradigm is the current Marxist model in both intent and outcome anywhere it has prevailed *on this planet*.

- **That modus operandi is identical in *any* totalitarian system.**

- As it turns out, **political correctness** harbors numerous euphemistic and dead lying cover-up names <u>for the identical process</u>.

- It is *those specific* general directions and plans of the world controllers acting through their hand puppets of modern politics, we have come here to change.

As anyone can plainly see, the intent, mode of operation, and overall results of modern politics is squarely at the bottom of the Scale of Consciousness. The outcome *specifically* does not intend to include you, or at least not you <u>as human</u>. Strictly speaking, *it never did and never will*.

That's what you wanted me to see. **That is the "why" in need of repair.** That is why we are now sharing that realization in this book.

Now we are going to unknot the biggest misinformation tangle of them all; **how to vote.**

This will not include the Fully Informed Jury Vote at this time because that is not within the scope of this chapter. We honor and teach this subject organizationally. I strongly encourage you to look it up online, and learn all you can on the subject. When you can instantly quote what Thomas Jefferson said on the subject, you move **from asleep to teacher.**

- Find that literature, carry it about, and distribute it *profusely*, the same as one would gladly do for the Evolution.

I observe that the biggest thing most folks fail to see, is that every dollar engaged is in fact *a very powerful vote*. As a result, most choices are all but completely unconscious and except for barest survival, *random*. The unconsciousness and absence of direction, directly results in tragedies that should not exist *in a society claiming to be human.*

Here is how it works: What we vote for continues or increases, and what we do not vote for decreases and eventually discontinues. *There is no aspect possible this does not apply to.* **There is the key.**

What is missed, is the nearly unlimited leverage, and thus the vast personal power available at each and every **potentially conscious** choice point <u>involved in **monetary vote management**</u>. Once one realizes that, the objective is to switch every unconscious non-choice point into a <u>conscious</u> choice point *at every single event*. This is a learned thought process.

- It is how to live *in empowerment*.

- For most folks, moving that particular voting process from unconscious to conscious will result in a *massive* increase in personal *effect*.

Fortunately I believe that most of the reasonable folks reading *this*, have commendably made that particular transition. It's the *remainder* of the human race that we must help into aware voting, because they are not now conscious in their voting **at all**. Sadly, it is *astonishingly* obvious.

- As we evolve our consciousness, we evolve our empowerment.

One of the biggest leverage points with **the monetary vote**, is that it is generally employed roughly 365 times as often as the foundationally destroyed ballot vote. What I want you to do, is see and feel the massive <u>comparative</u> leverage presented here. The ballot vote choice has been taken away from us. That condition prevailed from the Federal Reserve Act of December 23rd 1913. In real-world terms, that eliminated the ballot choice. And by the way, that was the entire idea in the first place—<u>by *the bankers own admission!*</u>

- The tragic part is that we failed to believe them.

This is where the *conscious* vote employment of every spending choice point has the potential to greatly more than counter the {also} electronically nullified ballot vote. The star example is that for every person the Reasonable Party by way of your monetary consideration, is able to bring into awareness, the entire world is moved into a greatly more beneficial **Consciousness**. The leverage point is that such process is occurring *daily and globally*. Right there, *with forethought and sustaining pledge*, you energetically turn the leverage point from the world controllers **to you.**

- ...And that of course *is* Reasonable.

To the extent that you can see, understand and put to practice this otherwise discarded leverage point, you gain your own personal empowerment. Therefore, please grab hold of this highly beneficial concept *tightly*.

Perhaps an even *more* misunderstood and not consciously employed vote, **is the communication vote.**

All the above concepts fully apply to this crucial vote as well. The leverage point is; that the world controllers have <u>*even less*</u> control here. Now should one mentally fall into the mousetrap of verbally claiming the "lesser of two evils" or other unthinking *crap*, then even this leverage and empowerment point is thrown away. It is simply dusted to the wind as if it never existed. *This is a very, very important point to understand if the world and human race is to be rescued from the chains of perdition.*

When the world controllers can turn your *thinking*, usually through laziness, toward them, their dishonorable choices, then they have stripped you naked of the empowerment given to you of the power of the voice. This is the danger of any portion of mainstream political thinking, and the further one dances into that **trap**, the further one is stripped of power. In that model, one is voting in favor of international bankers and cartel no matter what, **and no matter what one thinks.** *This is an exceptionally important fact*.

That is the very trap their totally fake polarization is designed for. That trap is set to draw the unconscious buffoon into supporting human sacrifice no matter which way they jump. And it doesn't make the slightest difference anyway. **That is the whole set-up.** When one gets emotionally, egotistically <u>and</u> <u>stupidly</u>, caught up in either side of the trap, the results are *identical*. This is <u>*the*</u> definition of mainstream politics.

- It is now beyond the slightest shadow of doubt.

It is **THE THINKING**, *the realizations*, that must shift in order to reclaim this personal empowerment. It is the **Awareness** that must move from non-consciousness and upward into Consciousness to reclaim power. As long as any part of the thinking is given over to mainstream politics, the trap of powerlessness owns you, or at least a certain part of your body that rarely sees sunshine. And they will continue to violate it *as they please!*

To provide an example of understanding and reclaiming the power of communication, I carry on my person at all times, unless I momentarily run out through *very* active distribution, a supply of business cards for the Reasonable organization. I also keep a generous supply of cards with my transportation for quicker restock. That move has turned out to be a day, deal and very valuable contact saver many times. I also keep an even larger reserve supply of cards at home for the same reason.

Think of each communication possibility as **ammunition.** *That should do the trick. Your power point is in* **spending** *that ammo against slavery and in favor of Humanity.* Spend it like a Marine taking a hill, *that should do the trick.*

Why I do this, is that I understand and put to beneficial use, the power of the voice. The cards, flyers and e-tools are part of the power and leverage *process*. They also serve to facilitate Reasonable presentations and events. Ironically, they work if I say nothing or I am not there. Now *that's* leverage. That's **empowerment.**

For example, good folks have joined this organization from cards and flyers displayed by myself and other Reasonable members at places we may have forgotten. That is the multiplied leverage of the power of the *conscious* voice vote. The more we act as an organization, as one Energy, as a unit, as One, *as a focused, conscious,* **membership generating dynamo**, the more personal empowerment each of us will enjoy.

This vote, when *and only when* **correctly** understood and employed, **cannot be taken away**. How many times a day do I chose to use this empowerment point, I couldn't say, but often. Now, multiply the empowerment contacts in a single day by the number of days in a year, AND, **here is the real key**—the ever growing number of Reasonable folks doing the same thing. Right there is a mind-blowing, ever growing, and infinite leverage amount over and above slavery's *three way destroyed* ballot vote!

- Think on that for a while. Let it soak in. See its *Divine* advantage.

What I want you to see is the empowerment *you* give to *you,* and not the helplessness the system would have you believe or inadvertently participate in. Belief in the system of slavery and limitation was the error we made in the past. *It is time to cut away those chains of failure and poverty*.

I would also like you to see that the leverage point or shift begins with, *and remains at*, dropping any and all <u>mainstream</u> political thought, participation and support **no matter what**. The more one correctly understands and maintains that <u>specific</u> leverage point, the more one is headed directly into personal empowerment. The inverse is also correct. Reasonable is in the clear understanding of *both*, and the highly empowering use of *one*.

The bottom line is this: If anyone can be convinced and usually by rote din and dun, that the only vote is the ballot vote, that person is flatly **owned.** Their goose is cooked; they reside in the self-made illusion of abject helplessness. How incredibly sad that is; for again, *the angels weep*.

- Every prayer and envisioning is also a vote and *voting process* **that is exclusively under your control.**

- That is how manifestation is completed into the hologram of existence.

In her book Creative Visualization, Shakti Gawain instructs us that we are exceedingly powerful creators every moment. In the realization of that, the objective is to create *that which is beneficial*. This task is accomplished through the focusing of thought, prayer and visualization on the desired outcome in the knowing of our actual *and constant* ability.

"Every moment of your life is infinitely creative and the universe is endlessly bountiful. Just put forth a clear enough request, and everything your heart truly desires must come to you."
Shakti Gawain

- Every thought is a vote.

When we dwell in fear with thoughts *captivated* {key concept} by conditions not desired, that is a creation or advancement of that which is not wanted. **This is the main captivity of the present system.** This is what the entire system is all about: 1, convincing you that you are helpless to create and, 2, steering your thoughts into fear and thereby placing you on the side of energetically providing contributions to slavery, limitation, failure, poverty and the wrenching travesty of modern politics.

- This process is done by way of emotionalizing fear thoughts.

- The objective is to break to nothing that **systemized enslavement**.

When we dwell in thoughts of benevolence and emotionalize that, we create those condition held in thought. When we see and feel it as completed, it is on its way. It is <u>this</u> process when brought into *conscious activation,* that provides us an unlimited empowerment.

- This is what the system ***desperately*** does not want you to know.

- The objective is to know and use this empowerment *correctly.*

When we come to view every thought, every action, every word and every dollar as a vote and a prayer, then a sense of responsibility comes over us to be much better co-creators within the hologram of experience. The benefit is yours. It is *your* empowerment.

That which each of us experiences is not only a mirror of our thoughts at their average, it is the instructional feedback tool by which we are continuously offered an infinitely better existence. **It is <u>exclusively</u> at our command**.

- This concept is worth contemplating.

- Within this model, your empowerment is at hand.

- We consider it a very Reasonable gift to you.

- Thank *you*, for advancing into empowerment.

How many times have I taken someone to a movie that portrays Consciousness and awareness? Who knows? How many times have we shown or arranged the viewing of documentaries that showcase Consciousness and awareness? A lot. How many speeches and classes has this organization presented? How many books have we sold? The point is, that every event, facebook, twitter or like is a vote. And as many folks participated and evolved, that was this organization and those in it casting a whoppin' lot of votes and *thoroughly and knowingly* enjoying the leverage.

- The point is that you can do the same thing.

- You have the Calling <u>and now the ability</u> to greatly increase your empowerment.

- *...As often as you like.*   • It is *highly* Reasonable.

How many books on Consciousness and awareness have I loaned out or given away? How many have I recommended? How many authors are named in this book? Every event was a conscious and aware vote. If two people read this book and read but one mentioned author each, Neale Donald Walsch as an example, that condition counts for *four* votes and so forth, because of the leverage employed *and the resulting and reliable* **exponential shift in awareness.**

If I talk to three people, that counts for three votes. Every one of them from what I've witnessed, will outclass the essentially nonexistent ballot vote. This is due to achieving a position of greater awareness and higher Consciousness. In time, the ballot vote will straighten itself out anyway. This is because mainstream politics as we now know it **positively,** and simply, **_will_-_cease_-_to_-_exist_**.   Make no mistake; *that is the goal.*

- *Because it unlocks immediate and unlimited human and planetary benefit.*   **Got it?**

- If you do, then **now** you know how to vote—**Consciously.**

- And that concludes the chapter on The How and Why of Voting.

Chapter Six

Term Limits

Term Limits.

Term limits could be my favorite subject right along with tax limit, balanced budget, and absolutely no borrowing amendments.

- Actually, the above conditions are America's favorite subject.

Somewhere between 80 and 95% of the voters and non voters alike, *strongly* support those obviously human beneficial conditions. ***And*** at the same time, {**key concept here!**} the "elected" mainstream political leadership is somewhere in the neighborhood of 90 to 99% vehemently, adamantly, drastically, and virulently opposed to those *identical* conditions*!*

What in the ***Tarnation,*** possesses the average *idiot* of a voter, to re-elect a single mainstream political cretin*!??*

Sometimes I wonder when the light is going to come on, and the final rejection of mainstream politicians will gain its completion. Personally, I hold the belief such Evolution into human benefit shall mature *with this cause*.

With just cause, mainstream politics has earned its end. *Such is the real and actual Term Limits I'm referring to* **here.**

- And it is so!

Here is the crazy part: The identical dichotomy with the same underlying *modern political* intent of human sacrifice, exists for a good number of examples beyond the above four basic starter samples. Perhaps the problem is that as a species and electorate, we never add the whole thing up in order to see the larger picture. That's why *the human race* created the Humanitarian Code—to end the human slavery ***process***.

We continuously view one political dishonor after another in a lifelong string of exquisitely destructive dishonors. We view them one at a time and are correctly outraged. Yet in spite of the unbroken *long train* of in your face dishonor, we fail to see the larger pattern of the **mainstream political process** of continual dishonor. *This* insight is the awakening.

The pattern is one event at a time and therefore obscures the larger and very hard-set _frog in the frying pan pattern_ of mainstream *intentional,* [i.e. cartel purchased] **blood soaked political prostitution**.

- For most of you reading this book, none of this is *the slightest* new information. Virtually all of *you* have it down pat.

Human slavery is not ever sold as human slavery. If it were, then the American public would not continue to be its purchasing and funding agent.

- Continued human future depends upon *this* understanding.

I could with ease, and the same justification, write entire chapters on:

🍎 Sunshine Laws

These *enormously popular* and, mainstream leadership hated laws, range from open town hall meetings to open bid laws, to disclosure laws, to the Freedom of Information Act, internet tracking and much more.

The overwhelming supermajority in the same range given above, strongly support these beneficial laws. ...And by the same shame filled range, the mainstream cartel appointed leadership vehemently opposes the same Open Process laws. Mainstream politicians prefer to keep their dispensings of hell behind closed doors. They have well earned their public disapproval rate. This was a lesson learned at the Federal level. It is now becoming standard practice at all levels of modern government.

With little surprise, 100% of everything in this list and a great deal more, shares the same dichotomy of the general public support range and the mainstream political leadership opposition range. Election after election and year after year, we see each of these conditions piecemeal, but not all at once. Therefore we fail to see the long term **pattern**. That is *exactly* where the problem is. Its *undoing*, is the Great Healing into human success.

- And it is so.

Sunset Laws

Every law, and in the specific, every tax law, *desperately* needs a Sunset Provision. Sunset provisions are the bane and undoing of the tax and mindless spending mainstream political **universe**. This provision means that each tax increase and human limitation law gets voted on by each House and Senate member at each election cycle.

Ooh, I like that! And as it turns out, so does the general public. Just ask the hapless, taken for granted and extremely overburdened middle class taxpayer. They bear the weight of endless new and *sworn temporary* taxes and tax increases for the most inane crap imaginable. ...All of which have a rather mystical way of becoming **forever taxes** with forever increases—as is the real experience.

- **The real experience is the direct opposite of the promised experience.**

- Did everyone catch that definition of mainstream politics?

- Good.

This provision totally eliminates the "blame the other side" bullcrap that dominates and defines modern politics. Sunset provisions expose the blame game *swindle* for the utter falsehood it is.

Here is the game: Mainstream side A raises taxes for an unvoted war or some other hellish inclemency, and then mainstream side B keeps the tax in place by not being forced to re-vote it in to continuation.

- This allows bad law and tax increases to continue on forever by way of *an engineered* **design of default**.

The same sunset provisions can and will work for all the egregiously failed governmental programs.

- *Which program has **not** horrendously and shamefully failed?*

- *Right there*, is the question we should be asking ourselves.

The same provision shall apply to any of many egregiously failed laws.

Most of those laws have turned into calamities of Biblical proportions. They are of human destroyment one right after the other like clockwork. It is their cumulative and progressive results that *define* the modern political system of human sacrifice at the hands of international cartel.

How many times have we as individuals been directly torted by some government law or process that we come to learn is non-constitutional and therefore **not at all legal?**

- Non-legal now defines the vast majority of present government processes.

- Welcome to cartel owned modern politics.

How many times have we had involvement with government processes that were subsequently discovered to be ***professionally*** **non-functional?**

An example, one I have heard of way too many times, is the Juvenile Criminal "Justice" system. Apparently the process is *consecratedly* non-functional throughout the United States.

- Welcome again to modern politics.

Each of us as a result of personal involvement, gets to see one or two chunks of government in its non-functionality or its lawless anarchy.

Typically the non-functionality is every bit the equal of the juvenile criminal justice system. Or the anarchy is every bit as profusely lawless as say the IRS, one of countless agencies that no longer bother to ***pretend*** the laws as passed by Congress applies to *them*.

Tragically, we as individuals are unable to see all the failed and lawless government programs and policies *at once*. Thus we fail to see the true hue and scope of the process **of human sacrifice**. From that perspective, we often <u>assume</u> *that somehow, <u>as if by magic</u>, all other* government programs *might* work as advertised. They emphatically **do not**. The evidence is clear. Virtually any research turns up an overwhelming tsunami of one sided proof.

It is the process <u>of human sacrifice</u> that is in need of term limits. Each of the concepts mentioned in this list, and many more of human empowerment serve to do precisely that. *This is the truth that sets us free.*

🍎 Supermajority laws

A supermajority vote as particularly applied to new taxes and tax increases would make perhaps the ideal Initiative Petition in states that have such a process. Such is how popular supermajority is *and why*.

The process of Supermajority goes a long ways in stopping modern political side B blaming side A for the intentionally failed provisions and their underlying tax burdens shoved down our throats *by both sides <u>equally.</u>*

Few one sided ***dolts*** have ever stopped to notice that modern politics, like their car's wheels and tires, *are round* and, like a half of a wheel in a D shape, will not roll. What that means, is that every law and program claimed by one side as failed, was passed with a majority vote, that invariably by definition, had to include plenty *or all* of the 'other' side *in full capitulation*.

'Side' A and side B labels are upon examination, then seen correctly as indescribably meaningless. **This is the gospel truth of all mainstream politics**. The mainstream voter was never supposed to understand this reality. Due to the repetitive dunning of the partisan dog and pony show <u>fiction</u>, the mainstream voter has not made this basic connection. Shorn sheep is the definition that applies to this condition of senseless anarchy.

- Lemmings go over the same cliff, the difference is that they die with truth, honor and courage.

The Supermajority Process serves to bring the above process out into the light as opposed to the hidden in the dark corner it now enjoys. It flat puts the halt to present "they did it" *bullcrap* each 'side' now sells like hotcakes to their particular sheep. In other words, the blame game is a lie just like any other lie. I just happen to think that it is time to call that lie a lie *because it is a lie*.

- The ding-dongs taken by that lie have simply been *hustled*.

You see, Supermajority does not stop the mainstream process of dishonor any more than the standard majority requirements do. It does however stop the *lying about it process* professionally wielded by the mainstream politician. The mainstream politico has utterly snowed their particular 'side' equally, and for the most part, *profoundly*.

- It is time to put Term Limits to that particular nasty little hundred and fifty year long dog and pony show ***of professional fakery***.

 I happen to like **Government Prohibition Laws** a lot.

However, that's what the Federal Constitution, the Oath of Office, and each State Constitution are. And the mainstream political leadership ignores them *as if they were never written*.

Most of that particular condition is due to the fact that as Corporate Persons each of us is documented as; we fall under Maritime Law that bears no relationship to the Constitution. It also makes the Constitution not in any part, binding evidence in a court of law. Although that subject is fodder for another book, it is mentioned here so as it may be researched.

Such is the *precise* explanation of the non-existence of Human Rights that are not recognized under Maritime Law. This is what the gold bordered or tipped flag symbolizes. Many claim that Maritime Law is in fact, or at least in practice, Military Occupational Law, **and they are correct**. The events in New Orleans following Katrina would be public evidence.

What I am referring to here though, is specific, targeted prohibitions that block modern politics and therefore government, from specific areas or functions. **Bill of Rights Laws,** although civil in nature, more or less fall into this larger category and can cover a lot of ground in specific areas of institutional function. Other examples would include the term limit, tax limit, balanced budget and no borrowing laws as spoken of in the opening paragraph of this chapter. Each very Reasonable concept is at essence a government prohibition law. They are restrictions placed upon a government that from real-world experience, desperately needs to be operating under a sea of such human beneficial laws.

I would like to see foundations and Humanitarian institutions in dedication to moving one Initiative Petition after another into existence. We will see that benefit reasonably soon. There are literally scores of issues presently enjoying majority population support. It is no secret that the mainstream leaders as purchased by the cartel, are in opposition to 100% of those issues. **It is time to demonstrate who is in charge of our lives.**

🍎 Overview Laws

This general category includes Ombudsman Laws, Inspector General Laws, Advocate Laws, Citizen Overview Laws, interactive internet access to government processes and more.

Various civil Bill of Rights Laws can and sometimes do, depending upon their scope, include at least some provision of appeal for the individual with some form of oversight and/or review. Overview processes themselves are a highly beneficial but dramatically under-known and underused process.

The real world has taught us this much: An ever increasing number of government agencies are so profoundly lawless, that the only thing they understand is a "bigger hammer". That 'bigger hammer' turns out to be something akin to an ombudsman process, even if it may have different labels state by state to describe a similar function.

A particularly good example would be the **theoretical** overview and correction process <u>as required</u> by all federal and state legislative offices.

When a citizen is wrongly treated by some agency of wrong treatment, the *legal requirement* is that the Legislators of said jurisdictions are responsible for, and are well budgeted, staffed *and required to*, review, step in, correct the wrong treatment, **and cause restitution.**

Sadly, this is a nearly nonexistent occurrence in today's political paradigm of oppression. A Politian <u>paid to oppress the individual</u> is not going to help the individual. ***This is the reality of 100% of all mainstream politics.***

When the overview process pertains to the governor of a particular state, it is most often called the Ombudsman. It carries the weight and authority of the Governor. I believe all states have this provision. However it can and does employ different names for the same thing. The function of such office and process is to investigate *and correct* lawless acts and lawless patterns of agencies within the state.

- It would be nice if all of the above actually worked that way.

- However **it does not**.

You are now reading many of the reasons *why* that system is also nonfunctional. The laws are in place for such overview and correction, *however <u>the will and intent are not</u>*. As it turns out, such *process* is a very important distinction to be aware of. It is one of the foundational differences between human sacrifice and Human Success. It is the difference between being treated **as a slab of meat,** *or regarded a human being.*

The above condition, treating humans as slabs of meat, is the present foundational and defining characteristic *of all modern politics.* Often times it is <u>how</u> the law is written. More often, it is <u>how</u> the law is carried out.

Modern politics sees humans as objects, items <u>and targets</u>. As ever, it is cloaked behind oceans of politically correct, *that is to say lying,* **eye wash**. The process can even be polite—whenever the sugarcoat theatrics *turns out to be convenient* (as your freedom flies right out the window).

Overview exists in law. It is drastically underused. It needs to be re-learned and employed often. There needs to be more of it and it needs *drastically stronger correction provisions.*

Expect **zero** cooperation from the elected mainstream politician in this regard. Real world experience has proven this beyond any shadow of doubt. It is unfortunate but true, ***hence the need for this book.***

A good example of overview might be an internet broadcast {CAFR} budget detailed to the last cent. This model would apply to city, county and state government. Eventually, it will be subject to final approval **only** by the citizenry. This example came from *you*. It sounds Reasonable to *me*.

- Any suggestion in this book would make a good Amendment.

🍎 Initiative Petition

In the States and locale where such a thing is available, Initiative Petition is positively the best thing going.

Initiative Petition is the process where we cause *or end* our own laws. We bring it up to vote by way of petition, and then vote the fate of the law. Quite amazingly, due to the general absence of awareness and wisdom of how political things work in the real world, some of the time this process is used to actually *increase* human ruination. The entire objective of Initiative Petition is to *reduce* human ruination. I do not readily know the percentages here, however most of the time this wonderful process is used to cause greater freedom. <u>*That is its intended moral function*</u>.

🍎 Recall

This process is given to the people to remove a politician from office who "got caught".

- According to modern times, that would basically be *all of them*.

Recall has to be the single most underused human beneficial process in the entire world—right next to the Initiative Petition. For a particularly offensive law passed by a purchased legislature, the Initiative Petition process is one way of how that law is undone. For a particularly offensive officeholder, Recall is the process of removing the skunk from the office.

The problem starts when EVERY modern politician defines the north end of a southbound pole cat. ...And that brings us right back to the intended <u>non lawyer</u> citizen legislature. .. And the need for stringent {and short term} limits for all offices **both appointed and elected**. ...As both conditions are crucial to the process *of ending of human slavery*.

🍎 Judgments and Riders

As wildly different as these two processes are, they share the same energy. Under the greater scope of modern politics, it is all but exclusively the cartel purchased intention *of human destroyment*.

We all know about **Case Law** that sets the precedence of how things are in a particular jurisdiction and usually dictates the same for equal jurisdictions. This is the bailiwick "served" or perhaps "served up" by a particular court system. The courts do manage once in a rare while to cause human beneficial case law. Such rarity however, makes the rule of handing down purchased case law advancing cartel driven anarchy and violence.

In the cause of human slavery, the judiciary routinely steps out of its Constitutional limits of testing the constitutionality of a law. From there the judiciary moves into a new area of human sacrifice known as judicial legislation. This is where the judiciary writes the law as opposed to trying the law for its legality or helping to interpret the law. Sadly, this has now become *the* standard practice within the moral dive to human slavery.

The **Rider** is the most abused process of them all. It is currently employed profusely by the modern politician. When the mainstream dirt bag knows a large bill is going to pass, every manner of harm gets attached to that bill by the Rider process. Tragically, the ratio of harmful stuff to beneficial stuff is about two hundred to one. This proves *beyond the slightest shadow of doubt*, that every mainstream approved politician is nothing other than a *lying, stinking, slimy {colostomy} bag*, **as you have well stated**.

When we begin to once again elect Reasonable people to legislative and judicial office, then both processes could be used to bring about human beneficial conditions. It is the very opposite of how they are now employed by honor absent modern politics. By the same process of how bad laws are now created, good laws *could be* created, and bad laws retired. It will take **honorable people** to do this. To do that, **WE** will have to make **the binding decision** to no longer tolerate the legal status of humans *as farm objects*.

Like all other listed processes, <u>the intent and letter</u> of the Constitution combined with the Oath of Office, was intended to govern the process. That is no longer how things are *at all.*

❖ Ballot Access Laws.

And that will bring us up to the Constitutional {legal} intention of ballot access. It is to allow alternative party members and independents to run for, and have at least a snowball's chance, of entering and winning an election.

As it is now, **the opposite is the case**. Ballot access is presently employed by the mainstream political process as a sledgehammer to road block any and all competition. *And that is exactly how they use it.*

For an example, the petitioning requirements are set specifically high enough to effectively stop the process cold which it usually does. The overall process is geared up to drain the time, energy, money and will power out of the potential competition so effectively, that when the actual election comes about, there is nothing left in the tank to move forward with. That is consistently how it works. <u>It is the *dead opposite* of how the original process was intended.</u>

In place of the original intention of bringing forth <u>diverse viewpoints</u>, today's process of ballot access is used specifically to <u>suppress</u> any viewpoint other than <u>the cartel purchased intent</u> **of unlimited brutality**.

To add a great deal of insult to that abuse of power, the alternate and independent is rarely if ever, supported by cartel. This means they will enter races often underfunded by a hundred to one *or more.*

- This means that every election is outright purchased.

We have witnessed this cowardice and shame for generations of cartel purchased elections. We have seen elections featuring one criminally dishonest mainstream politician after another paraded forth like strings of stamped out plastic posies. We have suffered this condition literally for lifetimes.

- Each "election" being the worst choice **in history**, *every time*, **is your proof**.

Stone cold *further* proof of the purchased election resides in the **dollars to vote** *ratio*.

For the mainstream, this ratio is enormously high at oodles of dollars per vote, pretty much without exception. Millions and millions are typically spent on elections for offices that pay only a minuscule fraction of the election purchase.

- If you can say; the system is rigged, *you are correct*.

And the answer **is not** in immaculately dishonorable politicians voting themselves yet *another* pay raise while the rest of their constituency sees their pay value cut for the umpteenth time! That is yet another upside down picture in desperate need *of **immediate and unequivocal eradication**.*

Which politician has not voted themselves increased perks and additional pay raises in a long train of increased perks and additional pay raises? There's the question. The real question would be: What is our answer? The question is Reasonable. *May the answer also be.*

For the alternate party participant, operating with little or no funding and in particular, no cartel funding, the votes cast for them, as few as they often may be, are gathered in *at an exceedingly low dollar to vote ratio*.

Now this knowledge and awareness presented here is very important. I will explain it because of its *design of obscurity*. The mainstream media conveniently manages to block this readily available information out. The media would rather favor whatever sad misfortune or inane squabble, (drama-crap), they can dig up *or cause*. That fifth rate, fifth column trash is then in turn puked all over *you,* should you allow it. *I for one do not.*

The Moral of the Story is this: If the alternative or independent candidates were on equal *financial* footing, they would win every single election simply because of the astronomical difference in the two dead opposite **dollar to vote ratios**.

- Thank y'all for pointing that out to me.

This information, indictment, awareness and appeal is, as previously clearly stated, written as petition to the court of the Creator of all Creation, and indeed all Creation itself, as is the entire book. The objective of this book is Consciousness, i.e., the Human Event and the Great Healing leading up to the Human Event. In this case, the Creator will be the Judge, precisely as The Creator with spiritual Might, speaks to the human heart in terms of increased consciousness **and the personal resolve** *to move that unlimited benefit into reality.*

The dollars to vote ratio is available public information that anyone with net access can look up. Both the vote totals and the dollars spent are well disclosed in most locations. One is very easy to get, and the other may take a touch more looking. However, the bottom line is that the above information is readily available, unarguable, and **absolutely conclusive** proof of absolutely corrupt elections—*every single time*.

With even the smallest amount of research, it does not take rocket science to understand that each and every so called 'election' has been outright and easily purchased by corporate cartel. That much is not the slightest news to you. Working as a team, you desired to bring this information to the general attention of the *egregiously and horrifically uninformed* public. It is now so.

Once we know the game of slavery, we can then stop playing that injury-game by dropping support away, by any and all legal means possible, from the mainstream political process **of human sacrifice**. *Most often, that will be accomplished with the voice and e-mail vote in simply communicating the existence of this book and the Humanitarian Code. With that, we are the Healer of persons, Nations and Worlds. We are* <u>placing Term Limits</u> *on the process of intentional and purchased* **human ruination.**

- **The future and those in it, thank you for doing so.**

- It is the *least* we can do.

Chapter Seven

The Four levels of Awareness

The four levels of awareness:

In relationship to the extreme contrast between the abject lack of consciousness as found in the doings of human slavery and its opposite, the Creator Consciousness of Human Success, there are four macro steps of awareness:

1. Non-awareness or perhaps more accurately, anti-awareness:

This is the tortured world of the walking dead. Here the term anti-awareness is the best description. In today's world, this is the common and default level of horrendous mental poverty. It is blindness to real-world cause and effect. The perpetual dupes caught at this level invariably get their fantasy-information, their diet of lies, from the fk'n television. The TV, news papers and any mainstream media, explain both cause and effect of this *astonishingly destructive and inexcusably pig-ignorant phenomenon.*

- This explains the mainstream voter ***to perfection***.

This level is the rather suicidal thinking that mainstream politics is ok. This level of awareness is somewhere south of IQ challenged. It's *really* out to lunch. Such strange thinking is in the not wanting to know what the Devil is brewing behind closed doors. It is a pollyanic dream world. It is a Rome is not burning self-flattery. It is a go ahead to the good-old-boy cutthroat back room deals. *It is textbook clinical insanity.* Such level of thinking is on par with the idea that oxygen doesn't exist.

That mental vivarium is the mainstream party vote for either A or B. The resulting difference turns out to be nonexistent. This is the mystified thinking that the modern politician "will do the right thing". It is the same thinking that the coiled rattlesnake won't strike. It is a left handed matrimony of unlimited arrogance and unlimited ignorance.

- Truly the angels weep in grief at this level of omni-destroyment.

- It is *that* ignorance of the doings of mainstream politics which has facilitated human slavery more so than any other factor.

From the obvious destructiveness of modern politics alone, we can deduce that such non-awareness level is ballparkish that of the amoeba. Actually, the amoeba is smarter. The amoeba does not elect and then **bizarrely re-elect,** a firestorm of utterly moral void cretins, soulless clones, and murdering thugs who correctly and literally belong in prison *until dead*.

For perfect example, no amoeba would vote for the cartel driven destruction of the planet earth, for even the amoeba has some of the innate intelligence God gave a goose not to destroy its own world. That is because the amoeba and the goose, have lived for countless millions of years in perfect balance and harmony with Nature. The mainstream partisan voter fails *all* of the above tests. **It is the *illustrated* definition of foot shot.**

For an even better example, no amoeba would either vote for *or finance* their own destroyment as we now do. The average voter also miserably, miserably, fails this test as well. It is simply an IQ test. Technically stated, it is a Dumb-tax. Those who vote mainstream politics get the Dumb-tax of human slavery. We have got to become at minimum at least as smart as an amoeba **in order to survive!**

- *The Universe itself simply will not allow it to be otherwise.*

There are four basic requirements of slaves and slavehood:

1 Slaves must be mostly uneducated. With today's government education, this is definitely the case.

2 Slaves must be, and remain, politically unaware. <u>This shoe fits</u>.

3 Slaves must believe or at minimum not *actively* object to whatever lie they are told, <u>and that is a lot of lies folks.</u>

4 Slaves must fall for televised (slavery) propaganda and instructions.

The mainstream voter solidly meets all four of the above requirements of slavehood. ...And as our 'educational' system tested 18th out of 18 advanced nations, such a peculiarly destructive combination is the foundation of human slavery. *All doubt in this regard has been removed <u>by the results</u>.*

Because the above hapless condition is textbook and clinical unawareness, this particular level by way of obvious results, can only be correctly called *unconscious*. From there, only one question remains: How destructive and how obvious does the above condition have to get, before the human species *forever and utterly abandons it?*

- **The clue is that the awakening must be accomplished while the human race still exists.**

2. The next level is awakening consciousness:

The moment one arises to a greater level of awareness and consciousness, the sheer contrast between their higher station and the lower totality *and tyranny* of modern politics, causes then, the same morally absent politics to be repugnant in the extreme. The contrast itself manifests *from the utterly demonic results of modern politics.*

However, *and this is the key condition*, one then falls into one of three traps that maintain one's Consciousness calibration locked below Integrity. Below integrity is defined as living a lie. The first trap is a direct falling backward into the level one demonstrated state of non-consciousness or non-integrity. It is the tumble down default position of omni-destructiveness *as defined by the results.*

Such trap is correctly defined as the profoundly insane notion of voting the lesser of two evils when that mythical beast went extinct very near the Civil War when humans became legally converted into incorporated and registered human farm *possessions*. The identical trap is also correctly defined by the equally mythical notion of "voting for the best puppet"; for such woe filed inane error winds up with the same profoundly human destructive results. Translated; it means slightly different lie, **same results**.

A highly similar trap at this *below Integrity* level, is the notion of not voting, or not voting at every opportunity presented to do so, simply because that trap facilitates the identical human destroyment process. It makes no difference if this paradigm is the numerical and factually correct majority; *it is the resultant outcome that matters.* That particular outcome is *very* arrogantly **TWISTED** into a resounding endorsement for human slavery*!*

The simple reason that the above condition is below Integrity, is that at this level, one is at least aware of the outcome of modern politics, however one then *fails to act* in response to that earned or intuitive awareness. The result is human ruination. **This is the present station of the human condition.**

Yet, because of the felt consciousness contrast between you and modern politics, this stage regrettably, can only be correctly defined as awakening conscious. Sadly, it is not yet enough to fizzle a woodpecker. The consciousness calibration remains roughly that of a sow bug.

In fact, there are several tests the pill bug passes with flying colors that the average voter *indisputably,* does not. For example, the sow bug well knows there is no difference between the uni-intent mainstream political halves labeled A and B or anyone within the Statist Uniparty.

A fencepost knows that much. A rock knows that much! The wind knows that much. The rain knows that much. The grass knows that much. A turnip knows that much… However, the average voter apparently **does not**.

- Go on ahead and say "insanely stupid" and get it out of your system.

- From one end of America to the other, that is what you called it.

The entire world *and everything in it* except, for the Prince of the Power of the Air television and the continual deceit featured on it, is *desperately* attempting to convey to the profoundly unconscious average voter the above truth.

- **And**, that condition has been going on their entire life!

Please get it. Your life depends on getting it. It is not rocket science. Which funny person said: **"here's your sign!"** *That statement simply could not be more appropriate than for the above condition!*

- Mainstream politics is now defined as the great Nash equilibrium where by all players gravitate to the very lowest common denominator of unvarnished hate, theft and injury.

3. The level of demonstrated Consciousness:

Upon further gaining consciousness, mainstream politics and its now perfected human destroyment becomes **unspeakably repugnant**. Similar to the former addict, one then lifelong *and with the resolve of the gods*, <u>correctly</u> swears off the mortal injury of mainstream politics at every possible opportunity, **while rapidly making the opportunities to do so.**

The recovered alcoholic knows that much, why doesn't the average voter? They got rocks in their head or sand in their soul? You tell me.

As a direct result of the raw destructiveness of politics and government in general, the American Vote of smaller government, fewer taxes and greatest personal freedom emerges and takes a strong predominance. Here is where the human race bands together and become proactive <u>*as related to human survival*</u>.

This level *by results* is clearly, demonstrated Consciousness. It is not perfect. It is not yet ideal. It is not utopia. It is not the full human potential. It is however very Reasonable. It is an unlimited improvement in human **living conditions** by way of an efficient and determined reduction of human slavery. It is really important to understand *this concept*. Human survival depends upon the human race making ***this specific move.***

Only at this third level, that of demonstrated Consciousness, and the first level above Integrity, do we begin to achieve the ever so desperately needed quo waranto recovery of the cartel and lawyer hijacked public office. This very American action returns those offices to the rightful and legal owners, the one or two time elected Oath bound **citizen** legislature.

3.5 Please be keenly aware that each lower level of consciousness or lack of it, is blaringly obvious to any higher level of calibration. To those not quite so systematically brainwashed and therefore not trapped in a previous level, any previous calibration becomes so repugnant and *grossly ignorant*, as to be *sickening*, and correctly so. As Reasonable, we understand that.

Therefore, the Mission is to both elucidate <u>and</u> be understanding. A real easy solution is to let this book do the primary enlightening by way of gift *so as you don't have to*. Trust me that particular choice also saves on wear and tear in dealing with unconscious mainstream partisan simpletons, *who may or may not be reliable with either shoelaces or toilet paper.*

I've made that debate mistake one too many times myself, and I know how to save you that incredible hassle. In fact, that is one of the very Reasonable reasons this book was created; **to help you avoid that**. Got it?

- If so, then for Pete's sake **use it**—*the advantage is 100% yours*.

4. Human Success:

- "The larger portion of enlightenment is not the truths gained, *it is in illusions lost.*" Probably from the Tao

Beyond and above all that, and only through the three previous levels every last one of us absolutely **will** go through, we gain the fourth level of Human Success; *our own ownership.*

I have vigorously lived all the previous levels of awareness. I know I am guilty as sin of my own sordid and inexcusable, ignorant, sickening and *consummately stupid* past political rookie mistakes. We all are or will be. That infantile crap is how human slavery occurred. By the opposite action, we **now** know how to undo the same human destruction.

- The undoing of slavery **is** Reasonable.

- *It is through The Humanitarian Code.*

As the human race awakens and moves into the New Energy of Human Success, we earn and experience the *vastly* better, brighter future worth living in.

- **It is *very* Reasonable indeed.**

Chapter Eight

Third Rails and Compromised Organizations

Third rails and compromised organizations:

"One learned man is harder on the devil than a thousand ignorant worshippers."   Mohammed

The seemingly odd juxtaposition of third rails and compromised organizations begins to make sense in the realization that both share the same underlying framework. Let it no longer be a surprise: The framework is **slavery versus Consciousness**.

We are instructed by society and media <u>to not notice</u>; that ever more items, paradigms and energies are now "third rails" to modern politics and the modern politician. Speaking any form of truth in relationship to those areas results in withdrawn support either from the partisan sheep, or far more importantly, various cabal. It is the removal of **cabal support** that subsequently causes a failure to **install the opinion** into the sheep and therefore harvest *their television blinded and thus totally predictable vote*.

The compromised organization, association or movement is the one that supports the mainstream politician. The math on this is extremely straightforward. There is no wiggle room in the definition *whatsoever*.

The logic you are asked to believe is this: The organization proclaims that the problem is the cartel purchased mainstream politician just as all mainstream politicians are. **However**; the solution is to support cartel purchased mainstream politicians.

- What kind of crap is that?

- It is the story of mainstream politics and sold out organizations.

Now we tie the two conditions together:

- *Without truth,* **everything** becomes the deadly third rail for mainstream politicians.

- This is the precise explanation of the ***professional emptiness*** of all mainstream politics.

- Within Consciousness, nothing can remain insolvent as every subject becomes a delight and pleasure.

- *This is the Reasonable solution.*

In a vote that does not matter, one that will pass or fail with a certainty known in advance, the modern politician will normally vote your main issue as per your wish. <u>This is done because it does not matter</u>. That vote will not make any **actual** difference whatsoever. *Stay with me here.* ...And the politician in question will universally *empty* their franking privileges to brag those meaningless votes to high heaven. This ongoing **process** sets up the illusion that they might be on your side. <u>*It is absolutely a lie*</u>. That it is a well orchestrated and well used lie does not change the fact that **it is a lie.**

On the **rare** occasions when a specific vote might actually make a difference, the odds historically drop <u>under 10%</u> on **your** issue. These are not odds one would take to Las Vegas and hope to clean the house with. The other ninety percent or so consists of a condition called back stab, cave in, or yeller belly. The Republican "leaders" have that down *technically perfect*.

Oh, but there is worse, *much worse:*

The lying, sold away mainstream politician supported by the wrong organization, association or movement will destroy your human rights in favor of the cartel or cabal on all <u>other</u> issues with a regularity you can set your watch by. This is not 10% or 50%, **it is indistinguishable from 100%.**

- Got it?

These are the directions on how to stop supporting human slavery:

- The solution to both conditions **is in being Reasonable.**

Both conditions, the ever growing third rail phenom and the compromised organization phenom, *are caused by lack of consciousness*.

- Both conditions are solved **with Consciousness.**

In the lack of consciousness, either condition shares the intent and result of human slavery. With the application of Consciousness, the **absence** of either tragedy results in Human Success.

When the organization, association or movement supports mainstream politicians, **GET OUT NOW.** *Let the dead bury the dead*. The energy of **deceit** does not need your blind sheeply and mousely follow-ship. It does however need competition centered in the New energy of Human Success.

- The odds of anyone changing old energy gatherings from within are **zee-row.** (Nor is it in their charter.)

- Like reform to modern politics, if it could have happened, it would have happened in the last 100 years of not happening.

- When the cave is filled with smoke (lies), **GET OUT!**

- Presently there is a 95 to 96% chance your life depends on it.

Now the opposite is also true: **With applied Consciousness** we readily observe through the Ron Paul Revolution, that the standard cartel purchased politician is trapped. There becomes no subject that is not poison *to them*. Every lie they speak simply digs them into a deeper hole (example: Hillary). As the crowds enjoying the side of consciousness grow exponentially over time, the tear jerking dull, *paid* gatherings on the side placating one lie after another shrink to the point of comedy, *just as they did equally with Rama & Bama*. Either way, the classically instructed party lines **are** *obliterated*.

- It is however due to the fact they did not *actually* exist.

- And this, concludes the chapter on third rails and compromised organizations.

Chapter Nine

Slavery versus Consciousness

Slavery versus Consciousness:

"There is only one moment in time when it is essential to awaken. That moment is now."

Buddha

- **Slavery vs. Success is now the human debate.**

Deep within the <u>engineered deception</u> of the left-right baseline of mainstream politics is the hidden truth that both ends represent a Totalitarian, despotic, **and death laden** end result. The design is that no matter where one acts from within that paradigm be it left, right, *"independent"* or any point in between, the unfailing outcome **is human slavery**.

Within this paradigm or limitation, it is the **belief** that has been hijacked as surely as any other robbery or assault. Here is the paradigm that states; whatever the television says must be true. Now a shift in both communications and consciousness comes along, and we evolve to find out that the televised spin pertaining to the left-right paradigm is *fantastically false*. We find out that the left-right measurement itself is false, that it is an illusion, that it is a cunningly devised trap designed to destroy our humanity.

Here is a bit of background:

The world controlling cartel interest gave us the Civil War in order to create the corporate person we now all are. This 'citizenship' act transferred ownership of our person to international banking corporate cartel **as <u>chattel</u>**. Legally and literally, everything you do, everything you create, everything you own, and everything you are, belongs to cartel **including your children**. *They have full rights to claim any or all of it at <u>any</u> moment to use for <u>any</u> purpose including child abduction and its associated slave trade syndicate through well established channels.* ⇨In that present model *as is*, **you have no functional legal recourse** *whatsoever*.

- The Supreme Court has rigorously upheld that position.

This was the first and largest step of human slavery within our borders. A similar pattern under different names has been followed by every nation on this planet *that has allowed debt instrument monetization*.

This action, the 14th Amendment corporate citizenship effectively eliminated Human Rights. It is of importance to acknowledge that this action was done under the pretense of doing the opposite of what it actually did. It could be rightly said that such intentional deceit not only began the era of modern politics, but also sums up modern politics in a nutshell. The Federal Reserve Act was only the coup d'état to theft 96% of our wealth by way of an unvoted tax we call inflation. Inflation tax, usury tax and the income tax all belong to the debt sourced monetary system <u>underwritten by government issued birth certificates</u>. That is your title, **not owned by you**.

- *There is simply no better way to rain destruction upon any nation or people than the three way combination of inflation tax, usury tax and income tax as inherent to debt instrument monetization. All three share the identical result of human slavery.*

The next step of human slavery took place with the Rothschild banking interest driven Act of 1871. This Act formed the corporation of the United States, a paperwork entity wholly owned and controlled by foreign banking interest. This Act put in place *the vehicle* to transfer legal ownership of our person **as chattel** to various cartel. At the same time, this Act also transferred both ownership and control of our Nation to the banking cartel. From the first moment of our government schooling, we were and continue to be, taught a very different **and extremely false** story in this regard.

The next step into human slavery was the Supreme Court case of 1886 conferring personhood to corporations. This judicial legislative act conferred an unquestioned sainthood upon the various cartels. Effectively, this allowed the various cartels and in particular the banking cartel, to do whatever it felt like. And it has. To this date there is no effective oversight of *any* cartel. Compounded with a direct and literal ownership and control of all three branches of our government and the same for most governments worldwide, the forces serving **Satan** *and therefore* **slavery,** have majestically prevailed.

- This is the condition we live under today.

- It is loosely referred to as modern politics.

Those who watch the liars on television must now stop and ask themselves why the West has failed to make any serious plans for the world's future *other than warfare.* **This is the results we get when the house of Rothschild and Rockefeller control all aspects of mainstream politics.**

The condition of continual warfare serves the various cartel. The modern politician is only the sales hack for that warfare. It is this truth that breaks the illusion of the left-right paradigm. At this level of essence, there is no left-right at all. It is replaced with ever advancing **despotism**.

We are urged to notice that the left-right illusion of dichotomy forms a horizontal line and resulting perception. The greater portion intentionally left out, is any vertical movement toward Consciousness. The truth is; the whole line is morally lifeless even when labeled "independent" ***which is not.*** It calibrates equally low at any point along the left-right line or with any mixture thereof. Any move, action *or perception* whatsoever along that line abundantly furthers, fosters and increases **human destroyment**.

Within that paradigm, it makes no matter what the question is, increased government has turned out to be the answer. Ayn Rand referred to this condition as Statism. It is the concept of government as God. This is the experience we call modern politics. Ever so ironically, this condition is mostly independent of the fact that virtually every modern politician is *the* poster child for the Wall of Shame. There is no one along that line who is not sold to cartel. There is no turncoat along that line that gives the slightest damn about you. *There is no moral leader possible in that entire paradigm precisely as we have experienced.* **There is only one lie after another.**

- Across America, that despotism is spoken of daily. I have only provided a small sample of the scene behind the condition.

For one to stand out from that horizontal line of lack of consciousness to the point of notice as Rand Paul or Gary Johnson has, requires a calibration of consciousness somewhere above the flat-line of death and assumed limitation. The line itself is classroom of no show and F students, useless, bullying, lying and condescending, that do not give a flying fig about anything beyond their own spoils system we call modern politics.

"Experience hath shown, that even under the best forms of government, those entrusted with power have, in time, and by slow operations, *perverted it into tyranny.*" Thomas Jefferson

Benjamin Franklin nailed modern politics with this description of the falsehood found within modern politics: "Tricks and treachery are the practice of fools that don't have the brains to be honest."

- Ah ha!

- Four identical and recent Presidents fit that description. They are impressively myopic **asses**, and *way over the top* self-worshiping narcissists and incessant liars *in a very long lineage of the same.*

- I've discovered massive agreement on that.

For those who require further explanation, every politician on the left-right line is a member of the same club as described by Ben Franklin. With no surprise, virtually all are members of same or similar organizations singularly dedicated to the ending of Human Rights. They cannot even afford to be open or honest about the purpose and function of those organizations.

As it turns out, no mainstream politician can rise to a station of power without first being a *loyalty tested* member of at least one and typically several organizations specifically dedicated to the full termination of Human Rights. Very few people I've spoken to were unable to call this condition out.

- The words *loyalty tested* are highlighted because it is the key concept being presented.

- **This is *THE* heart and core of all mainstream politics.**

- It has become central to human species survival to understand this process *correctly*.

- It makes no difference where you stand on any issue, the mainstream political process *is very bad news for you.*

It is a rather pathetic state of affairs, however the above described conditions truth test. The awareness of the condition came directly from the countless contributors to this manual. The awareness, *and ability to accurately describe the condition*, was remarkably consistent across America. One did not have to be Tea Party to comprehend that particular horror show.

Along comes the Libertarians Godspeed, with a new dimension in the political landscape. The Libertarian's up and down overlay goes from the bottom in a description of the totalitarian and proceeds to the top in the condition of Liberty.

The new up and down tract can *also* be calibrated along the Scale of Consciousness. The bottom Calibrates at the condition of human slavery. It should by now be no surprise that such is the intention and result *of all mainstream politics*. **The intent *and* condition truth test.** There is *zero* wiggle room or escape there.

- The truth test is spot on consistent for those who can use it correctly.

- …And that is a prime indicator one is able to use it correctly.

- For those in tune with their intuition and instinct, the truth test brings forth to the outer conscious, data that is already known.

- For example, this book has only brings forth the *overwhelming* consensus as found across America, men and women alike.

The top of the up-down paradigm calibrates at **humanity**. Why this come as a surprise to many is the colossal failure of our educational system. It is a system that does not recognize Consciousness beyond providing an opposition deception-definition. *Orwell by the way, called that one.*

Why the Libertarians include the outdated left-right illusion even after vehemently proclaiming it an illusion for forty years straight, is anybody's guess. They have it correct enough to warrant a drawing overhaul from a diamond shaped political landscape, to a much more truthful vertical illustration of **Slavery versus Success**.

- Which is Reasonable.

- **Because it Truth Tests.**

Defining the primary shift of 2012, we have a vertical line of experience and effectiveness known as the Scale of Consciousness. The turn in the road defining 2012 and beyond, is our exponentially growing **awareness** of the conditions along that line.

Power vs. Force is saying the same thing from a spiritual and practical standpoint as Slavery vs. Success. In fact, the same condition is described as Truth vs. Falsehood, Life vs. Death, Slavery vs. Consciousness, Love vs. Fear, and Satin vs. God. These all describe the top and bottom of a vertical exponential progression of effectiveness, worth, livability *and benefit*.

Nowhere along that Scale of Consciousness describes an *absolute* absence of good or God, the Creator of all that is. Everywhere along the Scale of Consciousness describes an ego derived *and measureable* amount of temporary distance <u>in perception only</u>, from Source <u>and</u> the results if continued at that level, *(on which all prophecy is based)*.

All prophesy be it good or bad, is a projection of results of the overall planetary calibration *IF*— it is not changed post warning. Given the present ownership of the power structure of earth, it is no surprise that all prophecy is in the form of a **warning**. It is the definition of a no-brainer. {**However:**}

- We are in the midst of our grand opportunity.

- **The human race is rapidly moving upward in consciousness.**

The left-right illusion fails this test because it all describes Statism. The entire line and all points along the line **calibrate the same.** *To make a long story short, that is where humanity gets thrown under the bus by the illusion and all elements and aspects associated with the illusion.*

- <u>Virtually all of you understand that correctly.</u>

We are now apprised by truth test *and intuition*; that the left-right limitation of violence backed despotism **is an illusion**. We admit that it is a fantastic illusion. It has well served the function of human slavery. It is an illusion that has been around for a long time. None of that changes the fact that the left-right limitation *is an illusion*, *shame, tragedy* **<u>and brutal failure</u>**.

Up to now, that illusion has generated enough money a lot of people wonder why they did not think of it first. With little irony, this also describes most of the world's religious practices. *As with modern politics, the less actual substance and effect, the greater the monetary yield*.

Both "sides" are masters at pointing out problems *only to offer more of the same as the solution*. It is the eye for an eye blindness Jesus warned of. This condition grossly fails to move upward in consciousness. It is the paradigm of keeping the crabs in the crab pot of human sacrifice. It would be mighty convenient if that did *not* truth test.

"Woe to you, teachers of the law and Pharisees, you hypocrites! You shut the kingdom of heaven in men's faces. You yourselves do not enter, nor will you let those enter who are trying to." Jesus in Mathew 23:13

"With devotion's visage and pious action we do sugar o'er the devil himself." Shakespeare

"I detest that man, who hides one thing in the depths of his heart, and speaks forth another." Homer (circa 1000 BC)

- We just nailed most of the status quo right there with a three count pin to the mat *that truth tests*.

- **What then is left to define the human who is not *viciously* opposed to human slavery?**

Modern government has come to define itself as pseudo-legalized tyranny at the behest of the cartel and the élite. Why then should we call it anything other than that? The original intended goal of the federal government was to protect our liberty. It has now degraded to be the dead opposite of that. The federal government has now grown to be the chief destroyer of the condition of human for multitude generations.

When we come to realize all tyranny is done under the color of law, then the euphemisms we employ to pretend away tyranny all of a sudden fail to make any sense. At that point, tyranny becomes tyranny. It is seen for what it **is**. *This is the awakening*. We then drop the spin-euphemisms of tyranny away from our thought and speech. **We do this because of the devastating results of the endless <u>cover-up labels, loopholes and scams</u>**.

- It is the *ignorance* of this condition that defines public education.

- In all of human existence, there are only two directions;

slavery-and-Consciousness.

The hidden catch within the cutthroat universe defining mainstream politics is that in the same motion one supports mainstream politics to cut somebody else's throat, they cut their own throat. That process takes place in the reality that all mainstream effort *is in support of human slavery*. Every vote is in favor of the cartel. Every penny advances your own destruction. There may be a thousand labels, complex deceptions and ceaseless **smack talk** designed to make it appear otherwise. Yet in the end, only these truth tested and time proven realities remain:

- When the law can cut one throat, it can cut any throat.

- It is only a matter of a different puppet installed into control that cuts *your* throat.

- ...And they will not hesitate to do so.

- *That* is mainstream politics.

- As it is these realizations that differentiates the sleeper *from* the awakened, you now have the means to conclusively know which one *you* are.

The Reasonable message to the mainstream voter is: Because you obviously don't know how to fix it; *for God's sake, please stop breaking it.*

- **The mainstream voter has for generations proven to be highly unprincipled, astonishingly fickle and amazingly uninformed.**

- One of the functions of this book is to change that condition.

That was easy, now for difficult:

A message to mainstream politics from Source:

"Think not for one moment that all is not seen or that all will not be seen. Where is the evidence of that which you advertise? According to your own standards, you have failed. Why do you yet lie, cheat and steal? Have you no shame at all? The record of your Treason will outlive you for tens of thousands of years. You have well earned that infamy. Many of you shall not escape prison. The dishonor you live by has snared you. Like swine, you have been bought and sold by perdition. Your Consciousness is seared by a hot iron. You are thieves, traitors, fools, charlatans, liars, whores and inmates with demons."

A message to the mainstream voter:

"Where is the evidence of that which you claim you value? Why do you continue to allow your leaders to lie to you with every breath? What possesses you to remain asleep and blind to the evil of those you elect? This error is now recorded for the travesty it is. What possesses you to allow any of this shame to continue? Have you not intelligence greater than a mouse?

Has your courage also ran and hid? You have been used as patsies in every manner of treachery, deceit, evil and apostasy. Where is the humanity you claim? Is it found in warfare and slavery? Is it found in the thievery you demand? Is it found in the lies and liars you support or the traps they set?"

A message to the religionists of the world:

"Where is the evidence of your claims? Think not the warfare you have caused is not seen and recorded? Why do you continue to forcibly separate the human from the Creator in the name of doing the opposite? Think ye that it is not seen or not recorded? Ye serve fame, power, slavery, glitter and mammon but not the Lord who made you. You take stand directly against the path of Light and Liberty. Do you think that this will not be answered for? Where is the peace that all of you proclaim? Your haughtiness that has led many astray is recorded so that the record shall outlive your institutions and your buildings and your piousness that is repugnant to your Maker."

- The clearest present step we can take in Consciousness is when corporations are no longer people, and people are no longer chattel or corporations.

- Contrast *this* to the soulless cacophony of corruption we call modern politics.

- "No army can stop an idea whose time has come."
                                                                    Victor Hugo

"We are watching the beginnings of the defiant self-assertion of a new generation of Americans."   David Graeber

"I don't want to abolish government, I simply want to reduce it to the size where I can drag it into the bathroom and drown it in the bathtub."
                                        Grover Norquist

As a result of advanced human consciousness, modern politics and the world controlling cabal that owns modern politics, shall see their end post 2012. *That condition is in progress right now.* With all the information you have provided for this book, it is important that this transformation away from slavery be stated here <u>first, correctly, and conclusively</u>.

- **You have earned that honor.**

This more than any other thing defines 2012 and beyond. It also defines the consciousness shift in progress as they are one and the same.

By default, it also defines the forces of evil self-destructing through dropping themselves out of the emerging dimensional shift that is upon us. How we label it is not that important. The outcome however is. It is Creator Consciousness in action. It is Human Teleology. It is the ending of human and planetary rape, slavery and destroyment.

How this manifests into our perception is likely to take numerous paths. Many of those pathways will initially be below our outer perception just as the process of Evolution is now. This is due to the exceptional level of mainstream media's control *and fanatic aversion to consciousness*.

Many, many façades will be dropped. The institutions fostering human slavery will sort themselves out by sorting themselves...out. Highly dynamic, new and diametrically different energies will take their place. The purpose and function will however, have openly shifted away from slavery and into Consciousness. **The shift will be to the polar opposite direction.** As the result of a greater station of consciousness, their effect will be *multitudes* greater. *They will enjoy resonance with the human soul.*

The powers in the service of Satan are now within inches of checkmate by the infinitely superior power of human validation. The terrible and strange irony of this condition is that the forces that be, are in keen awareness of this condition. The standard votary most assuredly *is not*. If a more bizarre condition ever existed, I do not know what that could be.

Therefore we have identified one of the reasons for this book. It is this awareness that is in need of changing. *Fortunately it is.* As the old saying goes: 'There is a God'. Even that will change to: "There, is God." The latter reflects a much more accurate understanding **of good**.

The conclusion is that our very existence will be shifted or rather transcended, into a radically advanced state. This is a state where not only the larger picture is known by all, but the manifestation of good is advanced beyond present understanding. *All will know what the few now know.*

Within that paradigm, the old energy of human slavery vanishes in the shame and meaninglessness that defines it. That *shift* is Human Teleology. It is also an equally important shift in our perception of *the process* that brings it into the morphogenic field of existence. **That is to correctly announce we are in direct** *and unassailable* **control of the process.**

Simultaneously, the power-vanity obsessed of the world are consuming themselves with the lies, hate and violence of their own existence…that the remainder of the world is now seeing right through *and simply rejecting.*

- The bottom line is: *This is all good news.*

As Reasonable, we seek the kind of peace that makes life on earth worth living…not merely peace in our lifetime, but peace for all time, a peace that is sustainable and based upon Truth.

To understand Freedom is to understand Love for they are one and the same. As one and the same, both love and freedom operate the same as well. Both play into existence only when extended to others.

As witnessed by the List of Grievances to King George, this Nation's forefounders knew from experience and to the depth of their soul, that if government is not kept *rigorously chained* within limits, then government would become a repository for every manner of crime, criminals and assault.

- As history has repeated itself, our forefounders were proven *correct*.

It is entirely Reasonable for the mainstream voter to wake up to the fact that **any lie** will be told to them by the mainstream politician <u>to facilitate human slavery</u>. ...And that virtually anything told to them by the mainstream politician **is a lie**.

- We would do well to remind ourselves that once any dictatorship is set, the velvet wings of political correctness it crept in on **vanish**.

Mainstream politics is so bought off that virtually everything in their existence is falsehood. The general public is rapidly coming to realize that the words the mainstream politicians speak are the emptiest delusion possible. *We have come to realize that every mainstream approved politician has stubbornly turned against their own advertised standards in addition to shamelessly, continuously and mercilessly backstabbing their own party constituency as well as the human race and planet.*

- So much for the obvious.

The human crushing juggernaut of slavery and its lackey modern politics, have feet of clay. We are the diamond being thrown against those feet of clay to break them to dust *precisely as foretold*. That diamond is Truth and Consciousness. It is the indomitable Creator Consciousness living in all of us that can no longer remain silent in the face of slavery, death, ruin and the pandemic hate, injury and corruption that define modern politics.

- All we really need to know is: **We were not created to be slaves.**

- Any and all actions into Consciousness flow forth directly from that *correct* understanding.

Some may call this contest the contest between good and evil, and by no means would they be incorrect. However the far more accurate descripttion is the difference in outcome between Slavery and Consciousness.

- This is the basic realization this book was written to advance.

- That is why this book is subtitled *a book on Consciousness*.

Our spirit tells us we were not designed for slavery, however nearly everything presented to us by modern society instructs us that we are. One is correct. The other is incorrect. *Many* **are the illusions, subterfuges** *and shames* **that die with that understanding.**

With that, we come to see mainstream politics as it is. We come to see the orgy of human decimation and spam grade lies that define mainstream politics. We also come to see modern government as Satan's personal playground, and that has come to define modern government.

- Within the Evolution of Consciousness, we now observe:

- The élite know it is over for them, their reign of terror is finished.

- They have *this* offer to tip over their king.

- And it is so. *(There is not one of them that cannot be imprisoned.)*

"Come up O lions! Shake off the delusion that you are sheep. You are spirits free, blessed and eternal."   Swami Vivekananada

"Darkness cannot drive out darkness; only light can do that. Hate cannot drive out hate; only love can do that."   Martin Luther King Jr.

"What we do in life ripples in eternity."   Marcus Aurelius

"Imagine the universe beautiful, just and perfect. Then be sure of one thing: the IS has imagined it quite a bit better than you have." Richard Bach

"You never change things by fighting the existing reality. *To change something, create a new model that makes the old model obsolete.*
　　　　　　　　　　　　　　　　　　　Buckminster Fuller

- That is Reasonable.

"Liberty, when it begins to take root is a plant of rapid growth."
　　　　　　　　　　　　　　　　　George Washington 1788

"Life shrinks or expands in proportion to one's courage."   Anais Nin

"There is but one straight course, and that is to seek truth and pursue it steadily."   George Washington

"Conscience is the most sacred of all property."
　　　James Madison, **the chief architect of the Constitution**

"*We have it in our power to begin the world over again.*"
　　　　　　　　　　　　　　Thomas Paine in Common Sense

"There is nothing more powerful than a vision that has found its time."
　　　　　　　　　　　　　　Victor Hugo

"Common sense is the knack of seeing things as they are, and doing things as they ought to be done."   Josh Billings

"It is better to be making the news than taking it."
Winston Churchill

"When a man who is honestly mistaken hears the truth, he will either cease being mistaken, or cease being honest."   Abe Lincoln

"I have sworn upon the alter of God eternal hostility against every form of tyranny over the mind of man."   *Thomas Jefferson*

"When the power of love overcomes the love of power, the world shall know peace."   Jimi Hendrix

"You can choose to survive, or you can choose to succeed."
Jon Von Achen

"The moment the slave resolves that he will no longer be a slave, his fetters fall. He frees himself and shows the way for others. *Freedom and slavery are mental states*."   Gandhi

- All of the above describe the Reasonable condition.

- At Reasonable, we love humanity and the humans in it.

- **For those who love humanity, it is time to love those within it *including you*.**

- *It is also time you voted for you, and that is the Reasonable choice.*

Now we will look at human slavery:

"We can easily forgive a child who is afraid of the dark; the real tragedy of life is when men are afraid of the light."   Plato's Republic

"Under democracy, one party always devotes its chief energies to trying to prove that the other party is unfit to rule—and both commonly succeed and are right."   H. L. Mencken

"The human being who would not harm you as an individual will wound or kill you from behind the corporate veil."   Morton Mintz

- Or from government *which is also corporate*.

"To know what is right and not do it is the worst cowardice."   Confucius

"Unless we put medical freedom into the Constitution, the time will come when medicine will organize itself into an undercover dictatorship."   Dr. Benjamin Rush

Dr. Rush, the only medical doctor to sign of the Declaration of Independence described modern medicine *to perfection*. Dad gummed, *if he don't sound like Ron Paul*. Contrast *this* with the Rodham-Romney-Obama-<u>pharmaceutical cabal designed model</u> of a peculiarly nasty, illegal, and *intentionally* human murdering, **dictatorship.**

And more:

"The United Nations is run by a bunch of gangsters. A lot of world leaders have been bribed and blackmailed into obeying these people. *We need to set up new structures, new systems, and a new way of running the planet.*"   Benjamin Fulford

- That would be Reasonable.

"Now we have a four cent dollar compared to the dollar we had in 1913" *Dr. Ron Paul*

- This provides us with conclusive ammunition to end the Federal Reserve. We *would have been* **that much richer.** (Get that)

Modern politics:

"Insanity is doing the same thing over and over again and expecting different results." Albert Einstein

"He who passively accepts evil is as much involved in it as he who helps to perpetrate it" Martin Luther King Jr.

Appeasers believe that if you keep on throwing steaks to a tiger, the tiger will turn vegetarian." Heywood Brown

"It is useless for sheep to pass resolutions in favor of vegetarianism while the wolf remains of a different opinion." William Ralph Inge

"When I was in the third grade, there was a kid running for office. His slogan was: "Vote for me and I'll show you my wee-wee." He won by a landslide." Dorothy of the Golden Girls

- I can say that sounds like Bill Clinton, but only because that was not his given name. Anyone else see a few patterns there?

"In my many years, I have come to the conclusion that one useless man is a shame, two is a law firm and three or more is a congress."
  John Adams

- And thus we have defined the freakishly failed and hideously destructive world of modern politics.

- …Where government is now a synonym for *malevolence*.

- This also shall pass, because:

"…and where the Spirit of the Lord is, *there* is liberty."
2 Cor 3:17

- And *that* is Reasonable.

One more thing:

At every possible opportunity, remind everyone that the 'sales tax';

is now called a corruption fee.

- We go by <u>what it does</u>, *not by what it was formerly known as.*

- And this concludes the chapter on Slavery versus Consciousness.

Chapter Ten

Cloture and Metamorphosis

Cloture and Metamorphosis:

Cloture:

"The one thing you can count on from an elected Republican, is the voting record of an elected Democrat."

100 years of evidence has proven Will Rogers *stupendously accurate*.

The catch is that almost no hardcore Republican possessed in their hardcore-ness, either the sense or shame to admit this blatantly obvious truth. Their blindness extends past the point of supporting the very individual that wrote <u>*and enacted*</u> the Obama-care package, and of all things, calling that person "conservative". This is in spite of a career voting record that has virtually no traceable conservative in it. The sad part being; this is multiple choice *average*. The big government **tax and waste** liberalness displayed by their leadership is *consistent* almost to the point of *perfection*.

- Amazing and *amazingly ignorant*.

Barry Goldwater would have thrown that **revolting quack** *and loser* across the line and over to the other team he has been playing for all along. An easy seventy five dozen other "leaders" would have been tossed over with him. (…for a first half day warm-up)

- There is a balanced mathematical equation there that starts with 'Republicans', ends with 'idiots', and rhymes with *muther truckin'*.

On the other hand, this author observed individuals {the one or two I could find} who cast the negative vote for Obama, and then offered up something similar to this: "I count that among the worst mistakes I have ever made." "***But,*** he is better than what's his name ***asshole***, was/would have been." We have three definitive statements as related to the damage of the negative vote. *Present however, was the awareness to admit the error in the evidence of a devastating Bush clone policy record, an undivided contempt for the Constitution, altogether brand new record levels of corruption and a highly disturbed and exclusively self-serving whirlwind gross-out obsession of verbal masturbation.*

Ninety three years ago, *make note of that*, H. L. Mencken, a journalist and Democrat wrote these immortal words: "As a democracy is perfected, the office of the President represents, more and more closely the inner soul of the people. On some great and glorious day, the plain folks of the land will reach their heart's desire at last and the White House will be occupied by a downright fool and complete narcissistic moron."

- There it is. …And with no hope from mainstream politics to produce anything other than the same or odds on *worse*.

- The key here is the Oath of Office to uphold, protect and defend the Constitution of the United States of America that every public servant is sworn to.

This repentance was noticeably absent in the Republican corner even in the face of endless single minded enemies of the Constitution. Two Bush presidents alone proved that much betrayal beyond any shadow of doubt. I don't need to toss in the purchased kingpins of Nixon, McCain, Gingrich, Romney, Boehner or infinite etcetera **as *extremely* conclusive evidence**.

- Is there a single one of those insufferable asses named or a hundred other hand puppets just like them, ***not*** also closely identified with an all consuming *and open house* corruption?

Here is the situation:

In nearly all of our collective lives no matter our age, how many of us have made *this* statement as related to Presidential elections:

- **"This is *absolutely*, the worst choice yet."**

- Eighty and ninety year olds made this statement.

- Virtually everyone made this statement time after time.

- *And we have been making this statement all our lives.*

At the same time, the establishment tells us **without ceasing** that:

- "This is the most important election in history." (The scare tactic)

- **Yet both choices are identical** *every single time*.

In retrospect, we come to find that: Every {mainstream} politician is owned by cartel.   Every politician is a member of secret and satanic society. Every politician is a singularly dedicated enemy to the Constitution. Every politician has but one cause and mission; to destroy Individual Human Rights, to destroy humanness, **to destroy you as a human**, to destroy the concept of humanity, and to destroy America, American and Americans.

- Every mainstream politician has *rigorously* advanced human slavery.

- *Their entire political career.*   {Their actions betray their rhetoric.}

Seeing the illusion ends the illusion.

When the fourth rate mainstream political illusion is exposed, the luster is lost. Along with that, is the loss of the desire to pay for more of the same fully depraved **poison**.   No rational, aware individual would again fall for a particularly lousy theft-trick they know the mechanics of. This is however the entire theme of mainstream politics; hawking emptiness. The objective being to place so many retrograde choices out there as to snowblind the hoi polloi into an outcome of unprincipled apathy **that guarantees human slavery.**

- If we drove our vehicles in the same aimless manner we vote,
  all land transportation would cease in chaos, death and wreckage.

- No one would reach their destination in a clueless existence of
  savagery, backstab, revenge and debauchery.

It is difficult to fathom any ordeal more piss-pore pathetic or more outright destructive than the mainstream political illusion and resultant outcome. Those of you reading this have described mainstream politics as so, *and absolutely correctly.*

- From one end of America to the other, you have emphatically stated that the only rational thing to do with mainstream politics is to **bury it**.

- Hu-Rah!   (borrowed from an Amy Allen song)

- This is the closure that nearly every one of you reading this *specifically* demanded.

- The truth within the Humanitarian Code ends that consummately destructive illusion *forever*.

Here are some quotes that help us understand conditions now under transformation within the human existence:

Again:

"To know what is right and not do it is the worst cowardice."
Confucius

"You never change a thing by fighting the existing reality. To change something, create a new model that makes the old model obsolete."
Buckminster Fuller

- That would be The Humanitarian Code.

- It does help that mainstream politics has already made *itself* the butt of every other crummy joke <u>on earth</u>.

"Resistance to tyrants is obedience to God."   *Thomas Jefferson*

"Necessity is the plea for every infringement of human freedom. It is the argument of tyrants. It is the creed of slaves."   William Pitt

"We the people are the rightful masters of both Congress and the courts, not to overthrow the Constitution, but to overthrow men who would pervert the Constitution."   Abraham Lincoln

"I can only say that there is not a man living who wishes more sincerely than I do to see a plan adopted for the abolition of slavery."
George Washington

- That would be The Humanitarian Code **of Peace and Freedom:**

1 The only legitimate function of government is to uphold, protect and defend Individual Human Rights.

2 We stand at One with the Creator in the Humanity of Liberty, the condition of Human Evolution.

3 We stand united in the American definition of smaller government, fewer taxes, and greatest personal freedom.

- For it is so.

"The world is indebted for all triumphs that have been gained by **reason and humanity** over error and oppression." Thomas Jefferson

"An army of principles can penetrate where an army of soldiers cannot." Thomas Paine

"There are a thousand strikers at the branches of evil to the one who is striking at the root." Henry David Thoreau

- Likewise, there are a thousand wrong names for human slavery *and only one correct name*.

"It is curious that physical courage should be so common in the world and moral courage so rare." Mark Twain

- Frederic Douglass for two:

"At times like this, scorching irony is needed."

"Power concedes nothing without a demand. It never did and never will."

- Anais Nin:

"And the day came when the risk to remain tight in the bud was more painful than the risk it took to blossom."

"Oh men of ignorance, with what language shall I speak that all will carry the love of the Creator and beware of harming others and yourself?"
  Mehran Tavakoli Keshe of the Keshe Foundation

"If everybody demanded peace instead of another television, then there would be peace." John Lennon

"In times of universal deceit, telling the truth would be a revolutionary act." None other than *George Orwell*

"We are enslaved by anything we do not consciously see. We are freed by conscious perception." Vernon Howard

"Knowledge is the most democratic source of power." Alvin Toffler

"Those who stand for nothing, fall for anything." Alexander Hamilton

- **That would be defining mainstream politics.**

"A miracle worker is not geared toward fighting the world that is, but toward creating the world that might be." Marianne Williamson

- That would be anything **other** than human slavery.

"Our deepest fear is not that we are inadequate. Our deepest fear is that we are powerful beyond measure." Marianne Williamson

- Indeed we are. *This is absolute fact.*

"In the world of illusions, we are lost and imprisoned. In our natural state, we are glorious beings." Marianne Williamson

- *One,* of those is Reasonable.

"Government is not reason; it is not eloquence; it is force! Like fire, it is a dangerous servant and a fearful master."   George Washington

- I think we have learned this the hard way.

- And it is time to contain it.   • **This task has fallen upon *us*.**

Mainstream politics was best summed up by P.T. Barnum: "There is a fool born every minute." *The human species* has come to realize that human slavery consists of the corporate aristocracy and an entire planet of purchased, **utterly asinine**, *loud mouth*, dictatorial, condescending, *and consummately dishonorable* politicians. It is only as of this moment has the human species come to agree upon the cause. It is *this* realization that changes the equation. Seeing the illusion ends the illusion. <u>The entire planet for the first time, is working **as a unit** to end human slavery</u>.

- This is good.

Regardless of its name, the present model of human slavery insinuates that an actual God does not exist. Within the model of human slavery, the god <u>concept</u> however, becomes a wonderfully handy tool to manipulate the masses in any direction desired by the cartel. This is done primarily through our institutes of religion vigorously supporting human slavery.

As you have stated, divisiveness is chief among those directions. Then, the media cartel so well explains to us; only more government and less freedom can solve the problem. One hand washes the other and both hands wash out God's design of humanity—**the humane treatment of humans.**

Our religious institutes have shamefully, horrendously *and purposefully* failed to instruct that Individual Human Rights are God's design of Humanity.

Because of manufactured labels, the implication is that incorrectly labeled people have no Rights and are therefore not human. It is then perfectly ok to enslave, injure or slaughter them at will. These are the results we have experienced. **Any cartel desired resource worldwide—has resulted in extreme brutality, mass murder, warfare and genocide, <u>normally by way of religion.</u>**

- Two things are overlooked in that construct:

The first is that any government powerful enough to deny the humanity of one, **can deny the humanity of all.** These are the results we have *experienced*. Second, is the somewhat hidden fact that various international cartel and cabal including religion, drive the ongoing inhumanity to man.

These are also the results we have experienced. It is the 501 (c) 3 **purchased slavery endorsement** of instituted religion that causes this condition *here*.

Seeing the illusion ends the illusion.

When our institutes of religion fail us this egregiously, clear to the cost of our very humanity, we must ask ourselves as to what purpose and benefit do they serve? We throw money at them only to be heaped upon with sweet words, terrible lies and endless guilt trips *without the benefit of acknowledgement of the very condition of humanity;* **God given Individual Human Rights**.

- When the institutes of religion instruct that government must be rigorously obeyed as virtually all of them teach, that institute has been purchased.

- We are reminded that Adolph Hitler set up *identical* conditions for the identical reason of human destroyment.

- It is the 501 (c) 3 trade-off that dictates their de facto message of government replacing God, and this has been our *experience*.

Even as we come to understand, appreciate and embrace the Creator Consciousness within, we drop away from the religious institutions that preach separation and are a key portion of the model of slavery. Nearly all of the same institutions would forcibly reject and vehemently condemn if not scream for the murder of, the *actual* person **and message** of Christ.

- The *identical* conditions and outcome prevailed many years ago.

- The more things change, the more they remain the same.

The same institutes of religion not only fail to instruct the true capabilities of mankind, but also act as a blockade for those who are in the process of discovering those capabilities. This has also been our experience.

- That is the old energy; human slavery and the illusion of limitation.

- We now recognize it as is.

A prime example of the New Energy, **that of God's Design of Peace and Freedom** is from Ezekiel 11:19: "And I will put a new spirit within you." The true humanitarian knows from Philippians 1:16 they are within the Creator's Design *of Peace and Freedom:* "Be confident of this very thing; that He which hath begun a good work in you will perform it until the day of Jesus Christ." We are the workers restoring **the humane treatment of humans.** This is our God given Individual Human Rights.

- We respect ourselves and others as human.

- These are the messages from all of you, even as we clearly understand that the task of restoration falls upon *us*.

- And we understand the survival of the human species is at stake.

"The most dangerous thing any nation faces is a citizenry capable of trusting liars to lead them."   Andy Andrews

- We *absolutely* have that.

⇨ "Permit me to issue and control the money of a nation, *and I care not who makes its laws.*" ⇦ *!*   **Mayer Amshel Rothschild**

- This has been our *experience*.

- This is the Slavery we shall end.

Along with the purchased shame of religious institutes worldwide, we have evolved to discover that the present model of human slavery has *three* main elements:

The *first* element is the corporate aristocracy known by various names including the illuminati, the cabal, the cartel, the world controllers, the élite, the banksters, the powers that be and several other labels. Virtually all appear to either be members of satanic society or have satanic/Marxist causes and practices. Here is where the fruit does not fall far from the tree and the various causes and practices clearly identify **their master**.

- The basic world model of the cabal is simply total brutality by way of numerous labels specifically designed to hide human slavery.

The *second* and now obvious element is the purchased and honorless politician worldwide. Everyone reading this book is likely to be keenly aware of this fact because it came from you. On this day, few nations enjoy much of an advantage or disadvantage in this regard. Every mainstream politician is purchased by the cartel. Every mainstream politician has sold their last vestige of honor. Every mainstream politician is a shameless puppet and prostitute *and nothing other* **than shameless puppets and prostitutes.**

The result of the political whoredom, is governments worldwide singularly dedicated to the destroyment of Individual Human Rights. We now experience a world of governments, few better than the other, that answer every condition with oppression, violence, brutality and murder. The contest is no longer who can provide the greatest freedom, it is who can answer any situation with **the most brutality**. That the United States **Corporation** is attempting to lead the model of instant brutality is a wrong that should never exist. The result is a calibration distantly below the line of integrity.

The *third* element is the purchased apostasy of the pulpit. Within this worldwide construct as experienced, no religious sect or label enjoys any particular advantage or disadvantage over any other sect. All are silent on Human Rights. All are silent on the humanitarian treatment of humans. All are silent on **God's Design of Peace and Freedom**, and how to achieve God's Design of Peace and Freedom.

- *The greatest silence of church remains; that the design of Individual Human Rights, is the humanitarian treatment of humans.*

- Virtually every religion has **caved in** to the design of slavery warfare and helplessness <u>as the way of life for the human species</u>.

- The fact that the *need* for slavery, warfare and helplessness *does not* pass the truth test seems to be irrelevant.

- The condition is that of teaching a pack of **very shameful lies**.

Seeing the illusion ends the illusion.

Many, are the religious institutes losing income and members for a very specific reason: The human intuition or instinct has clearly identified many of the above conditions even if the outer realization is just now making the connection. As a result of advances in Evolution and technology, the outer realization is rapidly catching up to intuition *that was correct all along*. The result is: The individual is advancing into Creator Consciousness *and therefore*, sees the various religious institutes <u>as a lost cause</u>. The fact that those institutes have lost their cause *is the cause*. It is a bone simple case of seeing the illusion ends the illusion.

Every detail in this book welcomes the Truth Test. We **know** where we stand. As every person's perception is in a perpetual state of evolution, it is of no challenge to us that an opinion may differ for the moment. With the truth test, it is known that "this also shall evolve." The ground we stand on at Reasonable is solid and unchangeable. It is lifetime and infinite. We are the *actual* humanitarians of this world. It is a very good place to **Be**.

- The benefits are unlimited. ***The life you own will be yours.***

- It is so.

- And we give thanks.

Metamorphosis:

In all of human existence, there are only two basic directions: The historical direction as experienced belonging to the Devil. That direction is **warfare and slavery**. The second direction, *the one not yet experienced*, belonging to Creator God. That direction is **Peace and Freedom**.

The first direction was facilitated by *the money changers* of debt instrument monetary supply, **alias fiat money**. Recall the quote by Mr. Rothschild. Fiat money defines human slavery because it is the primary architecture of human slavery. Human slavery is further driven by similar worldwide cartels of greed and slavery, and their media elected armies **of** *unwashed two dollar prostitutes.*

- We would do well to review the handling of the money changers by Christ. We would do *better* to emulate it.

The entire planet now knows, debt instrument monetization and the slavery it causes is no longer a survivable option. The paradigm of human slavery as facilitated by debt instrument banking is being brought to an end **worldwide** as of this writing through the Basel Accords, the currency reset, whirlwinds of arrests and convictions, forced resignations and many other directly related actions, way too many to list here.

- **By The Creator's Might, these walls of Jericho have fallen.**

- It is the ending of that cabal, and the now inexorable and **complete** termination of the very closely related worldwide corporate cabals, *that will facilitate human and world Evolution.*

- *It is up to us,* to eradicate the reign of terror and poverty lorded over us by the purchased and **utterly depraved** liar-politicians.

This chicken does *not* come before the egg. In order to end the reign of terror of various worldwide cabal, we must first elect individuals who will limit corporations to their original intended and *extremely limited* bounds.

- It is thus that corporations would serve the people and not the standard model of slavery; human sacrifice to the corporations.

Likewise, it is through electing good folks who understand and take to heart their Oath of Office that we will transcend the present model of warfare, violence, failure and the prevailing senseless brutality we refer to as modern government.

- It is thus that government will come once again to serve the people in place of the present model of slavery; the people subservient to government.

"You are a child of God. *Your playing small does not serve the world.*"
Marianne Williamson

"The truth is incontrovertible. Malice may attack it. Ignorance may deride it. But in the end, there it is."   Winston Churchill

"Greater is He that is in you than he who is in the world."
1 John 4:4

It is *this* truth; "Greater is He that is in you than he who is in the world.", that provides us with our first and most important direction to our Evolution. With that truth we discover that; "The kingdom of heaven is within you.", as stated in Luke 17:21 and several other passages.

- From whence doth that origin?

We find the Source detailed in Ezekiel 36:27 "And I will put My Spirit within you." Why was this done? The answer is given in Ezekiel 37:14 "And I shall put My Spirit in you, *and ye shall live*."

That is *the* showcase contrast between Satan's world and direction of slavery and warfare which is death which is modern politics, or God's Design of Peace and Freedom which is thriving which is Human Evolution.

The most important factor to notice is that in the first model, **Satan's model**, there is *specifically* no provision for Human Rights. In that model by way of the absence of Human Rights, you are not human. In that model you will specifically not be treated as human. There is no allowance in that law, Admiralty Law, for the condition *or concept* of human or humanity. You become many things, each a legalistic double-talk condition of **chattel,** yet there exists no provision for human *or* Human Rights.

Within this model **belonging to the great deceiver**, we must be keenly aware that the words "human rights' are often mouthed, but only as a smoke screen, subterfuge and scam. The words themselves are waved about as cheep eyewash and nothing more. In that model, the **words** 'human rights' are a cosmic joke to test our tolerance of *the absence* of Human Rights.

In that model, we may or may not have civil rights as modified or removed by government at the demand of cartel. That whole model facilitates the predatory agendas of the various cartel. Satan's model however is specifically void of Individual Human Rights that define both human and the condition of humanity as given and designed by the Creator God. Again, those Rights define human *and the condition of humanity*.

Within the model of civil rights, there exists only one inexorable direction: That direction is the unchanging, overall experience of **the removal** of civil rights. In the end, there remains only slavery.

Here is the chief contrast:

- In the model belonging to Satan, there is no human. There is no humanity.

- The Creator's Design is the intention and outcome of humanity **through Peace and Freedom**.

- Both these conditions have been true from the foundation of human existence.

This Nation was founded upon Individual Human Rights for all the reasons given so far. In our collective disgrace of government schooling and the purchased deceptions of our religious institutes, the general public has forgotten this truth. Yet those of you reading this have not forgotten, and that is why it is in this book. *You presented it to me.*

All master teachers in human history have instructed the truth that God is within. All master teachers in history instructed the truth that we are Spiritual in nature. God is a part of us, and we are a part of God. In truth, there is no separation. There is only <u>awareness</u> or <u>unawareness</u> of the truth of Unity *and ability.* **It is Consciousness.**

If God is everywhere, point to the place God is not. Should we point to ourselves, then God is not everywhere. Has God suddenly lost that power? Can God then be confined to a tin can to be shaken and poured forth only when convenient? When math of this simplicity can be used to prove Christ's direct instructions of the Creator Consciousness within, then it behooves us *to accept the fact*.

- With that, we begin to understand the benefits of *humanity*.

Individual Human Rights are the basic respect afforded from one to the other that we are a portion of the Creator and that the Creator dwells within each of us. It is the Creator that made this condition to manifest the Creator's Design of Peace and Freedom. It is the truth of God given Individual Human Rights that is the acknowledgement demanded by the Creator to honor the portion of the Creator within all of us.

Individual Human Rights are the cornerstone of human to human respect. This is the Design of Peace and Freedom. This is the Design of facilitating Human Success. This is the Design of the humanitarian treatment of humans. This is God's design. *Anything other than that is slavery, warfare, poverty, brutality and faultlessly proven failure.*

This is why Individual Human Rights are correctly described as inalienable and inseparable from human. It is also the condition of humanity; **THE HUMANITARIAN TREATMENT OF HUMANS***!*

- The same theme of humanity versus slavery was instructed in many of Dr. Seuss' books with Yurtle the Turtle being lead among them showcasing the easily demonstrable absurdity of tyranny. Seven year olds get this, yet the mainstream voter *repeatedly fails*.

- The cause of **humanity and empowerment** is the *singular* constant among 100% of all writers of the New paradigm.

With the truth of God within-ness, we have many important conditions: The first is the construct of Human Rights, the condition of humanity. The second is our untapped and unfathomed ability. Name the individual who stated: **"And greater things than these shall ye do."**

- As but one example, we shall end human slavery.

What is the point *in failing* to believe The Lord's instructions? Time and time again we witness the extraordinary and we are aware of the extraordinary throughout history. With honesty and attention, we also observe the many and various miracles and healings in our lives. Some of us observe the Truth; that our every moment is a miracle and only exists by the grace and power of the Creator.

There is the function of this book; to restore the reality of our actual ability. We accomplish this benefit through knowing the Source and methods of the ability. Amazingly, it has defaulted upon the people themselves to discover and live these humanitarian truths.

- And so we *are*; as All humans are driven by Design **to thrive**.

With awareness, we observe that every day new records are set. Every day a former limitation is surpassed. Every day a new ability is discovered. Every day brings about a new technological wonder. Every day someone somewhere constructs new ways to better serve their fellow humankind. Every day brings with it a new efficiency, a better process, a superior product, a cleaner methodology and New organizations. Every day causes a new inspiration within the individual who is in tune with the Universe.

- How can it be otherwise when that Consciousness is of *Creation?*

- As a part of the Creator, is it not part of our description to create?

- How can we *not* be inspired to cause something better?

We shall again quote John Lennon: "I believe that what people call God is something in all of us."

And we learn from Helen Keller: "Although the world is full of suffering, **it is also full of the overcoming of it.**"

- Reasonable, is the process of coming out of the Egypt of human slavery—*precisely as foretold, and precisely as asked of us*.

I intend to use a series of quotes to paint a very important picture. **That picture is Human Success.** We draw this lesson from one of God's creations, the caterpillar. The caterpillar is content to crawl about, eat and exist. At that stage, not much else is known to the caterpillar.

That describes the present status quo condition of human slavery. We are to crawl about, eat if fortunate and exist. The fact remains that without a government to uphold, protect and defend Individual Human Rights, we, like the caterpillar can be swooped upon and gobbled up, meaning destroyed, by "authority" for any so called reason or no reason. Many have suffered this fate. I have. You probably have. It is why you are reading *this* book.

Then comes evolution. Within that evolution there is a period of reorganization. To the uninformed and afraid, that transition is labeled as chaos. The reality is the clean-up of chaos. It is in fact the opposite of chaos. The key is **seeing through** the labels as given by the system of human slavery to protect the system of human slavery. This is what our intuition and our inspiration tells us *in advance* of our eyes informing us of exactly the same thing. **Understand this**: It is faith lived. It is courage experienced. It is the table turning of outcome from bad to good, *and the table has turned.*

With the caterpillar, that would be the stage of the chrysalis. How informative a lesson we observe in that what could be called chaos by the uninformed is actually part of the Creator's Design of Nature. We then observe that there is nothing wrong or bad with it at all. It was only our *understanding* that was incomplete. There was positively nothing wrong with Nature after all. It is only a very desirable *energy transcendation*.

The discovery itself is the evolution. It is our release from fear. It is the beginning of the metamorphosis *of the human race*.

- And then we have the lesson not yet experienced by the majority; the lesson of the butterfly, and the benefit of Evolution.

Our instinct, inspiration and intuition inform us in no uncertain terms; there is a better way of life above and beyond the present model of human slavery. We sense a degree **of direct benefit** almost, but not quite, *beyond our comprehension*. We can easily envision bits and parts of the evolution, the pieces entrusted to each of us individually, but not quite the whole.

How are we to enjoy the sum of everybody's contribution to Human Evolution, the ***process*** of Human Success? The answer is, we are privileged to know the co-Creator Source of our *own* inspiration and vision. Therefore, we can come to know the Source of all inspiration. As we come to know our own enthusiasm, we can come to know Enthusiasm itself.

This is the butterfly. The butterfly has the distinct advantage of knowing that it is a butterfly. The strangest possible irony is that the human for the most part *does not yet understand human*. It is the system of human slavery that has very carefully blocked out this vital understanding.

We have glimpses of freedom, visions of freedom, yearnings for freedom and constant built in thoughts on freedom, *yet we lack the freedom itself*. As individuals and as a species we are clearly designed for freedom yet we operate without freedom. **We barely survive *when we could thrive*.**

Within Evolution, the Creator's Design of Peace and Freedom is to soar far and wide as opposed to crawling near and slow. We have only lacked the proper vehicle to get there. What is the *one* model that can take the human species into the Creator's Design of Human Success?

I present to you **The Humanitarian Code of Truth and Success:**

1. The only legitimate function of government is to uphold, protect and defend Individual Human Rights.

2 We stand at One with the Creator in the Humanity of Liberty, the condition of Human Evolution.

3 We stand united in the American definition of smaller government, fewer taxes, and greatest personal freedom.

- This is the vehicle to the human future if there is to be one, and it is the future itself, **the future worth living in.**

- We say it is so, because there is a truth test involved.

- The good news is that the Humanitarian Code *passes the Truth test*.

Genius level IQ is not required to discern that Freedom and the condition of Humanity is vastly further up the Scale of Consciousness than the present model of slavery, failure, limitation and the now prevailing attribute of random brutality.

Therefore the Humanitarian Code is the vehicle. It is the process. It is the means to the future worth living in. It <u>is</u> the future worth living in.

- Strange as it may seem, only freedom can deliver the benefits of freedom.

- This is what we are specifically *not* taught by the system.

Slavery on the other hand, can only deliver the woes of slavery, <u>for there exists no actual benefit</u>. There are endless illusions of benefit that turn out to be false advertisement all, yet no *actual* benefit. **There is only the inexorable, permanent and perpetual loss of benefit.** It is important to understand this concept correctly: *It is mainstream politics*.

When modern politics and in the specific, mainstream politics has been over and over described as simply the modern day Sodom and Gomorrah, then several things become abundantly clear. The first and foremost is the removal of the basic right to self defense, your First Right.

- Make no mistake that the modern political model is the intended removal of any and all Human Rights. **That is THE central and ongoing product of all modern politics.**

The complete removal of the right to self defense against false arrest, misprision in the first definition, drumhead trial and false imprisonment *is the precise key*, now almost entirely in place, to terminate the last remaining thoughts that the human race ever had anything related to Human Rights to begin with. The same moment self defense is eliminated, the remainder is automatic. One can consult Adolph Hitler or Pol Pot on this subject if there are any further questions or doubt.

With this information, you now can correctly understand mainstream politics *in its entirety*. Without a doubt, mainstream politics will lie about any and all of this. At that point the truth test becomes simply the unbroken track record of mainstream politics being un-honorable about all aspects of their existence and performance as well as their intent. The self evidence on that is rather abundant, *precisely as all of you have clearly stated*.

The pertinent question presented here, particularly from an energetic standpoint, is this: Why has the description of mainstream politics being the modern day Sodom and Gomorrah persisted for at least three full generations that I know of? *It's a good question.* The answer comes right back to the energetic direction of slavery versus Consciousness.

During the time of Sodom and Gomorrah, humanity experienced a strikingly similar erosion and removal of Human Rights. The end result manifested in a somewhat different manner than today. However the underlying slavery construction used to perpetrate those results, the absence of Human Rights, **is identical** to today's model of cartel controlled modern politics. There is your *correct* answer.

- When we see that, the obvious then snaps into focus:

- Dehumanization *is* mainstream politics.

- You can call it anything you want, but in the end only that fact and unbroken direction and pattern remains.

- This is the *precise* biblical "Egypt" of dehumanization we are called to come out of.

It is now essential to the very continuation of the Human race to understand that and understand it clearly and correctly. It is now just as essential to be able to articulate the matter in terms and language suitable to correctly communicate these concepts to others. The human species itself is being meticulously destroyed by the all of mainstream politics even as we now speak. This is what most of us now present upon this planet chose to come here to prevent, undo ***and publically witness.***

What else is there to bring cloture to? What other evidence is there pertaining to mainstream politics that needs cloture?

There is plenty. One good example is that we have witnessed a full generation of White House occupiers and squatters who have clearly demonstrated the emotional maturity level of very spoiled little children. They have exhibited behavior utterly selfish and utterly self absorbed, fully expecting the public to believe their fairy tales continuously selling human slavery. This is what mainstream politics has delivered. Truthfully, it is about the only thing mainstream politics actually has delivered.

Worse than that, there is a laundry list of mainstream candidates contending for the office of the presidency who have clearly exhibited the emotional maturity and general stability of a very spoiled child. This is the mainstream political process that continually guarantees "the worst choice ever" again and again, the next time the same as the last time *only worse*.

Mark Twain sums up the whole process with this quote: "It's easier to fool people than to convince them they have been fooled."

Obviously, that's the case. There is but a sample of the failures and disasters mainstream politics has put upon us, that we have came here to put an end to. These reasons and many more along the same lines are the reason you have provided the substance of this book. The quicker we can share these realizations and find our resolve to correct them *forever*, the easier the process will be.

- As of this writing and this moment, the momentum has clearly shifted in favor of the human race.

- *That shift shall utterly eliminate mainstream politics.*

- Call that what you will however, *that is the fact of the matter.*

- It is this step that unlocks the potential of the human race.

- And it is so.

- Better yet, it is now *absolutely* in process.

- This is the action that shall be done.

- More than anything else, *that is what you wanted this writer to see and communicate.* That part is now complete.

Reasonable holds that it is time to respond to human slavery as opposed to continuing to only react to it. Through only reacting, we experience disempowerment. That is *the system,* of enslavement and dehumanization. It is simply the process of human disenfranchisement that defines all of mainstream politics.

Yet through responding, which is what Reasonable is all about, we then experience our empowerment. It is time now to realize the difference between the two directions and cause a future worth living in. This is where we recreate ourselves no longer as objects, but as humans. This is the awakening to our empowerment. **This is conduct becoming human.**

- Modern government can now correctly be defined as the golden calf that failed to lay the golden egg.

- Modern government has turned out to be the great malevolent incubus that has yet to fail to ruin everything it has ever touched *and* has yet to *not* break every agreement it has ever made.

Here is the lesson within those two **correct** definitions: On one end of the spectrum, is the loss of our humanity. On the other end of the spectrum, is the gaining of our humanity.

- One end of the scale is hate. The other end of the scale is Love.

This is really simple math, and here are some quotes to deepen your awareness, understanding *and resolve:*

"This is an extraordinary time to be alive." Because, as author Neale Donald Walsch instructs: "We're seeing a higher level of consciousness and many more opportunities for people to challenge their present ways of thinking and move into a grander and larger experience of who they really are."

- The key; *a higher level of consciousness.*

- And a grander experience of who they really are.

- Very Reasonable indeed.

"One can never consent to creep when one feels the impulse to soar."
Helen Keller

Here is one that is my experience: "As we become purer channels for God's light, we develop an appetite for the sweetness that is possible in this world." Marianne Williamson

"The most beautiful things in the world cannot be seen or even touched, they must be felt with the heart." Helen Keller

This is why and how, we have Creator and all Creation inspired visions of the endless benefits of conditions only a smidgen higher up the Scale of Consciousness. This is our personal heart-math connection. It is the cherished inspiration we have individually been given to enjoy. How ironic that the enjoyment itself of the vision *is the creation of the condition*.

Thomas Paine understood that principle: "The greatest satisfaction is through fidelity to a worthy cause."

As for our own limitations, Tony Robbins has this to teach: "What we can or cannot do, what we consider possible or impossible, is rarely a function of our true capability. It is a function of our beliefs about who we are."

- This is where we decide once and for all whether we are a slave race **or a human race.**

- The time has now arrived to experience **human and Humanitarian.**

One thing the Marine Corps did teach this writer, is that our limitations and capabilities are nowhere near where we once believed them to be. It is an interesting process to experience the 'impossible' transform into the completed. ...And it all seems for the better, once one discovers or creates beneficial applications.

George Washington understood the benefits of humanity: "Our cause is noble; it is the cause of mankind." (100% correct)

Again regarding the condition of humanity we find this truth: "If you bring forth what is within you, what you bring forth will save you."
Jesus the Christ in the Gospel of Thomas

- It is the Christ Consciousness within.

- The general direction is anything further up the Scale of Consciousness.

- The benefits are indeed unlimited.

- And it can be correctly described as the distance away from human slavery. It is the removal of the Devil **and the Devil's s crappy, twisted little servants**.

In this process, we notice Freedom, like Human Rights, like love, being one and the same, only comes into experience when extended to others.

Within that process, we discover a greater effectivity is gained by removing the focus from bad conditions and placing the focus on beneficial conditions. That is what causes the good conditions. You see, the pig likes to get dirty—*when the objective is to stay outside of the pig pen.*

Helen Keller teaches us the same process: "It is wonderful how much time good people spend fighting the devil. If they would only expend the same amount of energy loving their fellow human, the devil would die in his own tracks of ennui."

Within that process of moving upward on the Scale of Consciousness we are instructed of this benefit: "Blessed are those souls who have understood the true meaning of what has been said above and understand the beauty of what is waiting for the children of Adam in the concourse of the universe."   Mehran Tavakoli Keshe

Regarding The Humanitarian Code and the benefits from the condition of humanity we learn this: "When an idea reaches critical mass, there is no stopping the shift its presence will induce."   Marianne Williamson

- The desires expressed in this book came directly from you.

- Therefore we *are* at critical mass. <u>The point is to recognize it</u>.
  ...And live as a **human being** would live, *using every viable means*.

David Wilcock: "So many people are living in fear and terror of the future. We now have the science to prove that things are getting better, and in fact must get better—its written into the design of the universe, and it is a fundamental aspect of what we are going through."

And David Wilcock again: "I believe we are being intelligently guided through a planetary awakening at this time—and as we move through 2012, it seems that the ***public* downfall** of the Old World Order will be a key part of that process."   Amen and Amen, ***as it is so***.

Part of that process is this fact: "The human soul is divine in nature and as such cannot be forever subjected to external authority."
Thomas Jefferson

In regard to the Creator's Design of Peace and Freedom which is Human Evolution which is Human Success we again find: "There is nothing more powerful than a vision that has found its time." Victor Hugo

"Conceive it and believe it to achieve it." Napoleon Hill in the Laws of Success

Dr David Hawkins instructs the process this way: "To be the most spiritually aligned person you can be is actually doing what you can for the planet and for humanity in general."

Marcus Aurelius explains it this way: "What we do in life ripples in eternity." (I have employed some quotes twice as for their *eternal* truth.)

Arthur Schopenhauer teaches us this: "Thus the task is not so much to see what no one yet has seen, but to think what nobody yet has thought about that which everybody already sees."

Joel Arthur Barker teaches us: "Vision without action is merely a dream. Action without vision just passes time. **Vision with action changes the world.**" **That**, is Reasonable.

"A human being's greatness is in being able to remake ourselves."
Gandhi

"No man in his sense can hesitate in choosing to be free, rather than a slave." Alexander Hamilton

"The sun never shined on a cause of greater worth."
Thomas Paine

- And it is so. (100% correct)

From the experience of Jim Davidson we learn: "I don't believe in predestined fate. *The future is what we choose it to be.*"

- It is so, and that is but *one* of our abilities.

"The best way to predict the future is to create it."   Peter Drucker

Henry David Thoreau provides this insight: "I know of no more encouraging fact than the unquestionable ability of man to elevate his life by conscious endeavor."

And in Mathew 7:7-8 we find: "Ask, and it shall be given to you; seek and ye shall find; knock and it shall be opened unto you; for every one that asketh shall reciveth; and he that seeketh findeth, and to him that knocketh it shall be opened."   Fact.

As we look at the Scale of Consciousness and its rewards, we find this truth: "But seek ye first the kingdom of God and His righteousness; and all these things shall be added unto you."   Mathew 6:33

- Which says exactly the same thing as much of the above.

Said differently; Reasonable holds forth; that Consciousness is our undiscovered benefit.

- **...It is the distance away from human slavery.**

- And thus it is on this fine day.

And that concludes the chapter on cloture and metamorphosis.

Thank **you** for both.

Chapter Eleven

CAFRs *and The End of Taxation*

CAFRs *and The End of Taxation:*   (*fasten your seat belts folks.*)

"The first step toward freedom involves a sorting out of the false from the true."   page 34, A Course in Miracles.

"The knowledge that illuminates not only sets you free, but also shows you clearly when you *are* free."   page 18, ibid.

What's a CAFR? Technically, it is a Comprehensive Annual Financial Report. There are other names and acros for same function. That doesn't really explain much of anything does it? And there is the entire concept. **You**—are *not supposed to know anything about it.*

Unless one works for the government in a decision making or financial capacity, most will know nothing of the concept. That of course is the whole intention. It is the entire purpose of the label **and the cover-up.**

So what's a CAFR?

The correct answer is one of *essence*. The truth resides not in what a CAFR *is called*, the correct answer resides in what a CAFR *does*. We shall address **that**. The correct pronunciation is calf-er.

Now to the point: The function of a CAFR is to mislabel and thus cover up and hide every manner of third world corruption known. This is real simple. It is real-world. It truth tests. *It is the present intent and reality.*

Basically all governmental entities, some 200,000 of them in the United States alone carry **two sets of financial books.** This is not Chinese books. It is not mafia books. It is not even bookie books or the ones my truck driving friends employ *because they are forced to.* However, **it is the same thing**. Basically every contractor I know of also has two sets of books; one that is the truth, and the one presented to the government *jackals*. There is no possibility most of them would survive otherwise. I am certain there are exceptions; I *personally* haven't met any.

Most small businesses do the same thing. The giant corporations don't have to. They have vastly more effective ways of removing your money **through the vehicle of government.** We shall address how *in this chapter.*

Part of the deal is the realization that in avoiding scrutiny, we are little better than the devils in government. *The government however, lacks any right to do so in accordance with the intent of the Constitution.*

In the field of double books, the government has taken the deception to entirely new levels. The amount and nature of the dishonesties hidden within the CAFRs knows no bounds. Any competent research in this arena soon reveals an all encompassing widespread, rampant, blatant, corruption.

- That corruption starts with Marxism.

The first set of "books" as rubbed into the public's face is called the budget. **At best**, *the budget is a half truth and a collection of half truths.* It is usually called a quarterly or annual budget. It is the cunningly ginned up *and pretend*, **and pretend, and pretend,** presentation-lie, ⇨ *that all* **taxation is based upon.**

Right there is the rub. The taxation, in fact all taxation, *is based upon a patently, blatantly, and monumentally false premise.*

- The false premise, **the lie,** is that the government needs one single penny of your personal money to run it.

- **Because it does not.**

⇨ *There, is an interesting revelation.*

The second and hidden set of books is the comprehensive annual financial report. It contains information that can be readily and directly traced to massive, pervasive and fantastically illegal corruption. That is only *one* of the reasons why this information has remained hidden from the public.

- **The other reason is that taxes only apply to slaves (period).**

- It is not hidden *entirely* from view, it is however *mostly* hidden from view.

- ...And not instructed in government *de-education*.

- ...Or mentioned in the media.

- ...Or spoken of by the mainstream politician.

- ...And what else is new.

- That is why it is Reasonable to bring this information forth **here**.

And now we present the good, the bad and the ugly of CAFRs:

Once upon a time, some genuinely bent team of lawyers came up with a very crafty lawyerly-witchcraft idea: As with all things of this nature, *it centered upon mislabels.* The time began early in the 1940's and continues to this day. The concept was to steal a lot more of your money. Nothing is new there. Most of the project to steal your money was sold as a "rainy day fund" however both the project and its original label quickly removed itself from the public view. This is because the motivation sold and the motivation actual, <u>are two entirely different things</u>—*per normal.*

- As with all taxes, that tax remains to this day.

The hidden model paid for by the taxpayers in the form of a pervasive and pernicious overtax, resulted in massive funds over the course of time and the magic of compound returns.

The concept became so successful in terms of theft, super easy money for the plucking and systemic, open season, all consuming corruption, that basically every government agency in existence above dog catcher jumped on the bandwagon. *Endless insiders were given a very lucrative free ride.*

But that's only the beginning.

The sales label was a "rainy day fund". That however was not at all the reality. As with all mainstream politics, the label is far different *and normally the opposite of the actual function.*

- The more things change, the more they remain the same.

The actual and truth tested intent was to find and "sell" a way for government to siphon **taxpayer** money into the major international corporations. The intent was, and remains, to take your money and literally gift it over to the cartel. This is accomplished by way of the standard legal twists and inversions that define corruption, deceit and slavery. Here again, there remains not one politician **not purchased,** *and it is all of them.*

- And again mainstream politics is defined.

- ...Boring in its repetition but factual in its content.

- **This model is the standard ticky-washy of all mainstream politics.**

- know that. Know it well. *Get this chapter down pat.*

Keep in mind that these major corporations, large cap all, are the exact same corporations who have masterfully failed at creating a single new total domestic job count in at least three full generations. *This is very important.*

Marxism is defined as government ownership of the means of production.

- And it is so.

- *The Devil*, woe, ho, ho, now exposed, *is in the following details:*

As the lawyer-witchcraft story further unfolds we find that within virtually all CAFR funds, there is ownership of a usually wide selection of various major corporate stocks.

As a rule, no CAFR owns any one large stock. That might be seen as imprudent in the blue chip world of a diversified portfolio. The exceptions however abound profusely in the endless *and bottomless* brother-in-law wheels and deals expertly covered with names and labels so crafty as to merit concurrent Oscar nominations *and* Guinness records.

- ...And the five million dollar retirement packages for ONE year of public service.

- ...And the list of corruption goes on and on and on.

This begs the question as to why NOT ONE **mainstream politician** has brought this prime source of <u>magnitude unimaginable</u> theft and fraud to your attention so as to perhaps reduce the presently unlimited, *corruption*.

- The question is a Reasonable one.

- The answer, well, *is what it is. (SSDD)*

- <u>The largest possible shame is in not ending it</u>.

Further unfolding the story, we find that in the sum of around **two hundred thousand** or so CAFR portfolios each owning large cap stock, *we expose the ACTUAL intent:* <u>That phenomenon is the fact that nearly all major corporations are owned by the government</u>.

- *That* is Marxism.   • Bet you weren't taught that in school*!*

Oh yea, the government as owner also instructs their corporations how to mini-manage business. Translated into English; it spells **the dead end of innovation.**

- If you can say "bureaucratic nightmare" you have spoken correctly.

But the story does not end there.

- **It gets worse.**   (as your jobs fly straight to China):

The primary customer of virtually all of these corporations is, drum roll, YOU GUESSED IT; **government**.

<u>Now the story **gets worse**:</u> There is to no surprise, a built in *stupendous* profit margin with the government-customer. It would be illogical to suppose otherwise with the set up of government-owner and government/taxpayer-customer. **This is Marxism.**

Marxism was never anti profit. <u>It is just anti profit for anything not paid for by the taxpayer</u> *as captive audience*, (as the monkey on the string).

- *This is a very, very, very, important distinction.*

- know the difference. Know it well. <u>Know it thoroughly</u>.

This is the precise source of the legendary thousand dollar hammer, the collection of roads to nowhere, and a here to the moon list of strikingly similar items.

- Fundamentally, almost *any* price is acceptable.

- Fundamentally, almost *any* project is acceptable.

- The fact that most of it fails to make any sense *is irrelevant.*

- The mainstream politician is not going to step in and say no.

- ...Because their *personal* campaign funding would *instantly dry up.*

- Ah-ho! (<u>*This is the key that unlocks the puzzle*</u>.) **Get that.**

This is why **any** mainstream vote is *strictly* a vote cast in the favor of HUMAN SLAVERY. Any vote *or non vote* <u>not specifically stopping the process</u>, is understood by the mainstream politician as an endorsement and demand *just as they clearly tell you*, **for additional oppression**. That is how the horribly uninformed general public voted. That is what the horribly uninformed public received. *And it is presently so.* This is the heart of the present operation of the corporate aristocracy. *This is the alter that all mainstream politics and politicians worship at.*

- The soulless mongrel of mainstream politics does not dare to bite the corporate hand that serves it every-single-election.

- *It is important to understand that,* **it is their god.**

- *The readers of this book, the intelligent early adopters, get this.*

- *It is time now to bring this information to the rest of the world.*

Now with a captive **customer-monkey** who is the taxpayer by way of government, any price is a good price *and the higher the better.*

- *This is the company store as spoken of much earlier in this book.*

But the story gets worse: If a cartel can sell a gadget or a radio for virtually any price, why would they bother to spend a penny on innovation?

- Innovation is not in their interest.

- *Government contracting however is.*

- I know you can say "lobbyist".

- Why not say it, after all you actually *did* pay for it.

- ***The elimination of competition becomes the single minded goal.***

With that goal of eliminating innovation, we receive therefore the vast majority of all modern regulations. This chapter is simply the Paul Harvey, the rest of the story, on the present state of regulations.

"...Upon thousand dollar hammers we seriously vex, as well as African Harry Beetle Bug sex."   (from The Complete Tax Book by this author)

- Both items were one time major scandals.

The point of that quote, is to demonstrate how your money is taken by the government and subsequently *gifted* to the cartel.

- You are now looking at how that is accomplished.

- **This is the standard modus operandi of A-L-L modern politics.**

The CAFR has one and only one function; unlimited corruption, oppression and Marxism. There is no irony that unlimited corruption, oppression and Marxism are one and the same as identical **and ever were**.

- There is now no remaining deception otherwise.

Said differently; the one and only function of the CAFRs is for the rich to get richer and the poor to get poorer.

- This is the reality and the truth of the situation.

- *This is a model and main key of human slavery.*

- Read this chapter as many times as it takes until you *clearly understand it.*

- Because *this book* is the textbook of the New Paradigm of a humanitarian experience worth living in.

That was interesting. *Now for the rest of the story:*

There is an organization called CAFR1. The function of that organization is to increase awareness of the situation just spoken of. More importantly, their function is to return both **ownership and control** of the funds to the correct owners, the folks who paid for it, the public. There are local organizations springing up from coast to coast working on this *specific* situation. Further evidence of conditions found in this chapter is at CAFR1.

There is a group I am honored to call my friends working on this project right here in Kingman Arizona as this book is written.

But, wait a minute, it gets even more interesting:

Here is a key leverage point *of personal empowerment* that the shift of 2012 is all about:

Step one is raising awareness. This step strips bare the corruption that mainstream politics *is*. You **demanded** a way to put the soulless bastards **into prison forever**. This is it—delivered on a silver platter. *This whole book is all about your empowerment simply awaiting for you* **to step up and demonstrate it**.

Step two is putting this money **into the community where it belongs.** Here is where we take the direction of benefit away from the cartel entirely. This step places it into the ownership and control of the local community right down to the precinct, house to house *and individual* level.

But wait, it gets even MORE interesting:

Here is **the** shocker: The SIZE of the average CAFR fund is between eight and forty times the *entire* annual budget of the government entity that now pisses you money straight to the wind without rhyme or reason.

- **That my good friends, is a whoppin' lot of money.**

But wait, it gets even *MORE* interesting. *Now we get down to what you wanted to know:*

Because the fund is a "programmed" or force-backed high yield, the interest-income alone, *as separate from the principal from which it derived is:*

- **USUALLY ONE AND A HALF, TO TWO TIMES THE ENTIRE ANNUAL BUDGET.**

- That is to say there is no need for any form of taxation ***whatsoever***.

- *WHAT-SO-EVER.*

Know this well:

Taxation only applies to slaves—**and we've been totally, royally, utterly, CHUMPED**.

- It is time to decide between the experience of slavery and the experience of human.

You ***demanded*** a handy way out of taxation (*all taxation*). Here it is— <u>delivered on a silver platter</u>.

- **True humanity awaits only the decision only you can make.**

Here is the very reason government shall soon wield one tenth, *or far less*, of the size, scope, power, cost and influence it now has.

- Nothing could be more Reasonable (or beneficial) than that.

You ***demanded*** a way to return commerce, industry, innovation, thriving and absolutely top paying and safer jobs back to the local community. ***This is it.*** <u>*This is how it shall be accomplished*</u>. It is up to you.

We place the entirety of this funding into the local community from which it came and belongs, to gain superior function and benefit.

- Now how totally *Reasonable* is that?

- It is called **legal**. Technically, we own it ***entirely***.

- It is called **EMPOWERMENT**. (I knew you would like this chapter.)

- *It is the causation of a future worth living in.*

And this concludes the chapter on CAFRs <u>**and the end of taxation**</u>*!*

- Special thanks is given to the great American hero Walter J. Burien Jr., who for over twenty years worked tirelessly to *singlehandedly* bringing this information to the public.

Chapter Twelve

The Final Chapter of Human slavery

The final Chapter of Human Slavery:

This Chapter, THE turning point of the past, present and future human history, is being written right now, by you, *and through this book and intent*.

As the human species shifts into ever greater consciousness, the comprehensive failure of human slavery and its cankered prostitute of politics become both flagrantly evident, and profoundly intolerable.

As a species and as a planet, we are presently faced with but one all inclusive and exceptionally clear choice: Either the human race writes the final chapter on human slavery, or human slavery **and its hell born politics** *will write the final chapter on the human race.*

- Both are now in equal up full progress. (...for a huge improvement.)

That might not at first appear to be a whole lot of choice and it isn't. However, it is the very choice we as a species *are now looking directly at*.

- **The present choice is either extinction or Evolution.**

The Creator's Light at the end of the species length tunnel is our own upward Evolution into Human Success following the Great Healing. Going and gone forever, will be the highly despotic and dictatorial devil's brew of a Socialist-Fascist Corporatocracy and its unlimited murder and brutality. That is what we have come here to uncover and end. All the polite and trite cover up names for human slavery are so results identical as to render all the associated labels to be no more than an exercise in cutting smelly intellectual wind. No matter its deception-name, the condition of human slavery *shall cease.*

Daniel Quinn's just under 600 pound Ishmael informs us in a very understated way, that our present taker society laws are largely useless, widely ignored, deeply despised, and capriciously changed (to suit whichever cartel is jerking the political strings that day). In addition and a hell of a lot worse, the same cartel protection laws and regulation as pertaining to their enforcement, present the textbook definition of arbitrary. Their actual effect is *exclusively and directly* dependent upon which socioeconomic, <u>and thus political protection class</u>, one is in. **It is absolutely classic Marxism.**

The government itself however remains not only above the same laws, but is also by far and away the worst unchecked offender perpetually. The poisoned drinking water at Camp Lejeune is but one example among endless. These are the laws and regulations you are required *at gunpoint* to obey. All of the above conditions and trends are also growing exponentially worse and exponentially *routine*.

Modern politics has now been exposed. Political despotism has now been exposed. Human slavery has now been exposed:

- *They are one and the same. They are identical and inseparable.*

A good portion of ending politically planned genocide is awakening to the present reality that government, the supposed protector of Human Rights, has been for many generations the chief destroyer of those same conditions of human. The deed is done at the direct bidding of the upmost malevolent of global monopolies starting with the banking cartel.

Except for Doctors Paul, it is quite safe to say all mainstream politicians are now, and have been for multiple generations, purchased vassals and handmaidens to oil, drugs of both kinds, agri-business, union, military, banking, auto, and several other global cartels. There is no room for even *imaginary* consideration, for the politically unpowered human {meaning you} in that model.

Your job in that model is to shovel your time, talent and money to the cartel. It is accomplished either directly through a mandated purchase as many purchases now are, or indirectly, by way of the government where it *also* winds up in cartel hands. {CAFR as one example ***among many***} Make no mistake about the extreme viciousness of the controlling monopolies. We shall do well to remember that, of all the vicious monopolies worldwide, **government is by far the worst and most omni-destructive monopoly of them all.** *This is beyond any shadow of doubt.*

- Presently, government is by far and away the most lawless monopoly of them all.

- That statement was consistent enough across America as to again remove any doubt *whatsoever*.   **The Jury *has* spoken.**

For those who might yet believe that government can solve *any* problem that ends that insanity for-ever. Part of government's job is to break up monopolies, and they damn certain aint doing that. As it turns out, the government is the chief protector of the same monopolies. There is a great myriad of modalities by which this treason takes place. Every monopoly protection scheme is more human and small business destructive than the last. *It is the specific design of human slavery.*

How embarrassing it must be that the top whatever number of corporations combined, have not produced a single numerically new job at home for at least *three full generations.*

How amazing that small business, the one thing *savagely maligned* and viciously opposed by government, Marxism, television, media, union *and* modern politics, is the singular engine for 100% of all countable new non-gov jobs. The small business is the present sustaining grace of this Nation and the full world economy *in no uncertain terms.*

Perhaps the political picture is so *drastically* wrong, the average voter simply cannot believe their eyes. The proof is right smack in front of them. It is staring them right in the face in twenty foot tall, brightly lit flamingo pink neon sign-hood. It is blasted in both ears through 1,000 watt loud speakers!

- *Why,* they still don't get it would be the rather complete *eradication* of original thought from *way* too much television.

It follows that the political sales pitch for the body of cartel protection laws, by definition must be of inexhaustible falsehoods. After all, the average voter, **which aint saying much**, must be swindled and defrauded clear to the point of *physically* purchasing their own destruction. The mainstream voter has produced destroyment, slavery, suffering, servitude, endless violence, poverty **and non-life by cartel.**

The *correct* explanation, is that the entire insane and deadly scheme is entirely *and directly* dependent upon the deceived, swindled and profoundly betrayed voter. Fortunately, with all our considerable communication technology *and ever increasing awareness*, that massive body of shame and dishonor is being exposed *and set right*, as we speak.

- Every one of us will see the end of it, **as you have demanded**.

- This condition is directly resulting in a rapid loss of support to the mainstream professional liar and their mono-party of oppression.

The task now presented to the entire human race is, to break the cycle of ongoing human genocide at the banking, political and cartel levels first, foremost and immediately. We then follow that pattern in all areas of human experience.

- **This, is the Great Healing.**

- *And now we have the keys.*

Fortunately, the American if only by location, is now quickly gaining the *required for planetary survival* understanding that fundamentally every mainstream politician is very firmly in the pocket of special interest. And that would usually be defined as the corporate or union hold.

At that point any associated party names are rendered not just meaningless, but profoundly meaningless. The hate and the bribery that produced those lies, sees party lines as much as the Jet Stream knows it just crossed the State line of Nebraska. Said differently, there is **ze-ro** distinction. The truly sickening rhetoric that accompanies the mainstream party labels is simply one of the taxes the mainstream partisan voter suffers **for the exquisitely proven condition** *of uncompromising ignorance.*

From the same lack of honor, the Biblical proportions of current problems directly caused by mainstream politics will not in any way, be solved by the same politics and politicians who intentionally caused those problems to begin with. *Here is the key:* The all-consuming vested interest and re-election money rests in the problem. As it turns out, the more and the bigger the problems are, *the better*. This condition has officially been the case since 19 and 13 *at the sellout, one among countless sellouts.*

The money has never been in finding the solution (for anything). This lesson was learned with the Polio cure, when an entire sub-industry <u>and monopoly</u> worked its way out of a job. This explains multiple generations of "searching" for a cancer cure without plucking a single free herb of plethora that have enjoyed 30,000 years of peerless cancer eradication success.

- I'll say it in English: **It-is-an-absolute-scam,** *and always was*.

Fortunately, there is highly unlikely to be a single reader of this book that does not know that much clear down to their toenails. Score two points for having that awareness. The information came from you anyhow.

The sum of modern politics and, at the same instant, the underlying cause and intention, is a corporate and politically planned slavery and genocide **of the human *concept*.** Much of that intent is being felt now, not only here, but worldwide. *It is not a ticket to utopia*.

The key to the endless politically manufactured challenges, now indeed dire that presently face the human race is easy to understand: 100% all of it is dependent for its evil survival upon a very thick, and deeply entangled web of depraved, increasing, **and ever more *flatly blatant* political lies.**

The condition of one political lie after another has been ongoing for numerous generations. With debt instrument banking and its directly resulting pattern of ongoing manufactured globalized warfare, the pattern continues backward literally for centuries. All of it, is of purchased and **fully prostituted** mainstream, morally disease ridden politicians. (As you have well stated.)

- Providence tells us that it is time to change from that which does not work, *to that which does.*

- It is The Great Healing.

Human survival itself tells us it is well past time to become honest about modern politics. This is so, because when the problem [of unaware-

ness] lies with, and within ourselves, so then does the solution. And that is the good news: **It is entirely and absolutely within-our-control***!*

The same moment a certain number of people clearly understand that; human slavery *is over*. ...And **that**, is the Human Event!

Why then has the human race awaited to the last hour, perhaps the last moments of survival to finally act? Can the human species be that easily duped, blinded, deceived, ripped off, poisoned, maimed, ruined, backstabbed and slaughtered by prostitute-liars and their transparent and trashy lies?

The grand deception is not nearly of that high of quality. Of this writing, its coming apartness is horrendously exceeding its holding togetherness. It is by way of the sheer magnitude and momentum of mainstream political **greed.** The modern politics of human ruin is now its own downfall. That is what the entire human race is now very abundantly witnessing, correctly reporting, and is well in the process of *eradicating*.

Somewhere along the line, preferably now, we must find a greater faith in ourselves and in our honesty and ability. Did both Creator and all Creation bring us this far along, only to be extinguished as humans by rank, fourth rate and literally meth-junkie class political lies?

To me, such nature of sheer insanity does not seem like any kind of desirable way to go. Is the human race to continue to rush headlong into ever greater levels of suffering at the hands of political dishonor? Are we to live in abject slavery and be crushed lifeless by the planet destroying super-cartels where the pursuit of one more cent profit has caused unlimited murder time and time again?

The intended, vicious conditions **of human destroyment**, match far too well the rather glaring lack of consciousness of mainstream politics and politicians. Each politician now in power has morphed *themselves* fully downward in consciousness to become reduced to well trampled sluts. The one who has taken money from "the whole football team" is more honest (*and actually does something for a living*). The omni-destroying cartel puppet masters have much less conscious than that; *as virtually all of you have correctly identified.*

- All five conditions calibrate with unerring accuracy.

That mainstream politics is floating in the toilet is its own evidence, and it is time to flush. Right now, **that's the name of the game for human survival.**

- **Let's get 'er done!**

With no exception, every book on upward Human Evolution on this planet, has **clearly and correctly** condemned modern politics. You are now reading the reasons why. *All of them clearly and correctly understood the omnipresent destructiveness and brutal dishonesty of modern politics.*

Very few of those books on Human Evolution have bothered to explain the day to day workings of modern politics. Basically all books on Consciousness have however correctly pointed out that modern politics is the direct opposite of personal empowerment. Modern politics is shown *as the dead opposite of the condition of humanity.* That Truth is presented accurately and emphatically, over and over and over and over.

The reason behind that condition, the Paul Harvey, beyond its own extreme obviousness, is that the Scale of Consciousness truth test calibration of mainstream politics sets at the complete dishonor and whoredom of effortlessly purchased dishonesty. How then can modern politics, that is apostasy itself, be worthy of anything above ***immediate disposal?***

As modern politics cannot, and has positively no intent whatsoever, of climbing out of its own gladly self-caused pit of continual illegitimacy, it is time to let it go and leave it behind, the same as any other failure.

- If the milk is soured stinky, one does not continue to drink it down.

- The exact same thing applies to modern politics.

Even their egregious *and religious* dishonor may have been at one time somewhat plausibly tolerable. Presently, its complete dangerousness, openly attempting to conduct the extinction of the human race, has earned modern politics a yet even lower calibration on the Scale of Consciousness.

- Can you say: "Not good."

Very strangely, modern politics which is to say Marxism, *to this day* remains blind to the continual and massive purges inherent to Marxism.

Each and every purge claims a huge percentage of the upper hierarchy. The ever present purge process has virtually nothing to do with the strength of the belief in Marxism or "Revolutionary" commitment. In fact, those otherwise loyal attributes turn out to be irrelevant to the point of little or no consideration. (Example: Obama's cabinet, ministers and agency heads.)

- Life and death in any totalitarian model is *exclusively* dependent upon who, in power, favors you.

As it turns out, the one and only thing that matters, is political power or military backing. Lacking that corporal substance, even the greatest Marxist idealist enjoys any real-world security. Because of their idealism, they remain profoundly blind in an 'it won't happen to me' sense. The blindness remains regnant right up to their power plug being pulled, or their Vince Foster ending, *without the slightest warning*. **This is classic Marxism in past and current practice anywhere on this planet.**

If they are in fact *actual* Marxist devotees **as their voting record clearly shows**, neither will they have God or guides to protect them, or a better condition to transcend into. Pitiful lot if you ask me. I didn't say that it made any sense, only that it seems a tragic and wasteful situation.

When the true Marxist places no value upon their own soul, with all *begrudgingly allowed* human life being allowed ***strictly*** to serve the State, then it follows that <u>vastly less value</u> will be put on anyone else's life.

- That in a nutshell, is the entire Marxist {satanic} paradigm.

Anything above both human slavery and absolute poverty is rarely if ever allowed. ...Except for the State and those directly in it, who enjoy every luxury paid for, by those making roughly a 50 cent value against a 14 hour work day supplying the various international cartels with cute plastic, *pointedly designed to fail* widgets.

Hopefully by now, it *should* be patently obvious that any form of support or vote cast by the myrmidon in favor of mainstream politics, earns exactly the same consciousness calibration, culpability and obviously, results. This inescapable condition occurs regardless of whether the support was cast in the profoundly haunted train-wreck of partisan ignorance, or the results of human mouse-hood in the paradigm of the thunderously dominating, **and omni-damming** *negative vote*.

Dishonor, dishonesty, **slavery intention**, poison, betrayal and human extermination are the characteristics that now self-calibrate and define mainstream politics for all factions *equally*. It is also the ongoing results.

- It is time now to think about what we do want, and act accordingly to produce *that* outcome.

The unlimited mainstream political debauchery itself, is merely the thief in the night that slipped in to throat cut, so as not to be identified and held to count. It is the dirty political assignment done to the orders of the international cartels. **It is the act of the heartless and gutless mercenary.**

- And that, is mainstream politics; <u>***the very theory itself, that God is not watching.***</u>

The practical and learned individual residing in awareness as directly opposed to modern politically induced mind-rot, now asks this very telling question: Is there any form of government sourced abuse that cannot be readily, quickly *and correctly* solved by cutting the utterly unconscionable government's cost in both dollars and human suffering **by two thirds** again, and again, and again, and again, and again and yet again or again and again should the need to do so continue?

- Indeed, there is none!

Right here, are the <u>factually correct directions</u> and the only methodology presently left to the American people to bring government at any location into the Oath of Office required compliance and Constitutional Contract **legitimacy**. Anything other than **that process**, constitutes an absolute delusion. History has now proven this to the N*th* degree.

It would be convenient if any of this were made up. I'm really hoping that as but one large example, I do not need to point out what the sheer human cost of government has done to the economy up to 2012. Not only is that observation common sense, it is also a completely unavoidable mathematical axiom. It is two locations so far left politically untouched for multiple generations *as you have stated*.

Tragically, we have only begun to pay *that* piper. That leaves one choice. It is the American vote, and cutting the cost and scope of government sharply, *at this instant*, and in multitude.

The mainstream political slut as owned by the cartel, is not in any way capable, or the slightest part inclined, to suddenly flip and divest themselves of either lifetime dishonor, or of their lifelong drunken and asinine power and spending binges. Neither are any of them capable, as history has for multiple generations unanimously proven, of causing any other condition than ever worse, ever larger, and ever more *downright abusive* government.

- It is the unlimited violence of, by and for special interest.

Because that "special interest" turns out to be **human slavery**, it becomes imperative to human survival, to call it human slavery. We must call it that at every possible opportunity. We must also learn to create such opportunities. **As a species, we simply no longer have the luxury to *not* do so.**

One example among endless examples of "special interest" political influence, is that our anti-monopoly laws need to be changed, or far more accurately, enforced. This is so the mega-cartels **can no longer exist**. This condition should prevail not only in the United States, but to benefit human survival and well being, such action should be extended to the entire planet owing to similar, yet so far politically ignored (by way of baksheesh), anti-monopoly laws. (I do however, admire how Europe has outlawed GMOs.)

If anything, these monopolies, their poison, and their mile wide money trails expose <u>exactly</u> who the crooked, honorless, spineless, and hot iron conscious-seared politicians are. Unfortunately, it appears to be all of them—when the trail is well enough followed. This methodology is unerringly accurate no matter the cartel, the branch of government, or the party label, {what a joke}. It also matters not where the purchased double agent may be hidden deep within the bowels of government pay as is usually the case.

- We now have an establishment system dedicated *exclusively* to human slavery. It is composed of double agents and junk science.

- Particularly tragic, less than 1% of the so described double agents are in any way elected or accountable *except to cartel*.

- The Totalitarian model is thus defined.

Within this perfected example, the cartel purchased junk science alone slashes an unmistakable trail physically larger, and vastly more destructive than General Sherman's march through Georgia! Right there folks, is likely the world's finest example of just how preposterously easy and simple it is to sort out *to crystalline perfection*, who is on who's side, cartel or human race. It is time to open our eyes **and see**, preferably *before* our "caretakers" *remove the concept humanity* **from existence** *(for our own good of course)*.

- These well known examples are what modern, mainstream politics has brought the human race.

- Therefore, it is time to absolutely end modern politics.

Directly from result, mathematically and practically speaking, any form of support or vote for the mainstream candidate at any station, and in specific, **the incumbent mainstream politician**, can now be officially and correctly stated as the spiritual and practical role of suicide. Not only is the full human race coming to ever more clearly and correctly understand that, but also that the *fully mythical* 'lesser of two evils' does not now, and from 1913, technically/morally/practically has not existed **at all.**

1913, marks the start date of the Federal Reserve and modern uni-party politics. From that moment forward, any and all practical and real-world distinctions were by force of law and bribe removed from between the two rabidly anti-American political *sections* A and B. 1913, also marks the date of wholesale transfer of the power **of essentially all governing decisions** to international banking and numerous other mass murdering crime cartel syndicates. Thus we have *the correct* definition, outcome and methodology of human slavery and human slave trafficking.

It has been that way ever since, and will remain so until the moment we stop human genocide. We now know the results. Should one wish to know where political warfare comes from, *there is your truth tested answer*.

The question is: What do we do about it? We have a very Reasonable answer; it is called the Great Healing. It is the first step of the Human Event.

- See it and believe it, because it is present **right now;** *and you're looking at it.* ⇨ **And you created it.** ⇨ *Many of you know that.*

How strangely impractical it is that nearly the entire human species is keenly aware of the above mainstream Uniparty and their *rabidly* anti-American dedication. ...*Except,* for the asleep and goofy exception of the average mainstream, numb-skulled, **television advised** dolt of a voter. That condition is in contention for the most sad, tragic, *inexcusable* and outright destructive stories *in all human history*. It is so, if only from the resultant runaway human and human condition <u>destroyment</u>. Again, the angels weep in grief at the *horrendous* mental and spiritual desuetude.

Cartel commanded modern politics can now be correctly defined as not only the full intent of human slavery that truth tests, but also *the intent* of murder to annihilation of the vast majority of the human population worldwide that also truth tests. How such outcome is to be profitably accomplished is irrelevant. {However, western medicine very quickly comes to mind.} That such human destruction *does* get accomplished *is* relevant.

- *And that is the knife straight in your back, of mainstream politics.*

- Undoing Modern politics can and will, very likely save **your** life.

- Odds are now at 98% chance that ending modern politics will save your children's and grandchildren's **life**.

- *The mainstream idiot-voter must now weigh the preservation of their fantastic and morbid ignorance against the lives of their immediate family.*

- *...For it has come to be so.*

In summary; any mainstream political vote or support <u>*whatsoever*</u> directly **calibrates** at, endorses, causes, truth tests **and results in:**

- **A firm endorsement for ever increasing corruption.**

- A firm endorsement for ever increasing human slavery.

- A firm endorsement for human and world destruction.

- A firm endorsement for human condition destruction.

- A firm endorsement for corporate-military world domination.

- A firm endorsement for the end of Human Rights.

- A firm endorsement to be further reduced to the legal status *of possessions*.

- A firm endorsement to be further reduced to complete and presently unimaginable poverty.

- A firm endorsement for cartel national and world domination.

- A firm endorsement for an ***extremely*** **totalitarian** one world government.

- A firm endorsement therefore, for the human microchip implant.

- A firm endorsement for endless prison labor camps *for civilians*.

- A firm endorsement for warfare after warfare worldwide.

- A firm endorsement for further non-voluntary and unannounced human science experimentation.

- A firm endorsement for genetically modified misalliances.

- A firm endorsement for continued and increased drug, oil, *sickness industry*, auto and agri-business national and world poisoning.

- A firm endorsement for ever larger government.

- A firm endorsement for ever worse government.

- A firm endorsement for ever more invasive government.

- A firm endorsement for ever more intrusive government.

- A firm endorsement for ever more wasteful government.

- A firm endorsement for ever more aggressive government.

- A firm endorsement for ever more fraudulent government

- A firm endorsement for ever more violent government.

- A firm endorsement for ever more abusive government.

- A firm endorsement for ever more costly government.

- A firm endorsement for ever more completely out of control government.

- A firm endorsement for ever more government bureaucracy.

- A firm endorsement for ever more bureaucratic *insanity*.

- A firm endorsement for ever more governmental sourced *brutality*.

- A firm endorsement for ever increasing governmental injustice.

- A firm endorsement for ever increasing intentional destruction of the Constitution of the United States of America.

- A firm endorsement for ever increasing governmental lawlessness.

- A firm endorsement for ever worse and ever less government 'services'.

- A firm endorsement for ever higher priced government "romantic relations". *And you know what that is.*

- A firm endorsement for ever more insane, not working, unworkable, despised, dishonest, costly **and utterly corrupt,** foreign policy.

- A firm endorsement for ever more political abuse of power.

- A firm endorsement for ever more, ever bolder and ever more obvious political lies.

- A firm endorsement to not only be increasingly taken for granted, but also be taken as a complete fool, and be treated as a complete fool.

- Unfortunately in that case, *correctly so.*

- A firm endorsement for further turning every neighbor, friend, co-worker, family member, and passer-by, into a government paid spy and story inventing **liar-snitch.**

- A firm endorsement for further allowing, causing, and paying those spies an snitches to openly lie like a threadbare rug in a house of ill repute, *which an estimated 90% majority of them do right now.*

- A firm endorsement to further reduce every shopkeeper and small business person into primarily a tax collector.

- A firm endorsement to further reduce every police officer into a "revenue enhancement agent" or more accurately, **tax collector**.

- A firm endorsement to further cause all police departments to reduce, <u>and most often extensively</u>, any and all considerations of public safety or service in order to crank out 'revenue enhancement'.

- A firm endorsement for ever more laws and regulations that are utterly insane, flagrantly ignored, deeply despised, selectively, arbitrarily, **exclusively class based**, and politically enforced.

- A firm endorsement for ever more laws *viciously* counterproductive to the publicly stated sales pitch.

- A firm endorsement for ever more laws written by international cartel in order to favor international cartel.

- A firm endorsement for ever more laws dishonorably sold by Uniparty politicians who are paid extravagantly to **lie about all of it**.

- A firm endorsement for ever higher taxes, fines and fees that produce little or no *actual* service, have *no* positive benefit, and make no sense whatsoever except to screw you without mercy.

- A firm endorsement for the upmost bizarre, inane, unexplainable, foolish, fantastically tragic and utterly unconscionable dead end political pork barrel whims, larks, and *authentically* ill intended machinations <u>serving cartel</u>, **and therefore re-election**.

The most important part of it all, is the following realizations:

1 The above list has been the unbroken direction and comprehensive unreasonableness of modern politics from at least 1913. Many have claimed with faultless proof, that the above conditions started at or near the Civil War. Many now claim the end of America began the same moment, <u>foreign banking</u> was accepted to fund the first government related function.

- **Those errors handed the decision making power straight over to international cartel <u>where it remains to this day</u>.**

2 It is likely that the readers of this book are already aware of the above long standing indictments. I have only brought them out into the open, and thus into the forefront of awareness although you are, and continue to be the source of these rather obvious, observations.

3 There is highly unlikely to be a reader of this book who does not firmly agree with the above truth tested conditions. It is not only common sense, but also the lifetime experience of the American people.

4 There is unlikely to be any reader of this book who cannot upon reflection, easily add ten or three dozen points, to the above list.

- As but one example among endless, a *catastrophically failed* government "education" system comes to mind.

The directly resulting prison industry follows that. A Homeland Security that is 100% of everything *except* homeland security follows that.

A Revenue Service that is of no service at all and never has been, follows that. A Postal "Service" that has gone 'postal' with their prices follows that. *Each, <u>being a monopoly</u>,* **is the cause.**

Tragically, all of the above only *touches* a here to the moon list of the intentional and unvarnished energy **of human slavery**. Very tragically, that list now includes governmental unhealth "care". It is a condition that easily may prove to be the <u>by</u> <u>far</u> most expensive, wasteful, **fraud filled**, and intentionally harmful monopoly-dictatorship of them all.

- That Marxist paradigm is vying for one of the most *outright destructive* (and illegal) conditions in human history!

- *It is headed that way right now, and in a big hurry.*

There are three additional items associated with the cartel's "health care" system that you have brought to my attention:

A If you can force me to buy health insurance, I can force you to buy crappy spotted owl skin shoes. *You won't afford them either.*

B What happens to you should you hold a different and vastly more functional belief about human wellness? (As most of us reading this probably do)

C Oh yea, sorry about your luck if you are over 75. *You're shagged.*

- …And statistically, you probably voted for it. You definitely <u>paid</u> for it. Now you're likely to pay for that stupidity **with your life**.

- Like it or not, you are slated to be "legalized" into a "useless eater",

- *…and earmarked for benefit termination by way of death panel.*

5 All of the above, perfectly defines mainstream politics and its abominable calibration on the Scale of Consciousness. Needless to say; none of modern politics is human or planetary beneficial. Nor was it ever intended to be. Nor can it be. All of the above is highly *cartel* beneficial. However it is not **you** beneficial, <u>*although you foot the bill*</u>.

- Each of these conditions Truth test.

6 The moment we, as a species, develop the ability to see through the staged and televised Jerry Springerism of mainstream political rhetoric, the above long of train of abuse is the only condition presently left of any and all mainstream politics. It should by now, be *patently and pathetically* obvious— if only from the damage done <u>*so far*</u>.

7 All of the above conditions are *right now* generally accepted by the strong majority of the full human race as the correct definitions and descripttions of modern politics. It is indeed tragic that the average American *by location only* **voter**, is pretty much the last bunch on the entire planet to catch up to the above realizations. It is the direct *and amazing* opposite of how it should be. It is a textbook case of un-freaking-believable, but unfortunately and monotonously true. *That is the tragedy and results of government education.*

The double dimwitted average **mainstream party voter** could actually qualify as the dullest knife on the planet. For most of us reading this book, some of the confounded and corn fed cosmic idiots we have had the misfortune to argue politics with, they tripled it.

- I for one, could have been spared *that slough of despondency*.

8 Each of us now has various levels of emerging Consciousness and realizations *rapidly* catching up to our ever stronger intuitive voice.

This energetically defines 2012 and all beyond. We are evolving to clearly understand all or most of the above descriptions of mainstream politics. There are ever fewer exceptions to this as our awareness climbs into the condition of Consciousness.

A major part of the reason for this growing awareness, is that the above listed conditions are gaining in their openness, obviousness, and *unabated destructiveness*. The number of victims of modern politics has exponentially increased. That of course is the plan of modern cartel commanded politics worldwide. *The difference now, is in the obviousness.*

Those remaining few unawake exceptions, buried as they are in the old energy of human slavery, can now *officially* be classified as deceived. Virtually all will at some point, come out of that insanity. *Many will suffer destruction by modern politics first.*

- It is a lot easier learning the truth now.

- A very few, believe it or not, might take their mainstream political insanity straight to the grave, *right where that crap belongs*.

9 The Human Event begins with the Great Healing of placing the death spiral of modern politics firmly and forever behind us. We shall dump mainstream politics into the dust bin of history as mistakes made, lessons learned, and wisdom earned—with Consciousness, safety, self-ownership prosperity and Success awarded as the result.

10 Anything other than ***exactly*** that, is *fatally nonfunctional.*

11 Up until this moment, this book, this organization *and this movement* into a more Reasonable outcome and experience, there was not a damn thing any of us could do about any of the above except complain about it daily, remain very angry at the professionally dysfunctionalized and utterly poisonous system, and direly wish for a better condition.

12 Now we can do something about it. *This*, ***and only this***, is the Teleology of the human future. It is achieved through **The Humanitarian Code of Peace and Freedom**©.

13   *<u>Let's get 'er done!!!</u>*

Now that we have correctly examined the highly, highly injurious consciousness calibration *and results* of modern politics, let's now examine the consciousness calibration of the human race. **Right now** *today*, that ever increasing calibration and direction is the Human Event <u>in progress</u>.

- It is The Great Healing.

As an *outstanding* example, there are now almost endless oodles, distantly far more than any other moment in human history, of books singularly dedicated to ever greater human consciousness and upward human evolution. It physically and spiritually would not be *at all possible* to manifest nearly any of them into the morphogenic field of precipitated existence *unless*, the consciousness of the human species specifically and highly commendably **matched**, and thus allowed for, cultivated, encouraged and created their existence. They would have remained unsold as well.

Just as the growing awareness and consciousness level of the human species has caused *and created* this book, even two or three years ago it would not have been possible. The same thing holds true for countless additional books causing human species continuation, thriving, Evolution **and empowerment**. The New model is nested within a profoundly more functional paradigm of Natural living. It is the abatement of coercion. It is the absence of human slavery. *It is the breaking of Satan's force, facade and influence.* (…As we once again define mainstream politics.)

Likewise, and every bit as commendably, the human species is now person to person sharing a <u>greased lightening quick</u> growing plethora of videos and documentaries causing upward human Evolution. It is the distancing of ourselves both individually and collectively from the all consuming and insane destructiveness of human slavery **and its political whore.**

Furthermore and just as commendably, there is now a variety of major motion pictures intentionally showcasing some aspect of Consciousness. To the ever growing credit and calibration of the human race, several of those motion picture films, Avatar for example, have become record setting blockbusters.

In 20-20 retrospect, the success of Avatar could not have occurred even five years ago. Please understand **clearly**, that such condition is not due to technical whizz-bang tricks, but rather the dramatic upward shift in human consciousness.

This specific distinction is crucially important for you to perceive. The *correct* perception undoes mountains of ginned up *damage control* put out by the mainstream scientific publications. The deal is not about cutie-pie technical gimmickry. It is about Consciousness, ***period!***

Looking at Hollywood in general, with quite rare exceptions, the general bend for two or three generations has been a fanatical drive and well organized thrust into Marxism. The most accurate description of that intent and direction is <u>perpetually worse government as every solution</u>. Government is seen as an omnipotent end all, do all, be all. **Marxism, that is to say Satan's view, sees government** *as the direct replacement of God.*

Even without McCarthyism, the overwhelming preponderance of evidence very clearly demonstrated an omnipresent radical, and typically fanatical devotion to a Cuban, Cambodian, North Korean or Soviet style Marxism by Hollywood. The drive into Marxism is every bit the equal of generations of basically all major media, and nearly all of the so called scientific community. *The dishonesty alone demonstrates no boundary.*

Somewhere it is stated that to courageously shoulder the responsibility of one's mistakes is true character. Who among us could not deeply benefit from a lot more of such Evolution ourselves?

The point though, is that Hollywood for the most part, is now saying OOPS, you know what, we collectively, royally, totally, utterly, egregiously *and absolutely* screwed up! We have wrought human destroyment as opposed to human success. Now what must we do?

- *Plain and simple*, that represents a monumental shift in consciousness from human hate *to human respect*.

- We have discovered that the problem with any totalitarian paradigm, is that utopia cannot flow down the barrel of a billy club or gun.

- The catch voided of mysticism, is that the killers shall ever be the the next killed. **Labels at that point are stripped of any meaning.**

- Here is where everyone can learn from the evolution of Hollywood.

We can accurately call that the solid beginning of the Great Healing leading up to the Human Event. Know well however, that it started with the people of the human race, and *specifically not* the collection of strange and often amazingly self-destructive hun-yucks we call Hollywood.

Admittedly, there is a lot of talent and brainpower in that location and finally for Pete's sake, it is now beginning to be employed for beneficial purposes. Call that down payment **about a half a century overdue.**

- *It's a very good start.*

From that emerging realization, we now enjoy a rapidly growing list of big time actors, writers, film producers and sponsors all working day and night in the advancement of Consciousness. And yes, most of their work either in big or small part flatly knocks the crap out of modern politics and its concubine, modern government. It is accomplishing that hat dance as fitly as any John Grisham novel, and some of *them* have hit the screen big time.

That the New Energy sells as outstanding as it does is a monumental, upward shift in Consciousness. It is The Great Healing, pure and simple.

- And it is very, very Reasonable at that.

- What I am asking each reader to see is the larger picture; the worldwide upward shift *in Consciousness.*

Indeed, the Great Healing is the cutting away of the terrible, terrible chains of human slavery and the purchased, **actually demonic** workings of human slavery known as mainstream politics. Such exorcism is not only the right beginning, <u>but the factually correct location to start at</u>.

As it turns out, every day brings about an ever growing, heartfelt, loud, and *expressly dedicated* chorus of amens to the above statement. That alone is an important upward progression of awareness and rock solid proof of the New Energy of rapidly emerging Consciousness. In fact, the above condition is *irrefutable* evidence of the growing New Energy of increased Consciousness and the shaking away of the politics of human slavery.

- It is a very Reasonable *process.*

Yet the Human Event is a hundred, a thousand, a million times that. It is the experiencing of our own true, and heretofore mostly untapped, or more accurately, terribly misused and way not understood true potential in effective ability, manifestation of good, and co-Creatorhood Consciousness.

We are now one by one very rapidly developing huge new abilities and consciousness even if much of it is made necessary by the smoldering, twisted wreckage left behind by the grotesque failures of the old energy of man's inhumanity to man. This holds true even if those rather hideous failures are PC soaked and cloaked as they are, by dozens of slick, crafty, ginned up *political damage control euphemisms and trashy spin carnivals.*

- Has there ever been a media amplified political story that has <u>not</u> turned out to be false?

- Virtually all of you have *correctly* stated; **no.**

At what point in the disaster to disaster timeline do we come to realize, that from education, through Katrina to oil spills and a hundred poly-gate scandals in between, government will handle it the same way **every time.** The end result will be without fail, a scientific study in lies, mismanagement, totalitarianism, and all encompassing cartel greed. It will turn out to be a study in bullying, ruination, and **hideous failure**, <u>every-single-event</u>.

Indeed, a New Energy and a New Dimension is upon us. That New world is centered upon the basic human respect of a murder free paradigm. In the New Earth, there is no call for the political maiming or killing of each other. (The killing is done to supply passing amusement, bank account largess and betting entertainment for the higher up controllers).

- The butchery simply supplies the cartel their larcenies.

The murder by number paradigm that we call mainstream politics and modern government is simply human genocide. It is referred to as "population control" by the controllers. Nearly all cartel in existence has this agenda at or near the top of their list. You <u>specifically</u> are not included to survive. Nor does any part of the old energy recognize "human".

- **On this day**, **we move out from under the paradigm of genocide.**

The Human Event starts with that realization and much more importantly, <u>the experience</u> of the New paradigm of human respect and success. **It is the advancement into our truly unlimited human potential.**

- **It is the unlocking and the experiencing of, the unlimited human potential that is the heart, core and actuality of the Human Event.** It is *also* the absence of human slavery.

We have to do what we must as a species in order to survive. That condition is simply ending modern hate centered politics and its command mechanism, the world controlling cartels. Obviously, that includes numerous closely bound international cartels that order politicians worldwide, *particularly high level politicians*, about to and fro, this way and that like so many first day boot camp recruits.

- Nobody's heart is bleeding for the dirty bastards either.

As my editors are forever grousing for specific examples, I shall interject another, although it is generally to my distaste to dwell on failure. I strongly prefer to stay with the concepts, principles and compass headings into Human Success. I also strongly prefer to intentionally allow the *actual* outcomes and processes a rather complete freedom within the very fewest restrictions possible, such as harm no one with hate, and that's it.

This very construct then allows the true unlimited-ness of the human potential to emerge and cascade. It is that degree of freedom that I consider crucial to Hunan Success. The same moment one truly gloms on to that concept, that is truly gets it, there is no going back. It will change every cell and every atom of your existence and charge them with a high energy and thoroughly empowering New Vibration of self-ownership. When you get that, truly get it, then you understand the Human Event, the absence of coercion, **it is the treatment of humans *as humans*.**

*The experience of the Human Event is not from the head, it is from the heart. It is not from your physicality, it is from your Spirit. The message is from you **as a Human Being**. The message of the Human Event is simply You, attempting to communicate with, you.*

- By the way, it is fairly important to clearly understand that.

Now for the example:

Within the Great Healing, let's look at food supply *independence.* Within that now emerging condition, we break the fatal chains of the intentionally engineered **river of poison** as supplied by the present cartel.

Any of Kevin Trudeau's Natural Cures books state the sum total *food substitute* and sickness industry as it presently is. It is accurately stated as the sum total of our modern *illusion of nutrition* supply chain, **and applied kinesiology** verifies it to a "T".

- Hopefully, that's specific enough.

To learn more about the Truth Test, go straight to Dr. David R. Hawkins three books that are:

1. Power vs. Force

This magnificent New Energy book presents the foundational Humanitarian principles of any and all movements toward human Freedom and Success, that is to say; the Human Event.

Another New Energy foundational book, one that I've worn out from use, is the Handbook for the New Paradigm from Bridger House Publishing. The "authors" being one of the same sources this book was drawn from with myself as scribe. That by the way, provides me with the perfect excuse to write with a great deal of firmness. When I feel it and know it, I make the attempt to write within that knowing. When the certainty has come through, then and only then have I properly done my part as scribe.

2. Truth vs. Falsehood

This book details and brings to the forefront, the Truth Test. Ironically, or fittingly as the case may be, the Truth Test process is available in a self-adjusting sense, to only the roughly 15% of the population who have actively developed the learned ability to consciously set aside during the test, their ego and any and all preconceived notions, concepts and outcomes. ...All of which by definition strictly emanate from the vain-glorious, pumped up *and* **_extremely_ _easily deceived_ ego**.

The Truth Test is incapable of giving you what you presently believe to be the truth, it can only provide The Truth, and that is precisely why it will not work for most people, who by definition live squarely in falsehood. Gee, I think I may have just defined the mainstream voter. Yup, a solid ten-four there!

- And it is definitely so.

The truth test with practice, is only functional to those who have dedicated their existence to truth and therefore calibrate above the line or consciousness level of Integrity. No modern politician can use **_or compre-hend_** this test *because* they are bought, sold, Interchanged at will and smell like so much wet, happy hog dung. And you can forget the cartel paid to lie "scientist". Or the know it all religionist {and dictator want-to-be}, who for the dollar on the doughnut would just as soon see you shot dead as saved <u>and</u>, **body slams** the next religionist for doing identically the same thing.

- It is because the money flow is not going to *them*.   *Ah-ho!*

The lengthy laundry list of others below, and typically way below Integrity includes various hardheads, egotistical idiots, haters for sure, know-it-alls, holier than thous, and a great pile of others whose existence and world, the same as the pompous, hightailed polecats we call politicians, is *exclusively* <u>of the ego</u>. You don't want to talk to most of these folks, and their phonograph is invariably stuck. One end of the equation is *asleep*.

Universally, their stinking and one way Oscar winning piousness, is a dead reliable method of identification. Their general offensiveness and pushiness is also a sure indicator. The best indicator besides the closed mind that they all by definition own, is the cutting off of debate—simply because they know in their heart of hearts *<u>for certain,</u>* their argument can never stand up to the facts. And exactly that, is the mainstream politician!

The bottom line is that there is little or no possibility any of them are the least bit interested in actual truth, no matter how much that truth is in their face. This is simply because 100% of their ever so precious **re-election funding** is rewarded through maintaining a *<u>rigorous</u>* state of falsehood.

Those below Integrity maintain their falsehood almost as if their life depended upon it. Little do they know, *only their ego* depends upon it. Strangely and ironically, strictly due to the all fired ego, that condition is impressively easy to see in others, politicians for example, and almost impossible to see or perceive, without great effort, in one's self.

Such condition is the living example of the sliver and the plank. It is that condition, the ego driven inability to see one's own falsehood that holds into a *terrible* bondage, slavery and limitation, **all but the few**. And to add a lot of insult to injury, until they gain at least some identification apart from their imprisoning and tyrannical fear-ego, their life is nearly zero part likely to change for the better internally or externally. They are highly likely to continue to live within a very painful inward haze of self-pity, secret self-condemnation, victimhood, debilitating anxiety, *and dread of being found out*, *in addition to illusion*.   It is the *illusion* however, that winds up in the holder getting their tail end righteously kicked by reality **as many times as it takes**.

To digress and provide *the* prime example, we shall visit the genuinely tortured lot of the blind as a bat mainstream party proselyte. There we see great green eyed gorillas of all grimy green slimmed goofballs. For this example, we cannot help but notice that mainstream party X calls mainstream part Y, Statist *and rabidly dishonorable*. Neither one in this example possessing the first clue, yet hanging on like the local pit bull.

Ah, but both remain perfectly correct about the other, even in the pristine unknowing of why. Both, parties J and K, loudly and publically insist the other is delusional and hate inundated. Both are factually correct. How about them road apples that can never make apple butter?

Both "sides", *what a joke*, publically admit that modern politics is a total and utter failure. …That it is disaster and foundationally hopeless. Most, will forthright {and correctly} admit that modern politics should be bulldozed backwards into the pit of hell from which it spawned. Yet, *and this is the raving mad clincher:*   Not one of them will admit, or stop to realize **that they have a death grip on half a turd!**   Insane, Insane, Insane, Insane, Insane, *any questions?*

Even worse, is that the longer and harder those demented idiots hang onto their goddamn half a swirling turd, the worse off <u>they</u> wind up getting! Something, and I truly don't know what it might be, a light year beyond and below dumb, <u>might</u> cover it. You'd think, from the stink, that into their head it might sink! And then they elect another purchased fink! And I could rhyme it until I run out of ink and Rom-bamma belongs in the klink!

The above mainstream political scenario is a case of mental illness to the highest possible degree. I mean think about it, they mutually lay waste to themselves <u>as a life's mission</u>, **and still don't get it!!!**

Both 'sides' *so to speak*, <u>are in a mad frenzied throat cutting contest to see who can make government worst</u>. Unfortunately, both sides win, only to claim *the other side did it!* There is no longer even plausible deniability there, *or even close*. It's not even a half of a deck of cards or a half a bag of marbles. But, it is about a load of bricks short of a load of bricks, and an entire world short of honorable, honest, sane or workable. **It is human slavery.** It is the deception, *and disease*, of mainstream politics.

I do know that there is a world of poetry hidden somewhere in that mess and some of you will undoubtedly write it, seeing that unofficially, roughly 38% of us are underemployed right now {48% in my State}. The entire remainder of the planet sees all of the above and doesn't know whether to laugh, cry, puke, crap or croak. All they see is the United States flying headlong into a politically driven wasteland by the same bankers and cartel that have owned their governments, lock, stock and barrel *for centuries*. *This* is the prostitution of mainstream politics.

Moving straight to the chase: If "reform" of mainstream politics could have worked, it would have worked in the last **one hundred years** of NOT working! This concept is repeated because of its extreme importance. It is a foundational concept. *It is crucially important to get this concept clearly understood.* This basic thing should be patently obvious to the general public. I am trusting that this book will help make it so.

- *No matter which way one cuts it, mainstream politics is human ruination pure and simple.*

- It is now demystified once and *for-ever!*

Mainstream politics is an exercise and study in unconsciousness, futility, failure, profound dishonor, coercion, deceit, slavery *and nothing other*. It is crucially important to realize that very real-world present, and exquisitely well proven condition. The all consuming harm of mainstream politics alone tells us that much truth in very bold and direct terms.

- **It is time now to do away with the unmitigated disaster of mainstream politics that has centered itself exclusively in human destroyment.**

If you have that concept in your mind and that Truth in your heart, we will move away from that perfect example of human destruction and return to our discussion on the only solution there is: **Creator Consciousness.**

Notably, every new upward level of Consciousness will have its own set of perceived truths, many of which can be, and often are, different and sometimes drastically different than previous levels or dimensions of consciousness. The difference *in results* between levels of consciousness on the Scale of Consciousness are logarithmic and exponential. A small increase in Consciousness results in a very large shift in awareness, empowerment, benefit *and personal effectively.* It is attributable to personal consciousness work and the resulting evolution from that work.

Such outcome is not likely to happen by accident any more than one is likely to win the lotto without buying a ticket. The transition PROCESS is indeed through Grace, however it will not happen sitting in front of the mind and thought process destroying television.

Furthermore, the harder one hangs onto old notions even in the sure knowing that virtually everything the system of human imprisonment has ever instructed anyone is flatly false, the more impossible it is to achieve *and thus benefit from*, any upward movement in Consciousness.

In truth it is stubbornness itself, hanging on to **pure trash**, that keeps the vast majority of the human race below the line of Integrity and therefore in **terrible** bondage, suffering, and self caused *fear, paralysis and inability*.

Although both truth and falsehood is everybody's responsibility, falsehood is the necessity of the system of human imprisonment. Slavery, and the system thereof, has placed only falsehood on the instructional menu 24/7 lifetime for generations of generations. That explains international banking, the unparalleled dishonor of skunk butt politics, modern government, and the entire poison dealing cartel system **in full**.

Much of the human race is still laboring within, and mindlessly regurgitating **over and over**, the complete insanity of human imprisonment. Should one wish to view a real horror show played out, all one needs to do is take a good look at most people's lives that are lived out within the confines of *massive* system instructed, yet patently false limitation, disability and imprisonment. From that view, the unlimited tragedy (hell) of lived out falsehood and self-imposed limitations becomes excruciatingly obvious, and particularly so when measured against their own readily available potential.

That well paved road to ruin unerringly starts with the notion that the system itself is anything whatsoever other than intended slavehood. Or, more to the heart of the matter, that any mainstream vote is anything other than a demand for ever worse government and thus a wasted vote. Or that it will result in anything other than **increased tyranny**. *In that regard, history itself has offered no other outcome.*

If a person can get through and over this one so well historically established fact with a lifetime resolve not to continue to endorse human slavery, *one is then a Reasonable human being.*

And all that sets the stage for:

3. The Eye of the Eye From Which Nothing is Hidden.

This is where cool happens. The Eye of the Eye instructs us that, using truth testing, nothing whatsoever, no falsehood under any circumstances, can remain hidden. No political lie or doublespeak, no corporate cartel political money trail *or amount*, no shadowy, hidden, nameless *snake like* power brokers behind the scenes, no power abuse, no political bait and switch, nothing false whatsoever will be able to remain unknown or likely, un-broadcast *or unpunished*, ⇨ <u>*precisely as foretold*</u>.

Let's think about that for a while: Psalms 10:11 hits the modern, mainstream political belief right on the button:
"God has hidden His face that He will not see," Every single lowdown politician there is who destroys your Human Rights <u>in direct Violation of their Oath of Office,</u> and that is pretty much numerically all of them, have repeatedly and career lifetime, demonstrated <u>exactly</u> the belief that: <u>God is not looking</u>!

- **Oops. That train is now derailed.**

- Sorry mainstream political *illusion of* X.

- Sorry mainstream political *illusion of* Y.

- Sorry mainstream Uniparty of human slavery, *that gig is over.*

God is in fact looking. And one nightmarish hell to biblical proportions *worse* for the Slavery Uniparty, is that an ever growing portion of the general public is now *also* looking. For those who can Truth Test, no political lie anywhere will become anything other than *absolutely* laid bare.

Just for one example among *way* too many; how many endless times have we personally witnessed some disastrously mangle-managed government "benefit" which it ain't, drastically cut back *or away.* **And, here is the universal key to it all:** The same tax by whatever label without fail, ever, <u>not so much as once</u>, does anything except go right on being collected *for that which is not provided!*

I do not care if it is a water pipe upgrade or dental care in some kickback inundated "government care" insurance package. This one truth remains unchanged and **unnoticed**, simply because the ungodly dishonor involved was backed into place, *out of time sequence!*

My work is to bring it to your attention. The awareness is Reasonable. The bending over and back-jamming the public <u>for an utter pack of fools</u> is not. It is good to see the difference. The ability to Truth Test also reveals that the world controllers get a hell of a kick out of the fact that no matter what they do, the mainstream voter **just-does-not-get-it**!

The mainstream voter *to this day*, has no concept or understanding what is being done, or how it is being done by those same controllers. They *truly* , <u>tragically</u>, <u>pathetically</u> <u>and simply</u>, **do-not-get-it!**

- *If the mainstream voter did get it, they would no longer be a mainstream voter would they?*

- **There's your proof.**   *It's as simple as it gets.*

- At any rate, the price has arrived for the mainstream Uniparty politician in that every hand in the cookie jar gets caught.

- Every black budget will be viewed and every name will be named.

- Every double book will be seen, every dollar accounted for.

We are beginning to see that now, even though it has so far only earnestly begun with a now beginning *army* of whistleblowers. It is proof positive of the Great Healing in progress. This book is the **precise** essence of it. The Human Event disposing of slavery *and experiencing* the Greater human potential is its completion. *So yes, let's think about that for a while.*

Hmm, every politico in intercourse with the wrong spouse is popped. Every politico with a yard of coke is busted. Every politico in blood-handed bribery is nabbed and cuffed, booked and stuffed, nailed and jailed.

- Well now, it looks like we just about got 'em all!

It also looks like we got *almost* all of them on their own felony third strike *that they created for the rest of us—***who ain't them!** <(Key concept) (The reality here is that the controllers do not in any way, live by the rules they set for the rest of us, *nor do they pretend to*.)

The really, really scary part is that the above, is only *a few* random but somewhat *historically normal* offences on a list of who knows, perhaps ten thousand, twenty thousand...

- **The detestable bastards we ever so loosely call modern politicians, simply will not prevail in the New Energy of the Human Event.**

- Something I like about that.

- **It is breaking the chains of human slavery.** And that is, the Human Event.

Another up to date example is that the President-acting has made the United States the laughingstock of the entire world. Many nations the mainstream media abundantly condemned for their blood-bath dictatorships, are now pointing at our current political situation. To the last one, the bad guys are now saying: "Look at that self-absorbed ass." "Look at his utter contempt for the law." "Look how he lies continuously." "Look how he behaves as a child." "Look at his dictatorship and stop calling us the worst because we are no longer the worst." "We treat our enemies better than he treats his citizens." The latter is probably is not the case at all, ***but it is their*** *claim*. ...And the current Failure in Chief with his unlimited contempt for America has made that claim at least marginally *plausible*.

As heard behind every blade of grass, we have a wan-a-be dictator taking the lead in the dive through human slavery. The best quote I overheard summed it up thusly: "Obama is a perfect example of someone whose politics, policies and behavior belong in North Korea, *not the United States.*"

"Obamacare" is now described by various well recognized names as "incompetency from top to bottom", "incompetent throughout", "a failure by design", "an utter embarrassment for the Democratic Party", "another page from the Codex Alimentarius" and simply, "Big Pharma's wish list".
This author will surmise that the dictatorship going awry, will turn out to be just another study in uniquely unqualified cronyism, and an entire series of lies. We shall see if that's the case. Historically, the odds are with me right at 100%. With Several un-American administrations, piles of unqualified cronies, oodles of double-speak lawyers, endless excuse makers, spin masters and professional blame passers, *there is nothing new in this regard*. ...**And everything gets swept under the rug by bought off politicians everywhere.** It will be mainstream politics *as usual*.

What we have experienced there, is simply human slavery using political correctness as a human shield in the upmost cowardly fashion possible. We have also witnessed the Democrat and Republican parties equally, bow clear to the ground to that political correctness. We have witnessed the media play this outright shame *to stunning perfection*.

We expect this from Democrats, the home and heart of the Klan and Jim Crow because; well, *just because*. That is their explanation for the situation as there is no underlying discernible principle involved *whatsoever*. Apparently there is Right Turn Clyde the Orangutan driving *that* car.

That does however fit perfectly with the original Republican Party charter "To advance Socialism within the United States." The facts are; if you were not taught that—***you were lied to***. If one were to write a book on the Republican Party, the only truthful title for that book would be: **All Roads Turn Left**. The reason that is the case *is because that is the case*. Once again, the more things change, the more they remain the same. *At least now you know the reason why*.

- A *whole bunch* of mainstream dupes *just found out new stuff*.

As it turns out, the number one claim to fame for apparently all Democrats is the loudly stated noise that: "We are not Republicans." *Might as well be*. Every last one of your elected assholes owes cartel for their office. *Obama just happens to owe the drug pushers the most*. And you can have Lindsey Graham.

And now we have George Soros the foreign oil mogul in his at least fifth attempt to purchase the Presidency. But will the endless *and massive* skeletons in Hillary's closet prove to be the undoing of that dream? Could she turn out to be the most highly un-liked and insufferable (   ) on this planet? Could she have the most baggage of anyone in existence? Could Jeb Bush, Steve Forbs' talking-piece, be the agent of her installation as planned? At least it would be decent *stomping*. Stay tuned to your television sleepy folks, *and that is exactly the reward* **you will have earned**.   One could call it the ultimate f###-you from the Illuminati—the same as the previous *worst election in history*.

- After all it is, *all in the same family*,

- *Sick*.

And after providing those very specific examples, I will return the discussion back to the concept of food supply independence:

The best example of food {and health} independence is set in the book Anastasia of the Ringing Cedars Press. Her Dashnicks, Russian for organic gardeners, are both absolutely *and specifically* non-dependent upon the slavery system, but are also in total control of the price and infinitely more important; **the quality** of their food supply. Translated into the King's English, that would mean *detoxifying*.

Half of the point, is that the intentionally few books that I do call out by name out of oodles possible, are books worth studying. Any of them are quite capable of dramatically shifting awareness and consciousness upward, such as Lee Carol's The Journey Home.

Or, I could be talking about hydroponic or ariponic <u>independence</u>. Either one further breaking the **intentionally murdering** chains of over processed, over cooked, over engineered, denatured, *enzyme void*, sweetener stuffed, *addictiveness enhanced*, radiation hammered, bleach treated, insecticide loaded, human toxic, filler duffed, fat saturated, mineral depleted, calorie concentrated, hydrogenized, chemical crammed, preservative abused, hormone laden, antibiotic contaminated, heavy metal concentrated, machine manufactured, plastic packaged, toxin riddled, known cancer causing, known allergy producing, known acidosis causing, non-functional, **vibrationally empty**, *specifically hormone disrupting,* **Life void**, *fake*, and GMO ambushed *replacement of* nutrition and sustenance.

- Like it or lump it, this is the truth.

- Please say; *"**genocide**"*—and then learn your way out of it.

As a systems designer, I've seen some huge real-world and cost effective benefits here and had some fun with it. Yet the objective **as ever**, remains <u>Consciousness.</u>

- Or it could be a simple as outlawing chemtrails *for-ever.*

Consciousness, *first and foremost* <u>is what should be kept paramount at all times</u>. It is breaking the terrible chains of slavery and slavery's politically programmed outcome of genocide that matters. It is the starting point of experiencing true co-Creatorhood Design of our unrealized ability and potentiality. We thereby cause a future worth living in; <u>one of ***actual personal empowerment***</u>.

An <u>**organic**</u> non poisoned green, fresh, live **and natural** raw diet causes abundant health and wellness. This is known. The same also allows for and facilitates; **<u>key concept here;</u>** an upward shift in consciousness. It arrives by way of the cleaner-clearer human *condition* harmonizing with, and allowing the ever higher vibration, wisdom, morality, <u>mind function</u>, ability, outcome, **and genuinely unlimited benefit** of greater Consciousness.

That highly humanitarian *progression* allows one to escape, *in many very beneficial ways*, several utterly vicious, utterly satanic traps. They are all of; the under the thumb-ness of the system. One achieves distance away from the closely associated sickness industry for starters. Secondly, one rises above the *acutely diminished* ability **and awareness levels** the trap of human slavery has set just-for-you. *Right there*, is an extremely effective key to abundant health, wellness, empowerment and independence.

- Betcha **that** wasn't taught in school.

- If you can clearly state the reason why, congratulations, you are moving into awareness!

The same model of Creator sourced and co-Created **peace and freedom** applies to everything. As we as a species create our own Freedom and decentralization and thus our empowerment, we begin to view, understand and experience the unlimited joy and benefit **of our own ownership and potential.**

Benjamin Franklin who understood and clearly demonstrated the benefits of Consciousness, allowed us to benefit from this wisdom:

"Liberty is the noblest and deepest calling of the human soul."

- **And so it is.**

To become an empowered human being, draw **that** perfect beauty, wholesomeness, goodness, empowerment and grace of the Creator Consciousness prominently *into your every day awareness*. To gain stronger benefit, and be a participant in the Great Healing, employ all of the concepts given in this textbook on Consciousness. However, place the above Franklin quote in a place where it will be seen, *preferably in your own handwriting*, and actively choose to read it *at least* twice a day *every day*.

- Such Creator's Energy **of *Consciousness*** is not only very, very Reasonable, it is in fact, *the Great Healing*.

- "Never believe that a few caring people can't change the world, for indeed, *that's all who ever have.*"

    Margaret Mead

- *That, is the real lesson <u>right there</u>.* It is your empowerment.

So what have we learned from this book?

As we **as a species** close The Final Chapter on Human Slavery, we pause to review what we have learned and inferred from this book:

Indeed we have covered in real-world and truth tested fact, each of the defining insights listed at the very beginning of this book. It is thus that this book has fulfilled its first mission with truth. We have also glorified the Creator and upheld Creator Consciousness, thus fulfilling the highest possible cause any book could ever be written for.

We have honored the Creator Design of Nature for the wisdom it offers and as our physical sustainer. We have advanced humanity, the humane treatment of humans. We have also advanced humanity, being the calibration level of the humans constituting humanity.

This book has presented the *correct* steps standing with God, to human empowerment. Thus, the intent to move all there is toward the Light of the Creator is also fulfilled.

We have covered the **correct** path to the profoundly beneficial experience of the advanced human, and the profoundly beneficial experience of the advanced human race. It is thus we have defined, intended *and enabled* Human Teleology, the inexorable path of all of creation, *<u>including us</u>*, toward The Creator and Creator Consciousness.

That path is the opposite of human slavery. The reason so many do not recognize this condition is a combination of modern mainstream politics working in the unabated service of Satan, and the *horrifyingly failed* government school system. In the not too distant future, both conditions shall self-abate. You have demanded it, and now it is time for the Evolution to take place. It is time to claim it. It is *thoroughly* underway as we speak. **There is no possibility of stopping its fulfillment.**

- The key is to align *ourselves* into Creator Consciousness.

- And it is so.

We have correctly identified two immaculately clear cut paths that define the present human condition:

The past and present path is **warfare and slavery.** It is the direction rigorously maintained by mainstream politics. It is the path of deceit in the service of the author of deceit. It is the path of destruction by the author of destruction. It is the path of destitution by the author of destitution. It is the path of cruelty by the author of cruelty. It is the path *straight to hell,* by way of that same command structure *including all who advocate that path*.

The second path, *that of Human Teleology*, is **The Path of Peace and Freedom.** This is the path as provided by the Creator of all that Is, toward Creator Consciousness for the benefits of Creator Consciousness.

- How exquisitely simple both these directions and concepts are.

- It is the event of **the decision**, that causes the actuality to be just as straightforward as the concept.

None of this is rocket science or in demand of higher education to understand or produce. The illusion that might make it appear as so, is the fact that essentially none of the content in this book is instructed through the patently dishonest government-Marxist education that has very stubbornly centered itself on individual disempowerment and disenfranchisement. *This alone adds an infinite weight to removing government control of education*.

We have correctly identified the basic and omni-consuming facts of **all** mainstream partisan politics:

- Rule number one of modern politics: *You are a guaranteed victim.*

- In fact within all of mainstream politics, *that is your only role*.

- Rule number two of modern politics: *Everything is moved into human slavery.*

- This fact is longer hidden. (Several Presidents fixed that.)

- Rule number three of modern politics: *You are being lied to ceaselessly.*

- Like duh.

Along with that, we have likely uncovered the most *precise* definition of mainstream politics: **Something traded for nothing**. This was placed into the human genome (presumably) by Will Rogers about 1920. *Without a doubt*, he had gleaned this wisdom from earlier awareness. There are many *shiningly accurate* definitions of mainstream politics throughout this book.

For every definition of Marxist politics included, I personally heard at least two score. Most, although quite factual, contained words not fit for family entertainment. In that regard, the descriptions "cowardice" and "illegitimate" played the unwavering central role.

This author expressly encourages you to create your own definitions of mainstream politics and let the world know what it is. Perhaps we might construct a fun book on *just that, 'Defining Slavery'*. God knows, the ammunition has been well supplied. Here's another:

- Mainstream politics is now identified as the single-minded organization producing ruin.

We have also discovered there are many more basic rules of mainstream politics we *could have* employed. Each one would be just as real-world experienced as the first three. An example might be rule number four of modern politics: *All the politicians are purchased*. Although that much is self-evident, readily provable and glaring, it only serves to explain how the first three rules came into existence and continue **untouched** to this day. **The whole mess awaits only our resolve to end it.**

A fifth rule could be: *Everything serves the Cartel*. Again that is redundant. It simply states the obvious over and over.

There are many more rules mainstream politics lives by. **All of which are human slavery.** This author shall leave them up to you. We may use them to write the book, 'The Rules of Slavery' with. Lord knows I heard enough of them in my travels to construct a book with.

- The real point: Modern politics is a dead horse *that will soon be buried*. <u>Right there is where you gain your wish</u>.

We have correctly identified that in the entirety of the human condition, there is only one issue:

- **Human slavery or human<u>ness</u>.**

We have correctly identified that in all of politics, there is only one issue:

- **Human slavery or humanness.**

- Now, would be the correct time for your decision on this matter.

- And it is so.

"I didn't come here to tell you how this is going to end. I came here to tell you how it is going to begin." **From the Matrix**

We have correctly identified that The Humanitarian Code is the *concise*, modern version, **identical in all aspects** of spirit, effect and intent to Mosaic Law, The Magna Charta, and all of the founding documents of this Nation including The Constitution and Bill of Rights:

1 The only legitimate function of government is to uphold, protect and defend Individual Human Rights.

2   We stand at One with the Creator in the Humanity of Liberty, the condition of Human Evolution.

3   We stand united in the American definition of smaller government, fewer taxes, and greatest personal freedom.

- And:

- We hold these truths to be brilliantly self-evident as the foundation of all human success.

- Thereby we uphold Life and the conditions of Life in harmony and unity with All that Is.

- We literally are the Human Event and the Bringers of the Dawn of Humanity.

- Take note *that* is not instructed by either modern politics or government education.

- Take note that this truth is not only not instructed, but *vehemently* opposed, by the entirety **of the system of human slavery**.

- This is your key to *precisely* identify who is on which side.

We have identified that The Reasonable Human Movement and the Reasonable Political Party is **your** empowerment. It is **you** voting for **you**. It's **your** freedom. It's **your** life. We now include our nearly endless and greatly exploding number of sister organizations and movements, each centered *specifically* in the humanity of freedom. **IT IS THE CALLING OF THE HUNANITARIAN.**

- *These are very important concepts to correctly understand.*

We have clarified the *actual* definition of American. How incredibly poignant it is that *this* clarity may be the singular most necessary item this

Nation presently faces. Many are the outright lies and web of lies *now destroyed*—that went into opposing that basic truth.

We have summed and clarified the Basic Laws of Human Success by introducing The Humanitarian Code of Human Success©. From the results of that, we have introduced and defined Human Teleology, the gift and benefits of Creator Consciousness, Common Law, common sense **and actual moral integrity.**

In accordance with Prophecy, we have reviewed and employed "weapons they know nothing of". Actually that was easy: When we reviewed the concepts of truth, honor, integrity, common sense and justice that are a leading portion of Consciousness, we covered vast areas modern politics "*Knows nothing of*".

- I'm hearing unanimous agreement on that.

We spoke of Consciousness itself. In doing so, we pulled *ourselves* above the present state of the forces now running this world.

As this entire planet moves out from under black hat control and into a state of Consciousness, we experience that which is Human Teleology.

- The benefits of this are indeed unlimited, and almost unimaginable although nearly all of us have been given a small view of it.

- In that view, we see both the benefit and the Calling.

- And it is absolutely, Human Success.

Finally and most importantly, we have learned about ourselves.

Through our ever stronger inner voice, we learned we were not designed to be slaves. We now know that slavery is to nothing other than perdition. That perdition is tyranny and failure of the most proven order known. From that, we now know beyond any shadow of doubt that it can **and is** being relegated to the footnote of history. The *human species* is evolving above, and out from under human slavery *as of this moment*.

The main body and intent of politics has not changed in many millennia. It was the same when Baal ran the show with the iron hand of great cruelty. It was the same at the time of Plato's Cave that illustrated the bizarre absurdity and tragedy of the endless illusions of human limitation. It was the same when Sisyphus of Greek mythology first rolled his stone uphill demonstrating both the existing condition and bizarre absurdity of human slavery. It was the same when Christ tossed a few tables of the money changers demonstrating the bizarre absurdity of false exchanges, identical in spirit to the queered money even up to today. It hasn't changed at all, and will never voluntarily do so on its own accord because **it is human slavery.**

Because that same body of politic from the same blood line now has both the intent and readily available ability to destroy all humanity on earth if not the planet itself, it becomes the function of our survival to terminate *and eradicate* the main body of politic *as it is known today.*

- *Mainstream politics can now be defined as the throat cutting contest that has produced only blood to the depth of a horse's bridal.*

From the world of dishonor *and bitter failure* defining mainstream politics, we have learned their exposure is their demise. We have learned that such exposure now a stream, is very aggressively turning into a river *and then the flood of all floods*, to wash away every last portion of those same constituents of perdition.

- Like all Reasonable things, it is good news for humanity and bad news for the Devil.

- And that is a main point of the book.

I am no longer put off by unawareness to evolution: We would do well to remind ourselves that there is a losing team still on the playing field for a few moments longer, and that the only way they have ever played the game is dirty. As of *this writing* the final outcome is however, *published*.

- We have observed Satan's construct is warfare and slavery.

- We observe The Creator's intent is Peace and Freedom.

- *There is no remaining doubt as to the difference.*

We have learned this contrast is the present state of the human species. It is this *specific* contrast, the entire human race is looking directly at. We can call these two conditions anything we want, however the fact of the matter remains eternally intact. It's ironic that one of the above two conditions has enough mislabels to nearly outnumber the grains of sand in the sea and it *still* failed to hide either the author or the intent. Working together as a team, we have *caused* that particular author and intent to now be exposed.

- From that exposure, we have gained a nearly unlimited strength.

- We have learned that strength is our **Humanity**.

- **And so this is: The Final Chapter of Human Slavery.**

- And it is a *very* good day after all.   Because:

- The gates of imprisonment are wide open for all to escape through.

- Walking through those gates in resolve and courage into a vastly better, brighter future <u>***worth living in***</u>;   is,

The Human event.

Chapter Thirteen

This Shall Be Done   (epilog)

This Shall Be Done: (epilog)

In the old energy, we are forced to meet each other at our weakness.

- As Reasonable, we encourage each other into our strengths.

I had the most amazing fun writing this book, and that is how I live my life. It behooves us to daily and vigorously remind ourselves that the purpose of life is to enjoy it. It is very beneficial to not lose track of that. It is a most essential and enduring calling. In a very real sense, it is Freedom Itself, and the greatest human benefit of all.

So, if you would enjoy some good clean fun in kicking the system of evil and insanity in the crotch, that being, returning for once and finally, the many, many such "favors" as given to you by the system, then this strictly educational book and explosively expanding grass roots opportunity, is your best chance **lifetime**, to do exactly that. There is every benefit in self-ownership to gain from this inexorable and *exceptionally elegant* process.

At the same moment, a very freeing approach is to simply render the system non relevant to one's life and thoughts.

Such blessed freedom, that is always within reach, is the surest indicator of the evolved human who rarely lends *the human sacrifice system* the power, their power, of a single thought. The benefit of that quality is your empowerment through the key and critical process of your-keeping-your-power. The key to that power and Freedom, is staying so 110% involved in your calling, talent expression, and omni-beneficial outcome, that fun becomes your every moment just as it is now mine.

On the *then rare* interludes when human slavery rears its craven head, we fix it instantly and usually with a karmic clearing. That diffuses and dissipates the old energy. If done correctly it will remove and replace with Light, a portion of the old energy from the hate blinded perp as well.

It can be amazing to watch the process of a person going from blind to awake with that particular portion of the old energy crumbling to nothing even as you observe it do so. Now *that's* empowerment.

That of course being the exact last thought and power droplet handed over to uncut perdition and human loser-hood in the service of Satan.

Think of your thoughts, **that being your power**, as blood. That should do the trick of **not** handing it over to the devils who will bloody well gladly drink deeply of your life force! Spiritually, that is how it works. There is much more to that particular process than most are ready to understand, however that is the basics. It is important to get that much right.

Such error is the trap of entertaining the systemized emotion of fear. Therefore, courage is every answer not just that answer. It is of no concern what the question is. Specifically as related to ending the politics of human slavery, courage is the only *functional* answer, for that alone is the singular difference between bond and free, and likely now, *between dead and alive*.

Such is the knowledge and practice of the well human and any true healer. Courage to Be, (i.e. going Galt), is in truth the first and foundational step into human wellness, wholeness, enjoyment and Success.

Have fun with it. Experience the blessing of Freedom and fresh air away from the stench of slavery and mind control. And that's the whole point; fun, Freedom and fresh air. Gather your sacred empowerment right there, within easy reach. When done correctly, it is profoundly beautiful. It is free, and it is Freeing. **It is the Reasonable blessing of your Humanity.**

Except for The Three Immutable Truths of Human Evolution comprising Humanitarian Code, the three Reasonable action steps, and a few guidelines interlarded here and there, much of this book was intentionally written on a metaphysical level. Such is not one whit less Truth on this plane or any other, it is only deeper, timeless and much more beneficial Truth.

Test yourself, and see if you can read in such manner and find for yourself the manifold deeper and human beneficial insights. Most of the

New Energy is written that way and for a reason. It speaks volumes to your subconscious in Soul recognition terms.

In fact, pretty much all work in metaphysics exists to bring to your outer conscious, your true ability and thus empowerment and Freedom. It is the art, science *and intent* of communication to the effect of the outer conscious, subconscious and Super-Conscious working together *as One.*

My work is to bring to your outward conscious, that which you Are. You are designed by the Creator to be Free, not slave. If for any reason you feel that you are not Free and treated less than human, modern, mainstream, pigsty, and human dreadful politics, is *the perfected in ruin* reason why.

- The issue is human slavery **or humanness**.

- *In all of politics worldwide*, there simply and factually is no other issue.

Any and all other apparent issues or more accurately, illusions stacked upon illusions, *apparent* being the world-class word here, are only, strictly, and often amazingly wacky, subdivisions of that one and only First issue.

- That First Issue is human slavery *versus humanness.*

As it turns out, it has become all important to human survival to get that concept straight; because it is the endless and deliberate deceptions of modern partisan politics that *intentionally* placed human and earth into the political Baal, and the utterly hell bent superhighway we now experience.

- *Working forward from the First Issue concept,* **is the Truth that sets us Free.**

- And it is absolutely so.

In this book are an extraordinary rich diversity of heroes named or represented. They are far too many to list. In all likelihood, you probably recognized a few of their inputs and very distinct styles like *Stuart Wilde.*

Right there, is a bold leadership of how a seemingly impossible variety of backgrounds, time frames and viewpoints can peacefully co-exist just as they have on these pages. Each of them is profoundly appreciated for their paradigm shifting contribution to Human Empowerment. Fittingly, none are moved by this world's trivial rewards because they are Free and Masters.

Each hero, and the contributors to this book from every possible walk, if history is to revere them vastly after the shapeless, spineless critics and political hand-puppets are correctly and long forgotten or jailed, have one thing in common: They each had an unbreakable dedication to human Enlightenment and Empowerment, that which you Are—**the moment you make that decision.**

This book for example, is dedicated to your personal Empowerment and Ascension <u>which is One</u>. Exactly that, is the Great Healing, and, **the Human Event**. It is your self-ownership. It is your humanity: *It is the enjoyment of the <u>actual ability</u> of your very design.* A function of this book is to inform you that your ability is *infinitely greater than advertised*.

By not giving away power, one very quickly discovers who they Are by way of retaining more of who they were to begin with, which is Free, Human *and exceedingly powerful.* That is exactly why NOT buying into mainstream politics and its endless deceits and illusions, (and all of mainstream politics is deceits and illusions), turns out to be of vital importance to human survival and thriving.

Trust me on this if at first you must. For in not too long a time, this big as it ever gets <u>Light</u> will come on, and you will see and experience exactly what I am saying just as so many others already have. This book was specifically not caused by modern politics being the least part functional; and it is *one hell* of a lot worse any of the very rare times it is! That is now the world's largest clue, **right in your face <u>and dead obvious</u>**.

- Modern government is now defined as the billing department for somebody else's free-for-all orgy of corruption.

- *Modern politics is the process that takes place when everyone is out to lunch as to what is actually taking place.*

- Always remember that the Devil profits famously anytime anyone resigns that the only choice is the Devil's politics.

- This book accurately details the form, substance, intent and results of modern politics. At this point, *all of existence* is reduced to one question: **Are you awake or not?**

The following concepts help to drive home that essential question:

- When most of us say "poor mainstream party nominees" for the office of President, we are actually saying **"nothing that rises above the condition of puke"**.

- From coast to coast, that hit an enthusiastic majority agreement.

- This is the political Baal the world is presently dealing with.

- Every four years, and for that matter *every office*, the identical condition *and pile of illusions* assaults the human race.

- We think that it is entirely Reasonable to put an end to that crap.

- If the human race is going to survive, that is *precisely* where to start.

When the majority of mainstream politicians have made the majority of their salary through lying, there is no possibility that can morally be considered either a good resume or a good track record. It is that specific pattern that needs to be *eradicated*. These two overwhelmingly held concepts were *the* essential and central theme heard with virtually no variation from coast to coast. This book contains the correct directions on how to repair that situation. The time has come now to consider ourselves humans and begin to act as if we were human. As it turns out, that is the diametric opposite of anything so far offered or experienced with mainstream politics in any of our lifetimes *or our parent's or grandparent's lifetimes.*

- When you have a crystal clear understanding of the previous paragraph, you are probably on the correct team.

Much of the reason why our individual and collective intuitions are screaming at us, telling us that mainstream politicians are nothing other than and nothing above puke, is this:

To achieve power within modern politics, the mainstream politician must first provide superseding loyalty to organizations specifically committed to the full termination of Human Rights (as spoken of in chapter nine). *That prerequisite more than any other consideration, is what constitutes a mainstream approved politician as a mainstream approved politician.*

- As that is the center of mainstream politics, it is important to understand the paradigm working against humanity *clearly*.

The condition is an outgrowth of, and is strictly subservient to, the world controlling banks and cartels. This pattern also extends back to, and long, long before the British and Dutch East India Trading Companies. It is also a very integral part of that paradigm. It should be of no surprise to anyone that it is strictly human slavery. *It is also the heart and core of the United Nations which is one way in its advertisement, and the precise opposite in its reality.*

That loyalty is well tested *and continuously tested* through supplanting Oath, ritual, voting record, and the endless sales pitches defending human slavery. It is a new concept to few, that murder, mass murder, horrendous blackmail and all manner of utterly heinous crime is part of that equation. Nor should it come as any surprise that the blackmail runs in every direction, and that definitely includes the politicians self-committed to the forces of darkness.

The good news is that as the planetary control is taken away from the forces of Satan, any and all of such associated conditions will be brought to an end and to full justice. These are but some of the things that will be completed in dealing with, *and exterminating*, the old energy patterns of man's inhumanity to man.

Once cleared, the monopolies, the cartels and the satanic organizations shall be swept away. This shift, and it is *THE SHIFT*, **the** *primary metamorphosis defining this age*, shall facilitate Human Success in all aspects of the human condition. It is the achieving of *actual* humanity.

- It is the causal of a future worth living in.

Here are some other items learned from life. That is why it is in this textbook on human evolution. These items came from the public, yet had greatly more than enough agreement to warrant communication here.

We have learned that both politics and religion have a dominating history of solving their problems with suppression, oppression and murder. The objective is to be aware that such policy and practice is the old energy. *The endless piousness married to those rivers of Hell, fail miserably to excuse them.* Reasonable however, **is in knowing what the deal is.**

We have learned that a lie repeated a million times does not change the fact that it is a lie. We have also learned precisely that, *is the entire existence of mainstream politics*.

Is it just me. or is there a strange and inexplicable mystification going on out there? Have you ever stopped to notice that within mainstream politics, there is no such thing as a Dino, *yet with damn rare exceptions that can be counted on one hand, and half of them named Cruz, we have an entire countryside just chocked full of Rinos?*

We have learned many self-caused definitions of mainstream politics. There were way more than plenty available to publish a cooperative made fun book, *and we should*. Some definitions are incredibly funny *because of their truth*. Like the Dino-Rino observation or the Bama-Rama observation. A few were shared when they rose to the level of either unanimous or near unanimous agreement. Some of the definitions I heard of modern politics were incredibly sad *because of their truth*. I rarely share those owing to the fact that I prefer funny and so do you. Most of the items I heard were *not* included, however each of them were highly poignant, highly accurate.

Here is an example of sad just for general purposes: Mainstream politics is nearly the only thing left on earth that cannot legitimately claim a moral leg up on *child pornography*. For the record, that is not an endorsement of either one. It is a sad state of affairs that I had to include such clarification because some miserable reptilian connipulator out there would find a way to lawyer it inside out and stick it in Lamestream media with a label opposite of the truth. The pattern itself is self explanatory and life has taught us that also.

We have learned from a few lifetimes of experience that most of the folks who will be paid to criticize this book will not have read this book and it will probably be obvious. So much for the obvious. That by the way is the reason *they will be forgotten*. So much for that obvious to. I suppose that well worn pattern could be called sad as well.

- The good news is that the human race is going to *lay waste* to the sad patterns.

- You are looking at that process *now*.

We have also learned that with a few exceptions, the folks critical to the Constitution have never read the Constitution. A great deal worse than that is that many of the folks *supporting* the Constitution have *also* never read the Constitution. *Both conditions* are somewhere in the twilight zone short of honest. The good news is that the short version, the Clifford Notes of the Constitution, is the 48 words of The Humanitarian Code. You watch, some tongue wag who has not read either the Constitution *or this book* will say: "That's not the case." If they tripped over their IQ, *at least it would be a short fall*. Trust me, *it is going to happen*.

You can also bet your last cent they are going to get published. As you have told me, the mainstream media is not about truth at all. It is about supporting human slavery *period*, *exclusively*. Their sales are likely to continue to vanish because there is little possibility they are going to get the connection. That is just how sold and controlled they are. *The poison pill, they have swallered*.

- With the realization of what the broken parts *actually are*, we can proceed *to replace them*.

- Like anything else, they damn sure aren't going to fix themselves.

- And that is why *you* are reading *this*.

The humane treatment of humans, Individual Human Rights, is a main theme of this book. The dearth of practical knowledge on the subject raises some questions: Is Individual Human Rights, the treatment of humans as human, *the forgotten subject* as our education system has it? Or is the foundation of successful society *the forbidden subject* as political correctness would have it?

- Lets go ahead and define political correctness as that great collection of mistakes *that a dog 'd be ashamed of*.

- I *like* that.

It will be very interesting to see what the folks who are paycheck dependent upon defending human slavery have to say about the New Energy of Human Success. I do not believe that many of them will leave behind any doubt as to whose side they are on, at least *not if they like their paycheck*.

- As long as there is political correctness and a controlled media, **human slavery *will be fiercely defended.***

I just betcha the names are going to fly. The real simple reason is that political correctness as we have witnessed for a long time now, has virtually no other tools left in the toolbox. Said differently the inexorable sound bite name calling and hate bath, will be the clarion sign <u>*of terror-stricken desperation*</u>. I actually welcome it, because their End of Time has arrived
⇨ *precisely, as, foretold*.

- The stink all over that process, is only what is being *stomped out of 'em* by the truth.

- Hallelujah!   (I should spot 'em a dozen or so names—they've earned the need).

The human race is presently in a fight for its survival. Somehow and fast, **we must come up with the will to live.**

It is modern politics itself that is both the harbor and means of the now unabashed intention of human extinction. This sets up one of two conditions; either Satan's model of warfare and slavery shall prevail, or The Creator's model of Peace and Freedom shall prevail. Only one of those two conditions includes **the concept of human**, the other one does not. *The Humanitarian Code is now and forever the dividing line between the two conditions.* With that, it is real easy to figure out who is working for whom. This is where the wheat is separated from the chaff, also *precisely as foretold.*

- We are going to watch a sea of rats jump ship helter-skelter, just as expected and just as we are now seeing.

Those same rats are going to turn on each other in droves. This is mainstream politics as historically observed. The function of the human race is to sweep them off the ship with all haste, because they have *already* turned upon us with nearly every viciousness in their possession.

- Mainstream politics *owes the entire world* a debt it can only repay **by ceasing to exist**.

"The soul of everyone does possess the power of learning the truth and the organ to see it with. Just as one might have to turn the whole body round in order that eyes should see the light instead of the darkness, so the entire soul must be turned away from this changing world *until its eye can bear to contemplate reality.*" Plato

That is where the human race is presently at. With that understanding, I shall turn the conversation back to Ayn Rand:

Many terribly overpaid critics yet loathe Ayn Rand to their last pompous, condescending and universally Marxist fiber, just as she majestically out brain-powers them, and to this day, outsells 'em twenty thousand to two. In fact, she is every bit as popular and thought provoking, make that just plain provoking, as ever. The truly great usually are. It is because they refuse to exhibit cowardice. Ayn Rand damn certain passed that test. Her critics have displayed no earthly understanding of the component of courage. It is an inspired weapon "They know nothing of" *precisely as foretold*.

For the record, I shall now speak to the impossibly shortsighted and thick skulled ding dong critics for a moment: The reason Ayn Rand had the second bestselling book, next to the Bible, on the planet earth and in the United States in her day—and is enjoying a **massive resurgence** more than 50 years later is rather simple so please get it: The human Soul and construct is interested in Freedom and Empowerment, not your mindless and poisoned diet of helplessness, outright lies, half living, coercion, theft, abuse, bullying, arrogance, filth ridden poverty, spying, exploitation, rot **and endless human butchery.** One way or the other you have been paid to serve the Devil. *The human race* has had it with your senseless violence and ceaseless lies.

- **Got it?** " *'Nuff said!!!* "   ...*Oki Oil Man!*

- "*The shift is going to hit the fan.*"
  From the outside cover of the movie I AM

Could this book ever be as flatly feared as Ayn Rand? To be honest, I doubt it. Yet owing to its absence of grey, it is off to a very healthy and healing start. Could this no nonsense, no fancy stuff, and no damn chrome plating book change the course of human history as has a Thomas Paine, a Frederick Douglass or a Rosa Parks or a Martin Luther King? If it pulls but one human up and out of the pure hell of the deceit and devastating illusions of mainstream politics, then it has indeed made well, one critically important portion of the world—**you!**

To achieve Planetary Healing, the Great Healing, is strictly up to you. **You now have the *precisely* correct map.** However, no map has ever carried its owner over a single inch of the path. *The only thing that matters is action, intent and outcome.* **Let's make sure all three are Human Success.**

It will be achieved by a person to person transaction, the same as Anastasia, the Celestine Prophecy, the Code, Ishmael, Avatar, I AM, Thrive and so many others respectfully represented within these pages. Very similarly, **The Worldwide Human Empowerment Movement** has cut deeply across every culture, calling and land there is. Therefore it is off to an inspired excellence in that regard also. Yet the advancement of the human and planetary condition is <u>absolutely in your hands</u> **as of this reading,** *this moment.*

- *The future sincerely hopes it has entrusted accurately.*

The Humanitarian Code is the one and only process by which worlds are awakened and moved from past to present; thus from the pain of hate and slavery, to the Omni-benefit of peace and freedom.

- As it is so.

The World Healing Initiative and the Reasonable Statement of Intent:

"It is our intent that all opportunities, and challenges as equal merit, be met peacefully, legally, openly, honestly, and with full integrity, honor, respect, harmony and unity for the most beneficial outcome for everyone and everything concerned."

- And so it is.
- Peace be with you.

Please know, *fully know*, that you are now acknowledged

For choosing to be here during;

The Moment of the Great Healing.

We are One. We are Human. We are Free.

We are Healed, Whole and Empowered.

We are Reasonable.

And it is absolutely so!

Paracletus tells us: "There are three states of being. Mankind is only aware of two, the sleeping and awaking states. The state of full consciousness however *still remains elusive.*"

- **That is, until The Humanitarian Code *brought it to light*.**

- *…Making this a book on Consciousness.*

- *True Humanity, only awaits the decision only you can make.*

- **The decision is whether or not you are Human.**

- We believe you are.

- *By the Grace and Glory of God Almighty, these inspired words will change the course of the entire universe.*

Thank you *as Human*, for co-Creating and now experiencing <u>that which is 2012</u> and beyond—**The Time of the Great Healing.**

"For this cause we thank God without ceasing." 1 Thes. 2:13

- And so we do.
- …Which is entirely Reasonable.

"Practice yields outcomes while principles yield understanding."
From Burt Dubin's Personal Mastery Experience.

- The Great Healing is accomplished through The Humanitarian Code:

1 *The only legitimate function of government is to uphold, protect and defend Individual Human Rights.*

2 *We stand at One with the Creator in the Humanity of Liberty, the condition of Human Evolution.*

3 *We stand united in the American definition of smaller government, fewer taxes, and greatest personal freedom.*

- ***This marks the beginning of Humanity.***
- And it is so.

Thank you for reading and sharing this book.

- Fun, Freedom and fresh air is the Reasonable Experience.

- We are Personal Empowerment and Human Advancement through upholding Individual Human Rights.

- We observe that the Dawn of Humanity is through The Humanitarian Code.

You indeed are valuable, worthy and appreciated.

Because this is: *The Human Event!*

And it is right smack Now!

<u>*And you know it*</u>.

Gloria in Excelsis Deo!

Edwards Brothers Malloy
Thorofare, NJ USA
March 10, 2014